Communications in Computer and Information Science 1575

More information about this series at https://link.springer.com/bookseries/7899

Ashish Kumar Luhach · Dharm Singh Jat ·
Kamarul Bin Ghazali Hawari · Xiao-Zhi Gao ·
Pawan Lingras (Eds.)

Advanced Informatics for Computing Research

5th International Conference, ICAICR 2021
Gurugram, India, December 18–19, 2021
Revised Selected Papers

 Springer

Editors
Ashish Kumar Luhach
Papua New Guinea University of Technology
Lae, Papua New Guinea

Kamarul Bin Ghazali Hawari
Universiti Malaysia Pahang
Pekan, Malaysia

Pawan Lingras
Saint Mary's University
Halifax, NS, Canada

Dharm Singh Jat
Namibia University of Science
and Technology
Windhoek, Namibia

Xiao-Zhi Gao
University of Eastern Finland
Kuopio, Finland

ISSN 1865-0929   ISSN 1865-0937 (electronic)
Communications in Computer and Information Science
ISBN 978-3-031-09468-2   ISBN 978-3-031-09469-9 (eBook)
https://doi.org/10.1007/978-3-031-09469-9

This Springer imprint is published by the registered company Springer Nature Switzerland AG
The registered company address is: Gewerbestrasse 11, 6330 Cham, Switzerland

Preface

This book contains the best selected and edited papers of the Fifth International Conference on Advanced Informatics for Computing Research (ICAICR 2021), held during December 18–19, 2021 in Gurugram, India, in association with the Namibia University of Science and Technology, Namibia, and technically sponsored by the VNR Vignana Jyothi Institute of Engineering and Technology, India, Shobhit University, Gangoh, India, the Graphic Era Deemed to be University (GEU), India, and the Leafra Research Foundation, India.

ICAICR 2021 targeted state-of-the-art as well as emerging topics pertaining to advanced informatics for computing research and its implementation for engineering applications. The objective of this international conference is to provide opportunities for researchers, academicians, industry professionals, and students to interact and exchange ideas, experience, and expertise in the current trends and strategies for information and communication technologies. Besides this, the aims are to enlighten participants about the vast avenues and current and emerging technological developments in the field of advanced informatics and to thoroughly explore and discuss its applications. ICAICR 2021 received 220 papers, out of which 23 high-quality papers were accepted after the double-blind review process.

We are highly thankful to our valuable authors for their contributions and our Technical Program Committee for their immense support and motivation for making this edition of ICAICR a success. We are also grateful to our keynote speakers for sharing their precious work and enlightening the delegates of the conference. We express our sincere gratitude to our publication partner, Springer, for believing in us.

February 2022

Ashish Kumar Luhach
Dharm Singh Jat
Kamarul Bin Ghazali Hawari
Xiao-Zhi Gao
Pawan Lingras

Organization

Conference Chairs

Kamarul Hawari bin Ghazali	Universiti Malaysia Pahang, Malaysia
Dharm Singh	Namibia University of Science and Technology, Namibia
Ashish Kr. Luhach	The PNG University of Technology, Papua New Guinea
Sachin Sharma	GEU, India

Technical Program Committee Chairs

Pawan Lingras	Saint Mary's University, Canada
Xiao-Zhi Gao	University of Eastern Finland, Finland

Technical Program Committee

K. T. Arasu	Wright State University, USA
Rumyantsev Konstantin	Southern Federal University, Russia
Syed Akhat Hossain	Daffodil International University, Bangladesh
Sophia Rahaman	Manipal Academy of Higher Education, Dubai
Thippeswamy M. N.	Nitte Meenakshi Institute of Technology, India
Lavneet Singh	University of Canberra, Australia
Pao-Ann Hsiung	National Chung Cheng University, Taiwan
Mohd. Helmey Abd Wahab	Universiti Tun Hussein Onn Malaysia, Malaysia
Shireen Panchoo	University of Technology, Mauritius
Sumathy Ayyausamy	Manipal Academy of Higher Education, Dubai
Kamarul Hawari bin Ghazali	Universiti Malaysia Pahang, Malaysia
Dharm Singh	Namibia University of Science and Technology, Namibia
Abbas Karimi	Islamic Azad University, Arak, Iran
Upasana G. Singh	University of KwaZulu-Natal, South Africa
Ritesh Chugh	Central Queensland University, Australia
Pawan Lingras	Saint Mary's University, Canada
Poonam Dhaka	University of Namibia, Namibia
Ashish Kr. Luhach	The PNG University of Technology, Papua New Guinea
Indra Seher	Central Queensland University, Sydney, Australia
Sugam Sharma	Iowa State University, USA

T. G. K. Vasista	King Saud University, Saudi Arabia
Akhtar Kalam	Victoria University, Australia
Ioan-Cosmin Mihai	A.I. Cuza Police Academy, Romania
Abhijit Sen	Kwantlen Polytechnic University, Canada
R. B. Mishra	Indian Institute of Technology (BHU), Varanasi, India
Bhaskar Bisawas	Indian Institute of Technology (BHU), Varanasi, India

Contents

Computing Methodologies

Networks

Computing Methodologies

Worldwide Vaccination Report for COVID-19 Analysis and Visualization Using Deep Learning

Meenu Gupta[(⊠)], Rakesh Kumar, Shubham Gaur, and Puneet Kumar

UIE-CSE, Chandigarh University, Gharuan, Punjab , India
meenu.e9406@cumail.in

Abstract. Covid-19 is an ongoing pandemic, caused by the Acute Respiratory Disease Coronavirus 2 (SARS-CoV-2). The virus first appeared in Wuhan, China in December 2019. The World Health Organization announced the Public Health Emergency of International Concern on COVID-19 on January 30, 2020, and announced the epidemic on March 11, 2020. Due to high number of death cases the COVID-19 becames a deadliest pandemics in the history. The main aim of this work is to convey the analysis of various current vaccination programs around the globe by performing Exploratory Data Analysis on the scraped data present on the web. In the result analysis, the model visualizes and showcases the caused by Covid in different countries through the last one year and the progress of the vaccination program in various countries around the world. The result analysis shows that United States, United Kingdom, England, India and China are the top five country that are vaccinating maximum people in a day and Gabraltar have the most people vaccinated as compared to others.

Keywords: Covid-19 · Pandemic · Vaccination report · Visualization · Deep learning · Public health emergency of international · Exploratory data analysis

1 Introduction

The Covid-19 pandemic is the one of the most vital health disaster humans have encountered with [1] Covid-19 is spreading rapidly among humans as well as animals. Corona viruses are a large family of viruses that causes illness. The illness may range from common cold to severe respiratory diseases to even death. Corona viruses are classified as zoonotic, which means they can transfer between humans and animals too. There are several known corona viruses that are circulating in animals but not yet infected humans [2]. In 2019, a new coronavirus was identified as the cause of the disease outbreak among humans. The virus is known as SARS-CoV-2. The virus is thus known as corona virus disease 2019 (COVID-19). The outbreak spread at an alarming rate as a result of which the WHO (World Health Organization) declared COVID-19 to be a pandemic [3]. The corona virus infects your body's healthy cells. There, the virus makes copies of itself throughout the body. The virus moves down the human respiratory tract and latches its spiky surface proteins to receptors on healthy cells, especially lungs. This makes the hosts lungs to become inflamed which makes it tough for them to breathe. This may lead

A. K. Luhach et al. (Eds.): ICAICR 2021, CCIS 1575, pp. 3–14, 2022.
https://doi.org/10.1007/978-3-031-09469-9_1

to severe respiratory diseases to even deaths [4]. There are various methods introduced by scientists and people to know whether the patient is infected with Covid-19 virus or not. One of the methods include the study of the patient's Chest x-ray and chest CT scan, in which the doctors look out for shadows or patchy areas called "ground-glass opacity" [5]. Many health professionals, statisticians, researchers, data scientists and programmers have been tracking the corona virus outspread in different regions of the world using various different approaches. Data scientists have developed various algorithms which can identify whether the person is infected with corona virus or not, using the images of chest x-rays of that person [6]. The development of an efficacious COVID-19 vaccine has helped various countries all around the world to stand a chance against this pandemic. The rise in various vaccines developed by scientists have helped the countries to develop an immunization among their people against the Covid-19 virus. The vaccination programs are now ongoing in every major and minor city all around the world with aim to immunize the whole population against this virus [7, 8]. After the release of the first vaccine in January 2021, countries all around the world were trying to vaccinate and immune as many people as possible. But since March 2021, a second wave of Covid-19 struck various countries around the world. The Table 1 compares the new confirmed covid cases and deaths in various countries for 1st January 2021 and 5th March 2021, after they got struck with the second wave on Covid-19 [9].

Table 1. Covid-19 Data for new cases and deaths in various countries

Country Name	New Confirmed Covid-19 cases (1st Jan 2021)	New confirmed Covid-19 cases (5th May 2021)	New confirmed Covid-19 Deaths (1st Jan 2021)	New confirmed Covid-19 Deaths (5th May 2021)
India	20035	412431	256	3980
European Union	112548	106256	2296	2141
South America	47568	125704	912	4136
Brazil	24605	73295	462	2811
France	19348	260004	133	244
Japan	3257	4068	248	60
Nepal	426	8605	8	58
Thailand	216	2112	1	15

2 Related Work

In [8], the author has performed a study where the author tried to predict the progression of disease caused by COVID- 19 Vaccine. The author performed machine-learning models on the data collected at two hospitals, The Huoshenshan and Taikang Tongji (Wuhan, China) hospitals. Some patients were characterized as severe COVID-19 cases with fever plus one of SpO2 <93% or rate of respiration >30 breaths/minute in room. Then, in the dataset, the author selected the most representative features. using a feature selection. Factors which show differences between the two groups namely, critical and non-critical patients were selected by the author for the machine learning process. In the results, the author found that the patient's median age was 62.75 years, with more than 50% being male. The severe patients are much older than the non-severe patients. High blood pressure (>30%), heart disease(<10%) and diabetes (>12%) were the most common complications, and were frequently presented in severe patients. Increased levels of CRP, D-dimer and α-hydroxybutyrate dehydrogenase, lactate dehydrogenase (LDH), and a decreased levels of hemoglobin and albumin are found in severe patients.

In [9], the author has prepared a background paper on Covid-19 vaccines. The author has depicted how the various vaccines such as CoviShield and Covaxin works. SARS-CoV-2 infection induces both B-cell (antibody) and T-cell specific immune responses. T-cells are responsible for producing memory T-cells that remember the virus and B-cells are responsible for producing virus specific antibodies. Basically, both the cells combined prepare our body for future infection. The two most famous vaccines around the world that are being used by most of the countries are CoviShield and Covaxin. The CoviShield uses Chimpanzee adeno virus approach. When a person gets vaccinated with CoviShield, the vaccine doesn't inject the person with the actual SARS-CoV-2 virus, but instead the person gets injected with an adeno virus that infects animals, especially Chimpanzee. Adeno virus used in CoviShield is modified to carry a corona virus gene. When CoviShield is administered the adeno virus, enters the living cell and the modified gene instructs the cell to produce SARS-CoV-2 spike proteins and display it on the surface of the healthy cells. These spike proteins are then detected by the T-cells and B-cells and our body starts building immunity whereas, the Covaxin (BBV152) is an inactivated SARS-CoV-2 virus vaccine. An inactivated virus won't cause an infection in your body as it is basically powerless. It helps our body to make SARS-CoV-2 specific antibodies with the mechanism same as of CoviShield. In [10], the author conducted a study on the effects of the pandemic on the air quality of major Indian cities. The author reported that the COVID-19 has forced many countries around the world to declare a lockdown nationwide to further prevent the spread of coronavirus in the community. On March 24, 2020, India declared a lockdown nationwide. The author analysed the quality of air of three major cities in India, which are Delhi, Kolkata and Mumbai during the lockdown phase and compared it to before and after the lockdown conditions. The author looked at seven major air pollutants and analyzed data obtained from 56 stations under the Central Pollution Control Board present across the selected cities. The author has marked the air quality indicator and the local pattern for these pollutants. According to the author, atmospheric particulate matter 2.5, 10 and carbon monoxide are the main pollutants in India which have been reduced by a rate of 52%, 39%, and 13% in Delhi, 47%, 41%, and 27% in Mumbai and 49%, 37%, and 21% in Kolkata. This study shows that the temporary closure can result into a refreshing breeze in these big cities.

In [11], the author conducted an analysis of factors related to cardiovascular risks among patients infected with COVID-19. The author wants to analyse and evaluate the increase in factors related to CVD risks among COVID-19 patients based on the Framingham risk score, and to assess the correlation of CVD risk factors with clinical outcomes. In thae cross-sectional study, the author analysed 264 confirmed cases of COVID - 19 at King Saud University in Saudi Arabia. The electrical records of patients, including the ones in the age group 18–80 are recorded and updated. The patients are classified in three FRS categories mainly low, medium and high. In these results, more than half needed a treatment regarding the serious illness and 58 patients died, merely adding up to 27%. Pneumonia, shortness of breath and kidney damage was the most common complications that are found among the patients. In [12], an analysis is conducted by the author to gain information regarding the vaccination program among the population: a cross-sectional study is done by author from 1,449 people. The author wants to put across the point that the success of the vaccination program depends on the knowledge of people about the vaccines. By increasing the people's knowledge about the vaccine and strengthening the promoters, the acceptance of vaccine program can be increased among the population. The author performed the survey with the help of Google online survey platform. A total of 1249 responses are received, with majority from the age group >38. In the survey, the author found that most of the people have limited knowledge about the vaccines in groups already suffering from some conditions. Participants having age >45 years are more willing to take the Covid-19 vaccine as they believe that the vaccine is harmless. The younger generations maily from age group <30 are more concerned about the availability of the vaccines and their validity.

The researches spurred curiosity in me to work on the Covid-19 World Vaccination Analysis with the objective of understanding and predicting how the vaccination program is being conducted all around the world.

3   Material and Method

In this section the dataset used for analysis is discussed with proposed methodology.

3.1   Dataset

The dataset used in this paper is taken from Kaggle [11], which is been updated daily regarding the vaccinations done worldwide. The data used in the proposed work is being updated till 26th April 2021. This data set is further divided into 16 columns serving different purposes which will discuss later in this section. The vaccination data is collected for 195 different countries. The length of the dataset used is 13600 on the date it was taken from the Kaggle repository. A brief description of the dataset labels is discussed further in this section to understand the dataset and make prediction. This makes easy for us to understand the dataset and make prediction. The Country and Country ISO Code helps to identify the details of vaccination used for a country. The people are differentiated for covid-19 dose by anlayzing their vaccination report like, taken 1st dose or fully vaccinated (i.e., both of the doses). Daily vaccination column describes the number of vaccinations for that particular date/country.

3.2   Proposed Work

Data obtained from the Kaggle repository contains some missing values as it is data from the real-world. The reason could be many such as data entry errors or problems related to data collection. The dataset is first cleaned and the missing values are replaced with 0.0 in order to make the results more accurate. To implement the deep learning algorithm EDA, this work follows the following approach depicted in the Fig. 1

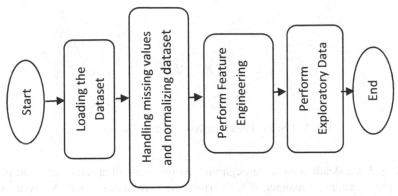

Fig. 1. Proposed model for analysis and prediction of Covid -19 on the basis of worldwide vaccination report

4   Experimental Results and Discussions

4.1   Analysis of COVID-19 Around the World

A brief overview of the Covid-19 situation, the daily confirmed cases and the deaths all around the world are depicted further in Sect. 4.1. In Fig. 2, the daily Covid-19 cases confirmed all around the world are shown. The figure shows data from 22nd January 2020 to 25th August 2021 about the new cases from Covid-19.

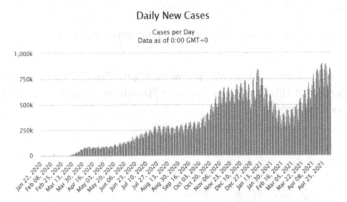

Fig. 2. Covid-19 new cases analysis through last one year

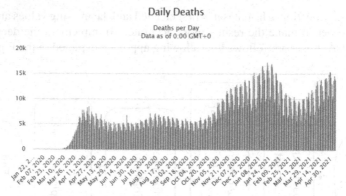

Fig. 3. Covid-19 death analysis through last one year

In Fig. 3, the death analysis through the last one year all around the world is been depicted in a graphical manner. After performing Exploratory Data Analysis on the collected dataset the results are shown with the help of graphs. For that, different libraries like matplotlib and seaborn are used. Given below are the results after implementing the algorithm:

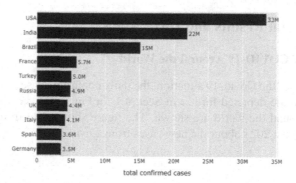

Fig. 4. Top 10 countries by total confirmed cases

In Fig. 4, the top 10 countries that are worst hit by Covid-19 pandemic are shown. The graph shows that USA leads by cases over 30 million. India and Brazil follow with 15 million cases reported.

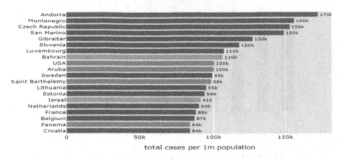

Fig. 5. Top 20 countries by total cases per 1 million population

In Fig. 5, the top countries with the greatest number of Covid-19 cases per 1 million of the population is shown. The graph shows that 14 out of top 20 are European countries, 4 are North American and remaining from Asia. Andorra is the country with most people tested positive for Covid-19. Also, 1 out of every 10 person in America has been tested positive for Covid-19.

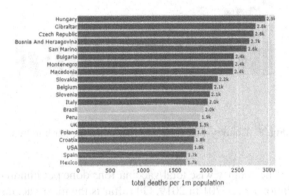

Fig. 6. Top 20 countries by total deaths per 1 million population

Figure 6 shows the top 20 countries having most deaths per 1 million of the population. Factors like age-group, chronic illness, healthcare measures and public awareness plays a crucial role in this. The graph has more European countries, 16 out of 20. Gibraltar has the greatest number of deaths as depicted in the figure followed by countries like Spain, UK and Brazil.

4.2 Analysis of Vaccination Program

After analysing the Covid-19 situation, this section discusses the analyse of the vaccination program is advancing in various countries around the world.

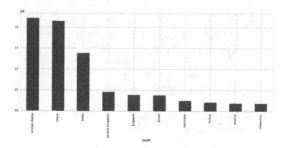

Fig. 7. Top countries in vaccination program

In Fig. 7, the graph shows that United States, United Kingdom, England, India and China are the top five country that are vaccinating maximum people in a day.

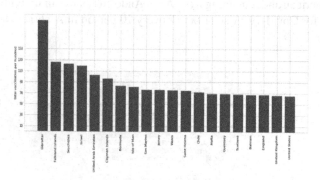

Fig. 8. Country wise total vaccinations done per hundred

Figure 8 shows the country wise total vaccinations done per hundred of population. Due to less population i.e., 33701 in 2019, Gibraltar is the most vaccinated.

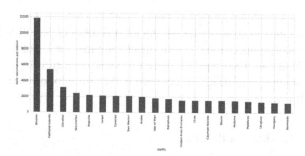

Fig. 9. Daily vaccinations in different countries in ppm

In Fig. 9, the graph shows the country in which country maximum people are being vaccinated in people per million (ppm). It has been noticed that Falkland Islands is the leading country having most people being vaccinated daily. Maybe, it's because of the low population of the islands, they cover most of the people to get vaccinated daily.

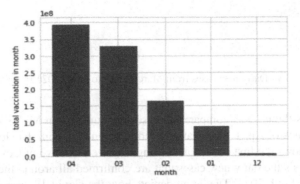

Fig. 10. Total vaccinations in a Month

In the above Fig. 10, it shows that maximum number of people got vaccinated in March all around the world. As most of the countries have the vaccinations in March, they tried to vaccinated as much as people as possible.

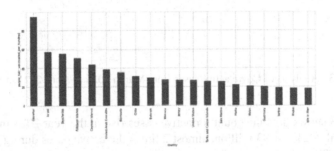

Fig. 11. People fully vaccinated in different countries

As a final result, Fig. 11 shows the countries in ascending order in which people are vaccinated the most. It is shown that because of the low population, Gabraltar have the most people vaccinated as compared to others.

4.3   Analysis and Comparison of First and Second Wave in India

India is country which is worse hit by the ongoing second wave of Covid-19. In this section, the deaths case of covid-19 in 2nd wave with the vaccination program in the country (i.e., India) is analyzed. From April – Sept, 2020, the ration of covid new cases came across the India was very high, its around thousand per day. After this tenure, the new case reported for this disease goes down. In mid of Feb 2021, the new covid cases encountered in India on daily basis and it reched to ~349k (April 24, 2021), which is

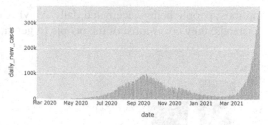

Fig. 12. Daily new cases from March 2020 to April 2021 in India

almost 3.5 times the case as compared to cases encountered in Mid-September 2020. After the first week of April, most states in India are under a complete lockdown.

Figure 12 shows the first as well as the ongoing second wave of Covid-19 in India. The graph analysis the daily new cases that are confirmed all around the country from March 2020 to March 2021. The graph depicts how the Covid-19 cases suddenly rose from under 100 k daily to more than 300 k between the spam of January 2020 to March 2021.

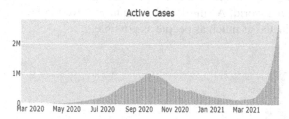

Fig. 13. Analysis of Covid active cases from March 2020 to April 2021 in India

Figure 13 shows how the count for active cases rise in the year 2021 in India. The count in April 2021 is 1.93 million, almost 2 times the active cases during the peak in September 2020.

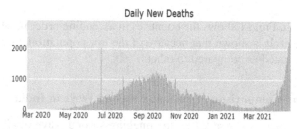

Fig. 14. Analysis of deaths by Covid-19 from March 2020 to April 2021 in India

In Fig. 14, the daily new deaths in India from March 2020 to April 2021 is shown. The graph depicts that the daily death toll is 1625 in April 2021, which is not more than 1.5 times the death toll during the peak of the first wave in India.

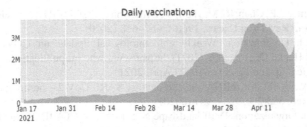

Fig. 15. Analysis of vaccination program India

In Fig. 15, an analysis of the advancement of vaccination program in India is shown. The number of vaccines being administered daily are increasing rapidly, with some periodic dips. Until now, 107 million people have received the first dose of vaccination and around 16 million people are fully vaccinated in India.

5 Conclusion and Future Scope

The Covid-19 pandemic is growing manifold daily. All around the world, the vaccination program is going at a high rate in order to vaccinate the people as soon as possible. In some parts of the world, the program is at a higher rate as compared to others. By using Exploratory Data Analysis, this paper has visualized and predicted the results and through graphs, United States, United Kingdom, England, India and China are the top five country that are vaccinating maximum people in a day. This work is not intend to develop a perfect predicting model but only analysis about the vaccination program in order to combat this disease. For future scope this research can be analyzed on the basis of dataset that is updated daily all around the world regarding the vaccinations done on daily purposes. Different Machine Learning Algorithms can be applied in order to improve the implementation phase.

References

1. Shih, H.I., Wu, C.J., Tu, Y.F., Chi, C.Y.: Fighting COVID-19: a quick review of diagnoses, therapies, and vaccines. Biomed. J. **43**(4), 341–354 (2020)
2. Chen, R.T., Pless, R., Destefano, F.: Epidemiology of autoimmune reactions induced by vaccination. J. Autoimmun. **16**(3), 309–318 (2001)
3. Kivity, S., Agmon-Levin, N., Blank, M., Shoenfeld, Y.: Infections and autoimmunity–friends or foes? Trends Immunol. **30**(8), 409–414 (2009)
4. Farez, M.F., Correale, J.: Yellow fever vaccination and increased relapse rate in travelers with multiple sclerosis. Arch. Neurol. **68**(10), 1267–1271 (2011)
5. Huttner, A., et al.: Risk of MS relapse after yellow fever vaccination: A self-controlled case series. Neurology-Neuroimmunology Neuroinflammation **7**(4) (2020)
6. Gudbjartsson, D.F., et al.: Spread of SARS-CoV-2 in the Icelandic population. New England J. Med. **382**(24), 2302–2315 (2020)
7. Huang, C., et al.: Clinical features of patients infected with 2019 novel coronavirus in Wuhan China. Lancet **395**(10223), 497–506 (2020)

8. Le, T.T., Cramer, J.P., Chen, R., Mayhew, S.: Evolution of the COVID-19 vaccine development landscape. Nat. Rev. Drug Discov. **19**(10), 667–668 (2020)
9. World Health Organization: Weekly epidemiological update on COVID-19–27 April 2021. World Health Organization (2021). https://www.who.int/publications/m/item/weekly-epidemiological-update-on-covid-19. 27 April 2021
10. Jackson, L.A., et al.: An mRNA vaccine against SARS-CoV-2—preliminary report. New England J. Med. **383**(20), 920–1931 (2020)
11. World Health Organization. Draft landscape and tracker of COVID-19 candidate vaccines. Genova, Switzerland: World Health Organization (2021). https://www.who.int/publications/m/item/draft-landscape-of-covid-19candidate-vaccines. Accessed 10 Aug 2021
12. Yi, Z.M., et al.: The implementation of a FIP guidance for COVID-19: insights from a nationwide survey. Ann. Transl. Med. **9**(18) (2021)

A Hybrid Filter/Wrapper Machine Learning Model for Classification Cancer Dataset

Ashish Sharma[1], Sandeep Vyas[1], and Anand Nayyar[2]([✉])

[1] Department of Electronics and Communication Engineering, Jaipur Engineering College and Research Center, Jaipur 302017, India
{ashishsharma.ece,dr.sandeepvyas.ee}@jecrc.ac.in
[2] Faculty of Information Technology, Duy Tan University, Da Nang 550000, Vietnam
anandnayyar@duytan.edu.vn

Abstract. Breast cancer is severe disease with high fatality rate in women. As per the National breast cancer foundation of India, one out of 5 casualties occurs due to breast cancer. Data mining techniques play a vital role in the identification of cancer cells in the early stages. In this manuscript, a comparative approach between two popular machine learning algorithms has been analyzed and results are compared in terms of future prediction of the disease. A prefiltering technique along with Support Vector Machine (SVM) and k-Nearest-Neighbor(KNN) techniques are used to enhance the performance of the model. The model is applied on Wisconsin Diagnosis Breast Cancer data set for classfication. The dataset having imbalance classes are difficult to classify because of the high probability associated with a majority of classes and algorithms classify the new data to the majority of classes only. This problem is addressed in the manuscript by introducing the refiltering of data to mitigate the effect that occurred due to class imbalance. The results are evaluated using 10-fold cross-validation. The performance of both techniques is measured based on important key parameters such as accuracy, precision, recall, F-1 score, ROC curve, standard deviation. The results are significant and competitive. The performance of both the algorithm reveals that both algorithms have significant advantages to predict and cure the disease but SVM based filterd/wrapper approach outperforms KNN approach with 98.18% accuracy in detection against the accuracy of 94.66% determined by KNN.

Keywords: Breast cancer classification · KNN · SVM · Data mining · Machine learning · Filter

A. K. Luhach et al. (Eds.): ICAICR 2021, CCIS 1575, pp. 15–29, 2022.
https://doi.org/10.1007/978-3-031-09469-9_2

1 Introduction

Machine learning has a wide variety of applications in the field of networking and healthcare. The healthcare sector mostly depends on output data prediction and visualization. Machine learning techniques may help doctors and researchers by reducing human error and improving accuracy. In health care applications, classification and prediction of diseases has always been challenging tasks for doctors. Breast cancer is one of the most common and deadly diseases among women. It affects almost two million women every year. Also, the research shows the fatality rate is highest in comparison to all other diseases. It has been reported that seven hundred thousand women die due to breast cancer every year. Among all types of cancer deaths, more than 20 women died due to breast cancer alone. The literature shows that there is no prevention technique is available to avoid breast cancer detection. Except early detection and diagnosis is the only way to reduce the fatality rate among the patients. In the initial phase, the detection of the disease and symptoms are not significant which causes diagnosis and treatment to be delayed. It has been also suggested by the National Breast Cancer Foundation (NCBF) that every woman with higher age than forty years, must go for a mammogram diagnosis every year. A mammogram is a technique used to find cancer cells using X-rays. This technique is mostly considered safe. The regular Mammogram offers a high survival rate of patients by detecting the cancer cells in early stages. Several techniques has been used to identify the breast cancer cells like biopsy, imaging techniques, physical examination. Mammography and ultrasound are imaging-based technique in which X-rays are used to generate the set images of breast cancer and the radiologist examines the results. In a biopsy, the symptoms are identified by extracting the samples from the body. These invasive surgical techniques sometimes left an impact on patient's health. Studies also reveal that 35% of results obtained using mass detection technique sometimes misleading due to poor image contrast and it is difficult for the radiologist to provide clear identification [1].

The number of researchers also provided the evidence that 70% to 80% biopsies are detected as malignant [2]. Thus, it is important to discover new techniques which provide efficient results. The Machine learning techniques with computer-aided designs may provide significant insights to the specialists (Doctors and radiologists) and can predict the result with great accuracy. Data mining techniques have become popular methods and show a wide variety of applications in various fields like bio-medical sciences, finance, and social sciences [3]. Recently, several classification algorithms have been applied to the medical dataset to predict and diagnose the patients [4,5]. As many algorithms are available in the field for the prediction and classification of the cancer dataset still a single robust universal algorithm doesn't exist. Also, many classification algorithms are don't provide significant results. All these analyses motivate researchers to explore and analyze the recently developed methodologies in the field of biomedical sciences to help the humans in early detection of fatal diseases. Many researchers also used feature extraction techniques based on various features like scale-invariant feature transform, elliptic Fourier descriptors, texture, and morphological features [6, 7]. Most of these techniques are very expensive for a common man. The texture and morphological-based classification techniques exploit the common texture features and fail to provide background features of the images. In the case of machine learning techniques, it is important to fine-tune the classifiers. In this manuscript, a comparative approach between two well-known states of art data mining techniques along with prefiltering stage is analyzed. The detailed empirical study on prefiltered support vector machine and K nearest neighbor were carried out for repeated households with 10 fold cross-validation on WBCD (original) dataset. The filtering approach is applied to abstract the most important features to reduce the computational complexity of CAD model. The proposed technique shows that by incorporating the filtered approach, the performance of state of art classifiers has been improved significantly in terms of performance measures. The findings in the paper indicate that filtered-based machine learning models are better to practice in the classification task. The results obtained from both the techniques are compared in terms of precision, accuracy, recall, and F-1 score. The preprocessing of data is performed using resampling filters. The results obtained in terms of statistical parameters are used to check the superiority of one algorithm over the other. In this manuscript, 7291 data instances of breast cancer detection with a dimension size of 9 rows and 698 columns are used. In summary, the original contribution of this manuscript is are as follows

- To present and demonstrate enhanced filtered based classification model with application in cancer cell detection.
- Comparative analysis between filtered SVM and KNN classifiers.
- To design a model which is able to discriminate benign and malign breast tumors using a public dataset
- To enahnce model classfication accuracy at least 90%.
- To provide a tool to a medical specialist, seeking to lessen the amount of misdiagnosis and contribution in early diagnosis of cancer.

The rest of the manuscript is oragnized in following way. In Sect. 2, a Literature survey about the various data mining techniques in the field of biomedical science is explored. In Sect. 3, various machine learning algorithms and their key parameters and performance index are defined. In Sect. 4, a comparison between the Support vector machine (SVM) and K nearest neighbor approach is illustrated after applying to the cancer dataset. Results obtained are discussed followed by a conclusion in Sect. 5.

2   Literature Review

Due to the complexity and severity related to breast cancer, early detection of the disease is always the field of interest among researchers and scientists. Recently, many classification algorithms has been applied to the medical dataset of the patients. All these algorithms show promising results and motivate researchers to solve the more complex and challenging issues of society. The literature shows that various types of techniques are available for the detection of cancer cells but still no single best algorithm exists. Recently, Alghodhaifi et al. [8] proposed a convolutional neural network-based model to detect invasive ductal carcinoma in breast histology images with an accuracy of 90%. Gayathri et al. [9] used the Relevance Vector Machine on Wisconsin original dataset for identification of cancer cells, and an accuracy of 97% was achieved. Khayra et al. [10] used the naïve based approach and used different weights to distinct attributes concerning their ability of prediction and achieved 93% accuracy. Gayathri et al. proposed a new model based on the fuzzy inference method called Mamdani Fuzzy inference model [11]. In this method, cancer cells are detected using Linear Discriminant Analysis for feature selection and Mamdani Fuzzy inference model is used to train the dataset. The model achieved accuracy of 93%. In the year 2007, Mohd et al. [12] compared several machine learning techniques using open source Weka software. This analysis was limited to introduction purpose only. Recently, researchers are also exploring the possibility of soft computing techniques in the field of cancer detection in the early stages. In this regard, Choudhury et al. [13] designed a soft computing model for the detection of cancer, heart disease and arthritis. Later the same author introduced the genetic algorithm-based approach in the detection, classification, and clustering of the lung cancer dataset [14]. In the year 2020, Solanki et al. [15] demonstrated a transfer learning-based model to improve the identification accuracy in breast cancer detection. Devi et al. [16] designed a very efficient fusion model of deep learning and image processing techniques in breast cancer diagnosis. All these studies reveal that breast cancer classification and prediction have always been the field of interest among researchers and scientist. Pathel et al. [17] introduced a new method for breast image segmentation based on the identification of micro-calcification. An adaptive k means algorithm was used but model accuracy was poor due to overfitting. Dheeba et al. [18] proposed a method based on swarm intelligence and neural networks for the detection of cancer. The result of this approach was better but the only drawback was high computational cost because of the possible solution given by several samples.

3   Materials and Methods

Machine learning techniques can be classified as the part of artificial intelligence which is capable of learning and understanding the system based on the training dataset. In literature, several techniques are available which enables systems to understand and learn. The techniques are data clustering, classification, deep neural networks, and decision trees, etc. Machine learning techniques are classified into three main categories [19], supervised learning and unsupervised learning, and reinforcement learning.

3.1   Materials

The proposed model is tested on famous Wisconsin Diagnosis Breast Cancer data. The details about the dataset is gven below

– Wisconsin Breast Cancer data set
  The model is tested on Wisconsin Diagnosis Breast Cancer data set down-
  loaded from 'UCI ML' repository. The dataset comprises 11 attributes and
  699 number of instances in which 458 are bening and 241 are malignant [9].
  In the WBC dataset, 16 records related to Bare Nuclei are missing so the
  preprocessing of data is performed to deal with the imbalance and missing
  values in the dataset. The important statistics are given in Table 1.

3.2   Methods

3.2.1   Classification Techniques and Other

Following are the fundamental techniques used for classification of the data. T

– **Supervised Learning**
  In this method, a function is created based on a labeled input dataset. Then
  the function is used to classify the future input data or predict the outcomes
  accurately. The supervised learning future is classified to handle two kinds of
  problems that is classification and regression.
– **Unsupervised Learning**
  In this technique, the algorithm classifies the input data based on patterns
  that exist in the input dataset which is not classified earlier. In this technique, the machine tries to identify the dataset by its mechanism. Unsupervised learning is more unpredictable. In reinforcement learning, the machine
  is trained in such a way that it generates a sequence of decisions. Machine
  tries to find the solution using trial and error methods.
  Reinforcement Learning
  In reinforcement learning, the machine is trained in such a way that it generates a sequence of decisions. Machine tries to find the solution using trial
  and error methods.

3.3   Support Vector Machine Approach for Data Classification

The support vector machine [20] classifies the data using hyperplanes in N-
dimensional space. Here N represents the N number of features. This hyperplane
classifies the data according to the number of features. Hyperplanes work as
decision boundaries that discriminate the data into several classes. The dataset
classified across the sides of hyperplanes is considered to be of a different class.
Figure 1 represents the process of Support vector machine classification. Here
three hyperplanes H1, H2, and H3 are used to classify the dataset based on the
features. In the proposed model, dataset is seggregated into training and testing for phase , the trining is performed on 1589 instances and 865 observations
have been used testing. The estimator is also set to 140 to ensure that every
observation must be analyzed and a prediction is made. The performance of the
proposed model is analyzed with the help of a confusion matrix. The confusion
matrix for the support vector machine has provided very good results. There

is a very less number of observation that identifies the value misleading in case of Benign and no observation is misinterpreted in case of Malignant and overall accuracy of the model is 98%. The confusion matrix of the support vector machine is quite promising.

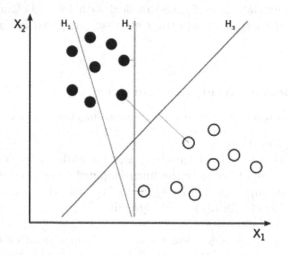

Fig. 1. A graphical representation of support vector machine

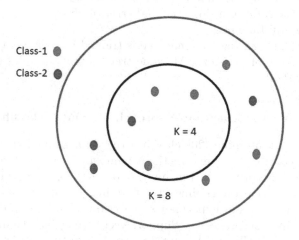

Fig. 2. Illustrative diagram of k-nearest neighbour approach

3.4 K-Nearest-Neighbor (kNN) Approach for Data Classification

k nearest neighbor [21] is another popular machine learning approach to find the data classes. In the K nearest neighbor approach, the datapoints are classified in K number of classes for training that exist in the near surroundings of the test data point. As the new data enters the nearby region, KNN collects all the data points close to it. The large degree of variation is the important parameter that helps in determining the distance vector. Figure 2 represents the simple classification model of the K nearest neighbor approach. Here the N training vectors are given, K nearest neighbor technique finds the number of K neighbors irrespective of labels. The KNN neighbor approach gives an accuracy of 94.66%. In this technique, only one observation is found misleading which is classified as Benign and observation is classified as Malignant.

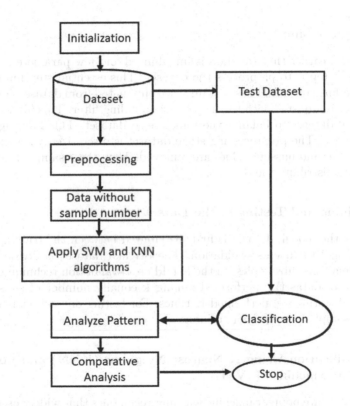

Fig. 3. Flow chart of proposed machine learning model.

4 Proposed Model

The proposed model comprises of various stages to classify the breast cancer dataset. Figure 3 represents stepwise procedure for proposed technique. KNN and

SVM performs well in most of the classification task but incase of overlapping or complex dataset results are misleading. In proposed model, resampling technique in preprocessing stage has been associated with the classification techiques to improve the accuracy of the model. A detailed discussion about every step is mentioned in the following subsections.

Table 1. Number of parameters used in the dataset

Dataset	Number of attributes	Number of instances	No of class
WDCB dataset	32	569	2

4.1   Preprocessing

As mentioned earlier that the data is imbalanced and few parameters are missing, the first step is to preprocess the dataset. This essential step improves the classifier performance. All missing values are eliminated from dataset. The imbalance dataset is adjusted with the help of a resampling filter. This filter generates the artificial dataset to balance the imbalanced dataset. This filtering stage is shown in Fig. 3. The preprocessing stage dataset is discretized with the help of a discrete filter and missing values are removed. Then the resample filter is used to uniformly distribute the dataset.

4.2   Training and Testing of the Datset

To evaluate the model, dataset is first distributed between the training set and test set using 10 fold cross-validation. The original dataset is divided into 10 different equal-size subsamples. In the K fold cross-validation technique, random distribution of dataset is performed among k equally number of subsets. The training and testing are performed K times. For testing one subset is used and remaining samples are used for training.

4.3   Classification Using K Nearest Neighbor (KNN) and Support Vector Machines (SVM)

KNN and SVM are popular machine learning techniques that widely used in classication purpose. Each of the algorithms has its advantages and disadvantages over each other in terms of classification performance which largely depends upon the dataset used. Table 2 represents the comparison between both algorithms. As shown in Table 2, the time complexity in the case of SVM is higher than the KNN. SVM comprises of N training samples with dimension d. For KNN algorithms, N training samples are N and K is a random number of samples at the node.

Table 2. Comparison between KNN and support vector machine

Parameter	KNN	Support vector machine
Time complexity (Training phase)	$O(n^2)$	$O(n^3)$
Problem type	Classification and regression	Classification and regression
Accuracy	Provides high accuracy with large data	Provides high accuracy with greater number of features
Model parameter	Non-Parametric	Parametric

4.4 Performace Measure

The output variable is classified as bening which comprises 357 number of observations or classified as malignant which comprises 212 number of observations. The positively classified variables are considered benign cases and negatively classified as a malignant cases. The results for both the techniques are also displayed in Fig. 4 and Fig. 5 in terms f the confusion matrix.

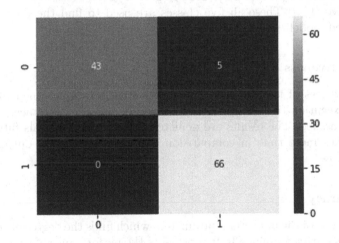

Fig. 4. A confusion matrix obtained in case of filtered SVM

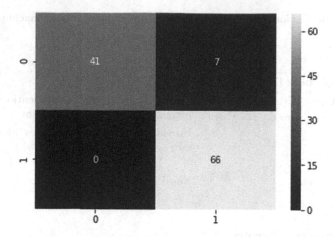

Fig. 5. A confusion matrix obtained in case of filtered KNN

The performance of the machine learning techniques is measured using various parameters [22]. A confusion matrix is one of the parameters calculated for both the actual and predicted class of the dataset in terms of five standard values called True Positive (TP), True Negative (TN), False Positive (FP), and false-negative (FN). These all five classes are used to find the performance of the proposed model.

4.5   Effectiveness

The effectiveness of the classification model has been determined in terms of accuracy, execution time of the model, correctly classified instances and incorrect data classfied. The results are depicted in Table 3, it reveals filtered SVM classfier takes more time in comparision to other models but outperfroms in other matrices.

4.6   Accuracy

Accuracy is one of the important parameters which finds the degree of correctness or exactness during training [3]. It represents the performance of the model. It is helpful in the identification and measuring of the correct prediction concerning wrong predictions. The mathematical formulation of accuracy is given as

$$Accuracy = \frac{TP + TN}{TP + TN + FP + FN} \tag{1}$$

The accuracy of the model is given in Table 3.

Table 3. Obtained parameters for the proposed model

Classfier	KNN classifier	SVM classifier	Filtered KNN classfier	Filtered SVM classifier
Correct instances identified	553	518	661	686
Incorrect insatances identified	34	33	30	19
Accuracy	79.3%	74.2%	94.66%	98.18%
Time	0.06	0.01	0.08	0.09

4.7 Recall

Generally recall is also called sensitivity. The recall is defined as the correlation between correct positive instances to all the measures instances. Recall [3] helps to measure the cost and predicting positives. It also helps in finding the effectiveness of the system.

$$Recall = \frac{TP}{TP + FN} \tag{2}$$

Recall value in case of all models are given in Table 4.

Table 4. Recall values identified from the proposed model

Classfier	Begin	Malignant	Average
KNN	0.94	1	0.92
SVM	0.95	1	0.925
Filtered KNN	0.96	1	0.93
Filtered SVM	0.97	1	0.985

4.8 Precision

The precision is used to measure the degree of correctness in positive instances. The degree of correctness is the ratio of true positive instances to overall instances [3]. It measures the system capability for positive instances and does not give any information regarding negative instances. The Table 5 represents the precision values of SVM, KNN and filtered SVM and KNN models.

$$Recall = \frac{TP}{TP + FP} \tag{3}$$

Table 5. Precision score identified from the proposed model

Classfier	Begin	Malignant	Average
KNN	1	0.92	0.89
SVM	1	0.90	0.85
Filtered KNN	1	0.95	0.0.97
Filtered SVM	1	0.96	0.98

4.9   F1 Score

F1 represents the weighted mean value of the precision and Recall. It considers only false values. The unity value of the F1 score is considered as a perfect score while it considers as a total failure when it is zero (Table 6).

$$Recall = \frac{Precision * recall}{Precision + Recall} \tag{4}$$

Table 6. F-1 score identified from proposed model

Classfier	Begin	Malignant	Average
KNN	0.96	0.97	0.91
SVM	0.97	0.97	0.92
Filtered KNN	0.997	0.996	0.997
Filtered SVM	0.998	0.998	0.998

5   Results, Analysis and Discussion

In this manuscript, a comparative analysis between two famous machine learning algorithms is performed using Support Vector Machine (SVM), and kNN (k-Nearest-Neighbor). The algorithm is performed on Intel core i7 processor-based Windows 10 operating system with 8 Gb of RAM. Several open-source Python libraries are used like Scikit-learn, pandas, and NumPy which are freely available. All the programs are implemented on Jupyter notebook. The testing of the classifier is performed by utilizing the K-fold cross-validation technique. The dataset is segregated using 10 fold mechanism and separated into 10 different chunks. The 9 fold has been applied for the training and the remaining applied for the testing. The number of observations for the training of the dataset is 465 and the remaining are used for the testing purpose out of a total of 569 observations. The results are displayed as shown in Tables 7, 8 and 9. Initially,

Table 7. Classifiction performance obtained from the proposed model

Experiment stages	Classification accuracy	
	SVM	KNN
Unprocessed dataset	79.3%	74.2%
Preprocessed dataset	84.6%	82.9%
After first resmpling of data D1	87.3%	84.3%
After second resmpling of data D2	91.66%	87.66%
After third resmpling of data D3	93.62%	90.89%
After fourth resmpling of data D4	97.50%	93.5%
After fifth resmpling of data D5	97.66%	94.5%
After six resmpling of data D6	98.13%	94.61%
After seventh resmpling of data D7	98.18%	94.66%

Table 8. Accuracy measure obtained from the proposed model filtered KNN classifer

True positive	False positive	Precsion	Recall	Roc curve	Std	Class
0.997	0.003	0.997	0.995	0.996	0.28	Bening
0.997	0.003	0.996	0.993	0.995	0.28	Malignent

Table 9. Accuracy measure obtained from the proposed model filtered SVM classifer

True positive	False positive	Precsion	Recall	Roc curve	Std	Class
1.0	0.048	0.989	0.997	1.0	0.56	Bening
0.961	0.000	1	0.997	0.951	0.56	Malignent

both the classification algorithms are applied original dataset It shows that the performance of the support vector machine has higher accuracy, precision, recall, and F-1 score. It clearly shows that the SVM technique outperforms the KNN approach in every parameter. Table 7 represent the performance of the proposed model in terms of classifiers accuracy. The results show a significant improvement in the accuracy when both the techniques are incorporated with a resampling filter. The reason behind this is that imbalanced data generate biased results. After the addition of the filter stage, it maintains the class distribution. As shown in Table 7, The accuracy also improves as the number of resampling filters increases. Support vector machine provides the best results and outperforms the KNN classifier in terms of accuracy. The results obtained from the proposed model are superior to the standard SVM and KNN approaches.

The results shown in Tables 8 and 9 represents in terms of accuracy measures. By incorporating the re-sampling and preprocessing stage before both the classifiers dataset, it is observed that the performance of the proposed model has been increased significantly.

6   Conclusion and Future Work

Breast cancer is one of the deadliest diseases among Indian women. It has been observed that one woman chosen randomly out of 12 is found infected with breast cancer [17]. Early identification and diagnosis is the only way to save the life of a human being. In this manuscript, a comparative analysis is performed between two well-known machine learning techniques for the identification of cancer cells. The SVM and KNN are wrapped with preprocessing filters and applied to Wisconsin Diagnosis Breast Cancer data set for the classification. Both the algorithms show significant results and it has been observed that accuracy in the case of both the algorithms is found more than 94%, for the identification of benign tumor or malignant tumor. The results are shown in Tables 8 and 9, it has been also observed that SVM has higher values of performance indices in comparison to KNN approach. The results obtained reveal that SVM along with preprocessing filters is the most efficient in the identification of breast cancer with the highest accuracy, precision, and F1 score over the filtered KNN algorithms. Thus the machine learning techniques are helpful in the field of biomedical science for the detection of cancer cells. It is also a promising field in cancer research and analysis.

From the result obtained from the proposed model, it is evident that pre-filtering stage before the classfication techniques could improve the classification accuracy, decreases the cost and computational complexity of the model. In future, prefiltering stage along with feature extractor and start of art classfication techniques could generate higher accuracy. Finally, Increasing the number of filtering stage with purpose of decreasing the error classification rate can provide the better accuracy of the model.

References

1. Cheng, H.D., Shi, X.J., Min, R., Hu, L.M., Cai, X.P., Du, H.N.: Approaches for automated detection and classification of masses in mammograms. Pattern Recogn. **39**(4), 646–668 (2006)
2. Rathore, S., Hussain, M., Aksam Iftikhar, M., Jalil, A.: Ensemble classification of colon biopsy images based on information rich hybrid features. Comput. Biol. Med. **47**(1), 76–92 (2014)
3. Darrab, S., Ergenc, B., Vertical pattern mining algorithm for multiple support thresholds. In: International Conference on Knowledge Based and Intelligent Information and Engineering (KES), Procedia Computer Science, vol. 112, pp. 417–426 (2017)
4. Asri, H., Mousannif, H., Al, M.H., Noel, T.: Using machine learning algorithms for breast cancer risk prediction and diagnosis. Procedia Comput. Sci. **83**, 1064–1069 (2016)
5. Saabith, A.L.S., Sundararajan, E., Bakar, A.A.: Comparative study on different classification techniques for breast cancer dataset. Int. J. Comput. Sc. Mob. Comput. **3**(10), 185–191 (2014)
6. Rathore, S., Hussain, M., Khan, A.: Automated colon cancer detection using hybrid of novel geometric features and some traditional features. Comput. Biol. Med. **65**(March), 279–296 (2015)

7. Rathore, S., Iftikhar, A., Ali, A., Hussain, M., Jalil, A.: Capture largest included circles: an approach for counting red blood cells. In: Chowdhry, B.S., Shaikh, F.K., Hussain, D.M.A., Uqaili, M.A. (eds.) IMTIC 2012. CCIS, vol. 281, pp. 373–384. Springer, Heidelberg (2012). https://doi.org/10.1007/978-3-642-28962-0_36

8. Alghodhaifi, H., Alghodhaifi, A., Alghodhaifi, M.: Predicting Invasive Ductal Carcinoma in breast histology images using Convolutional Neural Network. In: 2019 IEEE National Aerospace and Electronics Conference (NAECON), pp. 374–378 (2019)

9. Breast Cancer Wisconsin Dataset. Available at: UCI Machine Learning Repository

10. Kharya, S., Soni, S.: Weighted Naïve Bayes classifier -Predictive model for breast cancer detection, January (2016)

11. Gayathri, B.M., Sumathi, C.P.: Mamdani fuzzy inference system for breast cancer risk detection (2015)

12. Mohd, F., Thomas, M.: Comparison of different classification techniques using WEKA for Breast cancer (2007)

13. Choudhury, T., Kumar, V., Nigam, D.: An innovative smart soft computing methodology towards disease (cancer, heart disease, arthritis) detection in an earlier stage and in a smarter way. Int. J. Comput. Sci. Mob. Commun. (IJCSMC) 3(4), 368–388 (2014)

14. Choudhury, T., Kumar, V., Nigam, D.: Intelligent classification & clustering of lung & oral cancer through decision tree & genetic algorithm. Int. J. Adv. Res. Comput. Sci. Softw. Eng. 5(12), 501–510 (2015)

15. Anand, Solanki, A., Nayyar, A.: Transfer learning to improve breast cancer detection on unannotated screening mammography. In: Luhach, A.K., Jat, D.S., Bin Ghazali, K.H., Gao, XZ., Lingras, P. (eds.) ICAICR 2020. CCIS, vol. 1393, pp. 563–576. Springer, Singapore (2021). https://doi.org/10.1007/978-981-16-3660-8_53

16. Ajantha Devi, V., Nayyar, A.: Fusion of deep learning and image processing techniques for breast cancer diagnosis. In: Kose, U., Alzubi, J. (eds.) Deep Learning for Cancer Diagnosis. SCI, vol. 908, pp. 1–25. Springer, Singapore (2021). https://doi.org/10.1007/978-981-15-6321-8_1

17. Moftah, H.M., Azar, A.T., Al-Shammari, E.T., Ghali, N.I., Hassanien, A.E., Shoman, M.: Adaptive k-means clustering algorithm for MR breast image segmentation. Neural Comput. Appl. 24(7–8), 1917–1928 (2014)

18. Dheeba, J., Singh, N.A., Selvi, S.T.: Computer-aided detection of breast cancer on mammograms: a swarm intelligence optimized wavelet neural network approach. J. Biomed. Inform. 49, 45–52 (2014)

19. Quinlan, R.C.: 4.5: Programs for Machine Learning. Morgan Kaufmann Publishers Inc., San Francisco (1993)

20. Noble, W.S.: What is a support vector machine? Nat. Biotechnol. 24(12), 1565–1567 (2006)

21. Peterson, L.E.: K-nearest neighbor. Scholarpedia 4(2), 1883 (2009)

22. Hossin, M., Md Nasir, S.: A review on evaluation metrics for data classification evaluations. Int. J. Data Min. Knowl. Manag. Process 5(2), 1 (2015)

Segmentation of Tumor Region from Mammogram Images Using Deep Learning Approach

M. Ravikumar, P. G. Rachana$^{(\boxtimes)}$, and B. J. Shivaprasad

Department of Computer Science, Kuvempu University,
Jnanasahyadri, Shimoga, India
pgrachana@gmail.com

Abstract. Breast cancer is most common among different cancers that affect women and it is the second main cause for cancer deaths in women all over world. In order to increase the survival rate breast cancer must be detected and treated the earliest. Enhancement of mammograms is much needed in order to improve contrast of images which further helps in better segmentation. In this paper, method for segmentation using U-NET after enhancing the mammogram image with CLAHE (Contrast limited Adaptive Histogram Equalization) is proposed. A comparision analysis is carried out between proposed method and mammogram image segmentation without enhancement, it is found that enhanced mammogram image provides better segmentation results. Experimentation is done using publicly available DDSM (Digital Database for Screening Mammography) dataset.

Keywords: Enhancement · CLAHE · Segmentation · U-Net

1 Introduction

The average life expectancy of human being is decreasing gradually, affected by insalubrious food habits, lifestyle, gene mutation and hormonal changes which may result in origination of deadliest disease, cancer is one among such diseases. Breast cancer is the second most common cause of deaths in women around the world [1]. Breast Cancer being common among women must be detected and treated as early as possible, as early detection helps in increasing the rate of survival. Mammography is a widely used screening technique for screening breast cancer which can be done using low dosage x-rays to analyse human breasts. Asymmetrical breast tissues, adenopathy, density, microcalifications, and masses are some of the abnormalities that can be seen on mammograms. Breast masses are found to play a crucial role in the development of breast cancer.

Enhancement of mammogram images helps in better segmentation, which further helps in detecting subtle signs of cancer and makes abnormality easier to identify. In order to enhance images, spatial or frequency domain enhancement

A. K. Luhach et al. (Eds.): ICAICR 2021, CCIS 1575, pp. 30–42, 2022.
https://doi.org/10.1007/978-3-031-09469-9_3

techniques can be used, which removes noise, improves contrast and preserves edges. In the past few years, various algorithms for breast cancer segmentation have been widely studied, such as convolutional neural networks (CNN), these networks are introduced to avoid the problem of overfitting data that occur in multilayer perceptron and it is considered as its regularized version and U-Net is a one such convolutional neural network primarily developed to segment biomedical images. Its major advantage lies in usage of global location and context at the same time.

To provide a better understanding, remaining article is organized in the following order related work is discussed in Sect. 2, In Sect. 3 the proposed methodology is discussed in detail with enhancement technique with output images, and Sect. 4 discusses the results and Sect. 5 concludes the paper.

2   Review of Literature

For enhancement of mammogram images various spatial domain enhancement techniques and frequency domain enhancement techniques are used, such as logarithmic transformation [2], power-law transformation, histogram equalization [3,9–14], contrast limited adaptive histogram equalization [4,11–15], median filter [5], Bilateral filter [6], Butterworth filter [7], Gaussian filter [8], Dina A. Ragab et al. [16] in their paper used CLAHE method for image enhancement, Habib Dhahri et al. [17] and Anji Reddy Vaka et al. [18] in their methods used gaussian filter for enhancement of mammogram images during preprocessing.

For segmentation of medical images, convolutional neural networks are majorly used. Timothy de Moor et al. [19] presented a method that detects and segments soft tissue lesions in digital mammography using a u-net deep learning network. Shuyi Li et al. [20] presented the Attention Dense U-Net technique, which can separate breast masses in real time without the need for feature extraction and parameter selection manually as in classic segmentation algorithms. Using a U-Net architecture, Xiaobo Lai suggested a DBT mass automated segmentation algorithm. Md Shamim Hossain [21] introduced an automated approach and segments any micro-calcification in the mammogram images using modified u-net segmentation networks. Hui Sun et al. [22] proposed a novel attention-guided dense-upsampling network (AUNet) for accurate breast mass segmentation using a complete mammogram images directly. Vivek Kumar Singh et al. [23] proposed a conditional Generative Adversarial Network (CGAN) which segments the breast tumor present in mammogram images by segmenting the region of interest which certainly hold tumor region.

Compared to traditional segmentation methods, U-Net architecture provides multiple advantages, it provides pixel-accurate semantic segmentation, it is fast to compute, works well even with limited dataset and its architecture is easy to understand. Next section details the methodology.

3   Proposed Work

In this part, the proposed method for segmentation of mammogram images is discussed in detail and the block diagram for proposed method is given in Fig. 1.

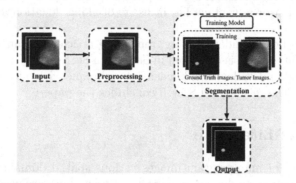

Fig. 1. Block diagram for proposed method.

3.1   Preprocessing

Mammogram images are obtained from DDSM dataset and are preprocessed in order to enhance the mammogram images. For enhancement different spatial enhancement techniques are used, in that CLAHE technique gives better enhancement than other spatial enhancement methods. Hence, CLAHE method is used in enhancement of mammogram images.

3.2   Data Augmentation

Since the dataset under consideration for testing is small. To minimise overfitting, we artificially supplement the training images to build a larger dataset. Geometrical operations such as translations, rotations, shears, and cropping are commonly used to create augmented images.

3.3   Segmentation

Segmentation is done using deep learning technique U-Net segmentation; the U-Net architecture is shown in Fig. 2. Input images are of size 256 * 256 pixels, which undergo processing through layers of convolutional networks and max-pooling, and then upsampling is done by concatenation of respective convolution layer and previous up sample layer. Finally, the segmented output accuracy is compared with output obtained with image segmented without enhancement.

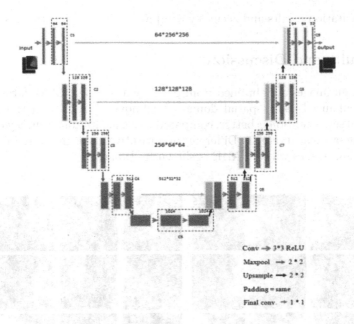

Fig. 2. U-Net architecture for corresponding input.

3.3.1 Encoding Path

The encoding path is made up of a series of stages. Each move comprises of two convolutional 3×3 filters for feature extraction, as well as a 2×2 max-pooling function for downsampling the input image and the ReLU activation function. Features are multiplied at each polling stage by breaking down the down-sampling into multiple stages. The final encoded footpath is large in size and contains a lot of data.

3.3.2 Decoder Path

Following feature extraction in the encoding path, the decoder path begins upsampling in order to build a segmented mask of dimension same as that of input image. The feature maps from the encoding path are copied to the decoding path. These feature maps are affected by the upsampling function's output.

3.3.3 Training and Optimization

In order to increase the number of input samples and to reduce the over-fitting problem, data augmentation is done. After augmentation data is trained and optimization is done using Adam optimization, which is used to minimize the cost function soft dice metrics. The ground truth masks are used in training and optimize by using cross-entropy loss.

$$L\left(N,m\right) = \sum_{p=1}^{q} R\left(m,p\right) logt\left(Q=p \mid N\right) \qquad (1)$$

The segmentation results and accuracy comparison is shown in the next section.

4   Results and Discussion

Mammogram images are obtained from publicly available DDSM dataset. Then they are enhanced using spatial domain technique CLAHE and the obtained accuracy of segmentation is better, compared to segmentation accuracy of images without enhancement Fig. 3. Different quantitative measures after enhancing mammogram images with CLAHE is shown in Table 1.

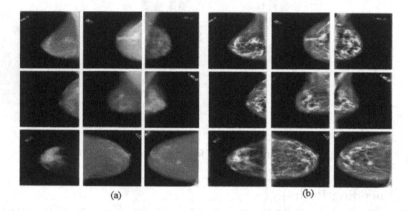

(a)   (b)

Fig. 3. Mammogram Breast images results of (a) original images and (b) enhanced images.

4.1   Segmentation Without Enhancement

Here, no preprocessing methods are used to enhance the image. Mammogram images are segmented with U-Net method. Results are given in Fig. 4.

4.2   Segmentation with Enhancement

In this, spatial domain filter CLAHE method is used for preprocessing. After enhancement, mammogram images are segmented with U-Net method. Results are given in Fig. 5.

Then performance measures of proposed method is compared with different segmentation methods such as (M1) SegNet, (M2) UNet and (M3)XNet. Below graph shows performance measures of different segmentation methods. Performance comparision is given in Table 2 and its respective graphical representation is shown in Fig. 6. The proposed methods performance is analyzed using different metrics such as precision, recall, accuracy and loss shown in Figs. 7, 8, 9, 10, 11, 12, 13, 14 and 15.

Table 1. Different quantitative values of CLAHE

Images	Entropy	MC	PSNR	SSIM	AMBE	NRMSE
1	5.94	1.0	11.18	0.69	34.86	1.0
2	9.89	1.0	8.89	0.45	61.38	1.0
3	6.77	1.0	9.28	0.63	47.97	1.0
4	8.44	1.0	14.02	0.56	24.14	0.99
5	6.99	0.96	11.65	0.65	33.08	1.0
6	8.44	1.0	11.16	0.55	40.88	1.0
7	11.29	1.0	7.2	0.35	78.95	1.0
8	7.77	0.98	12.08	0.59	35.36	0.99
9	5.83	1.0	9.6	0.68	42.55	1.0
10	7.05	1.0	8.25	0.61	54.91	1.0

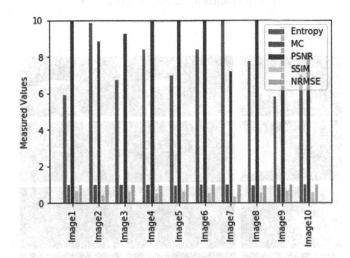

Fig. 4. Different values of CLAHE.

Table 2. Comparision of different segmentation methods for performance measures.

Methods	Accuracy	Precision	Recall	F1-score
M1	0.88	0.70	0.75	0.70
M2	0.90	0.75	0.78	0.72
M3	0.91	0.80	0.82	0.78
Proposed	**0.92**	**0.88**	**0.87**	**0.80**

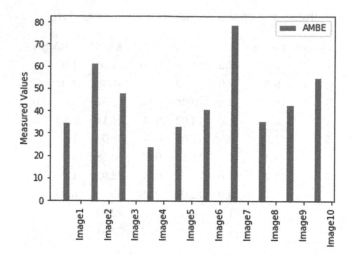

Fig. 5. Different values of CLAHE.

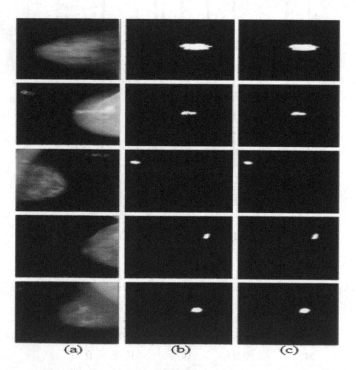

Fig. 6. Tumor segmentation results without enhancement (a) original images, (b) ground truth and (c) predicted.

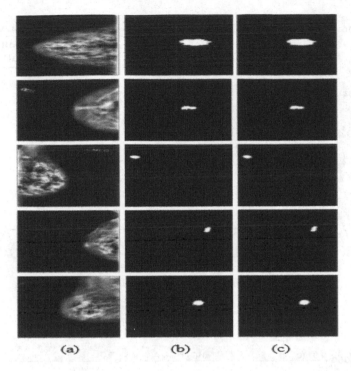

Fig. 7. Tumor segmentation results with enhancement (a) original images, (b) ground truth and (c) predicted.

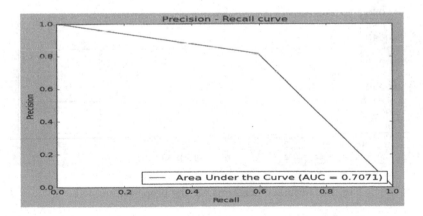

Fig. 8. ROC diagrams of the proposed work for segmentation.

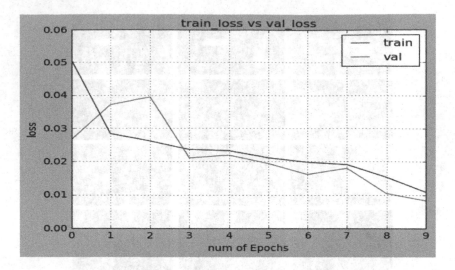

Fig. 9. Loss diagrams for the proposed method.

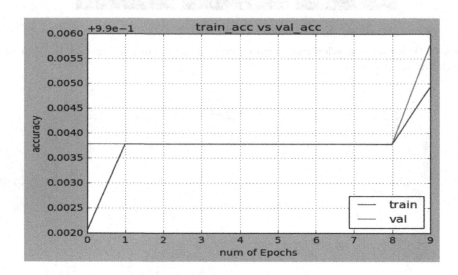

Fig. 10. Accuracy diagrams for the proposed method.

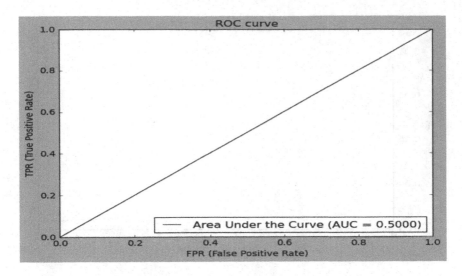

Fig. 11. ROC diagrams for the proposed method.

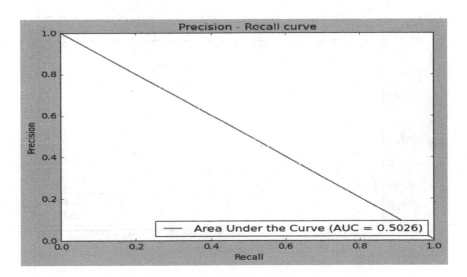

Fig. 12. Precision-recall curve for the proposed method.

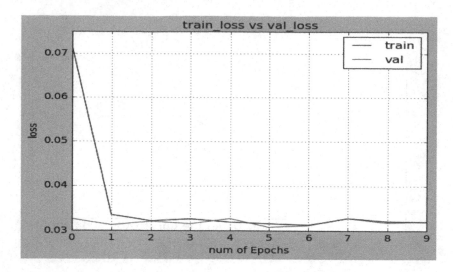

Fig. 13. Loss diagrams for the proposed method.

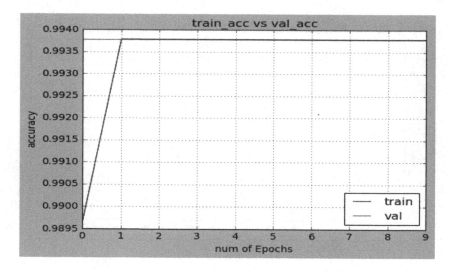

Fig. 14. Accuracy diagrams for the proposed method.

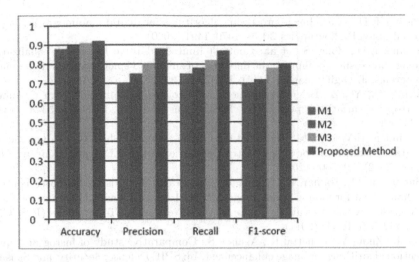

Fig. 15. Graphical representation of comparison between different segmentation methods.

5 Conclusion

In this paper, segmentation method using UNET after image enhancement is proposed. For enhancement CLAHE method is considered which was found better among different spatial domain filtering methods. It is found that enhanced images gives better segmentation results when compared with images without enhancement.

References

1. Fear, E.C., Meaney, P.M., Stuchly, M.A.: Microwaves for breast cancer detection. IEEE Potentials **22**, 12–18 (2003)
2. Maini, R., Aggarwal, H.: A comprehensive review of image enhancement technique. J. Comput. **2**(3) (2010). ISSN 2151–9617
3. Saini, V., Gulati, T.: A comparative study on image enhancement using image fusion. Int. J. Adv. Res. Comput. Sci. Softw. Eng. **2**(10) (2012)
4. Ali, M.: REZA: realization of the contrast limited adaptive histogram equalization (CLAHE) for real-time image enhancement. J. VLSI Sig. Proc. **38**, 35–44 (2004)
5. Ko, S.-J.: Center weighted median filters and their applications to image enhancement. IEEE Trans. Circuits Syst. **38**, 984–993 (1991)
6. Tomasi, C., Manduchi, R.: Bilateral filtering for gray and color images. In: Proceedings of the 1998 IEEE International Conference on Computer Vision, Bombay, India (1998)
7. Gairola, A.C., Shah, O.A.: Design and implementation of low pass Butterworth filter. IJCRT **6** (2018). ISSN: 2320–2882
8. Seddik, H., Braiek, E.B.: Efficient noise removing based optimized smart dynamic Gaussian filter. Int. J. Comput. Appl. (0975–8887) **51**(5) (2012)

9. Pisano, E.D., et al.: Image processing algorithms for digital mammography: a pictorial essay. Radiographics **20**(5), 1479–1491 (2000)

10. Pisano, E.D., Zong, S., et al.: Contrast limited adaptive histogram equalization image processing to improve the detection of simulated spiculations in dense mammograms. J. Digit. Imaging **11**(4), 193–200 (1998)

11. Wang, C., Ye, Z.: Brightness preserving histogram equalization with maximum entropy: a variational perspective. IEEE Trans. Consum. Electron. **51**(4), 1326–1334 (2005)

12. Abdullah-Al-Wadud, M., Kabir, M.H., Dewan, M.A.A., Chae, O.: A dynamic histogram equalization for image contrast enhancement. IEEE Trans. Consum. Electron. **53**(2), 593–600 (2007)

13. Sundaram, M., Ramar, K., Arumugam, N., Prabin, G.: Histogram based contrast enhancement for mammogram images. In: 2011 International Conference on Signal Processing, Communication, Computing and Networking Technologies (ICSCCN), pp. 842–846. IEEE (2011)

14. Lu, L., Zhou, Y., Panetta, K., Agaian, S.: Comparative study of histogram equalization algorithms for image enhancement. In: SPIE Defense, Security, and Sensing. International Society for Optics and Photonics (2010)

15. Sivaramakrishna, R., Obuchowski, N.A., Chilcote, W.A., Cardenosa, G., Powell, K.A.: Comparing the performance of mammographic enhancement algorithms: a preference study. Am. J. Roentgenol. **175**(1), 45–51 (2000)

16. Ragab, D.A., Sharkas, M., Marshall, S., Ren, J.: Breast cancer detection using deep convolutional neural networks and support vector machines. https://doi.org/10.7717/peerj.6201

17. Dhahri, H., Maghayreh, E.A., Mahmood, A., Elkilani, W., Nagi, M.F.: Automated breast cancer diagnosis based on machine learning algorithms. https://doi.org/10.1155/2019/4253641. Jinshan Tang

18. Anji Reddy, V., Soni, B., Sudheer Reddy, K.: Breast cancer detection by leveraging machine learning. ICT Express. https://doi.org/10.1016/j.icte.2020.04.009

19. de Moor, T., Rodriguez-Ruiz, A., Merida, A.G., Mann, R., Teuwen, J.: Automated soft tissue lesion detection and segmentation in digital mammography using a U-Net deep learning network. arXiv:1802.06865v2 [cs.CV], 8 March 2018

20. Li, S., et al.: Attention dense-U-Net for automatic breast mass segmentation in digital mammogram (2019). https://doi.org/10.1109/ACCESS.2019.2914873

21. Hossain, M.S.: Microc alcification segmentation using modified U-net segmentation network from mammogram images. J. King Saud Univ. - Comput. Inf. Sci. (2019). https://doi.org/10.1016/j.jksuci.2019.10.014

22. Sun, H., et al.: AUNet: attention-guided dense-upsampling networks for breast mass segmentation in whole mammograms. arXiv:1810.10151v3 [cs.CV], 6 August 2019

23. Singh, V.K., et al.: Breast tumor segmentation and shape classification in mammograms using generative adversarial and convolutional neural network. arXiv:1809.01687v3 [cs.CV], 23 October 2018

Optimized Analysis Using Feature Selection Techniques for Drug Discovery Detection

Abhay Dadhwal$^{(\boxtimes)}$ and Meenu Gupta

Department of Computer Science and Engineering, Chandigarh University, Punjab, India
dadhwal.abhay.abhay@gmail.com, meenu.e9406@cumail.in

Abstract. Machine learning is a tool with immense potential. One of the most important tasks of machine learning process is feature selection. To select best feature selection technique in Drug Discovery most studies could be noticed testing them with classifiers and selecting the one with highest score. But this study demonstrates that in such environment the features can be selected in a more effective manner to determine their quality. This study employs five feature selection techniques and utilizes their results collectively in a method called Priority feature selection. This method ranks the features and produces the most optimum set of features of this experiment. This standard is verified by testing this method by four classifiers where it produces results that surpass the performance of other feature selection techniques. This study also makes a big difference by producing and suggesting a feature selection method that attains maximum performance with all classifiers.

Keywords: Drug discovery · Feature selection · Classifier · Accuracy · Comparative analysis

1 Introduction

Small organic molecules that achieve their desired action by binding on a receptor at the target site can be called drugs. Their interactions are microscopic. It occurs in the molecular world. Drug Discovery as evident through the title is the process of finding possible new medicines. Subjects that encompass molecular theory like biology, chemistry, and pharmacology are covered in drug discovery. Ideally, experts and biologists would attempt to better understand the mechanisms of disease to build a molecule that can disrupt the disease agents. Yet, due to the presence of several complex interactions at the cellular level, it is difficult to proceed with the logical drug design process as good analytical skills are required. Some books provide great insight into the processes included in designing drugs [1]. Due to heavy resource consumption in drug discovery, success is noticed in high-yielding industries like cancer research lately. It is estimated that taking a drug from research to the market will cost an average of $2.6 billion and more than 10 years (can be seen in Fig. 1).

© Springer Nature Switzerland AG 2022
A. K. Luhach et al. (Eds.): ICAICR 2021, CCIS 1575, pp. 43–54, 2022.
https://doi.org/10.1007/978-3-031-09469-9_4

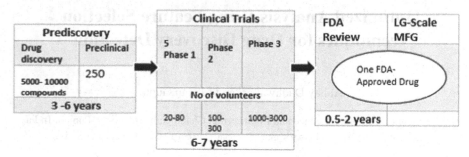

Fig. 1. Drug discovery pipeline

The need to stay relevant in the modern-day has pushed various industries [2–5] to practice machine learning techniques. Through the introduction of fresh concepts in AI like AlphaFold (AI algorithm of Google), Insilico Medicine, etc. the drug development job has seen a drastic change with work being reduced to days from years. A term called Synbiolic creates brand new molecules using Variational Autoencoder (VAE). Thus, significance of AI has become huge in Drug Discovery.

A wide variety of attributes or characteristics, such as topological indices, the characterization of three-dimensional molecular structures, quantum mechanical descriptors, and molecular field parameters, may be required to describe complex molecular compounds leading to tens or hundreds of thousands of characteristics. That is prohibitively high in some learning algorithms and in truth not all the features hold equal value. Therefore it is a good choice to choose the appropriate characteristics that are necessary to construct a quality model. Fundamental steps are still necessary, such as data cleaning and preprocessing [6, 7]. The larger the amount of unnecessary features, more difficult will be to find an acceptable decision function for the algorithm: the system may not converge to an optimal solution within a suitable period of time, or more data may be required to achieve a correct solution. To achieve best subset of features one can:

- Consider all features equally at first and calculate correlation value between target and every other feature.
- Select the subset that produces the most accurate result and also provides stronger generalizing power

1.1 Problem Statement and Contribution

In an environment of multiple feature selection techniques, recent studies could be noticed forming their results based on individual feature selection technique performance. They simply choose the technique that produces highest performance score out of all. But this study proves that it is possible to utilize multiple feature selection techniques collectively to determine the best set of features. It is carried out under the Priority feature selection method and the results produced prove that features selected through collective utilization deliver most optimum performance.

The individual and relative performance analysis of feature selection techniques is also demonstrated in this study as it always helps to understand more about the dataset in hand, for example, the relation between performance and feature-set size in general. The derived findings will lead to better future decisions especially in the field of pharmaceutical scientific research. In this paper most acknowledged feature selection techniques and classifiers are employed namely Pearson correlation coefficient, Chi-squared, Anova-F measure, Lasso and Tree-based (Random Forest).

Further sections are divided as follows Sect. 2 provides review of the previous studies and explains some areas where enhancements can be made. Section 3 acquaints with this study by describing the tools and techniques used. Section 4 presents the results obtained and the insights derived through their analysis. Final Sect. 5 summarizes the whole study by discussing important points and final outcome.

2 Literature Review

Since the recognition of the ability of feature selection there has been a lot of experimentation by researchers [8, 9]. The Drug Discovery process should be efficient; from cost to techniques applied everything should be efficiently sorted. Below mentioned are the studies that helped to familiarize with current techniques in Drug Discovery and to select the tools required for this experiment. Moreover, they helped to guide and define our research problem as described in the summary after these studies.

H. Shi et al. [10] and S. Redkar [11] laid the foundation for our study. They utilize feature selection methods for DTI prediction and also address the issue of class imbalance and high dimensionality. They employ WEKA tool and fewer number of feature selection methods are utilized and the ones producing higher score value are simply considered the final outcome. Choosing the available feature selection option from WEKA tool doesn't give much information about the suitability of features. More information on the selected features can make the process more robust in terms of performance. This forms the base of our study and is discussed more in the summary of this section.

T.Clifford [12] and K. Zhao [13] contributed in drug discovery domain by working on the feature space of dataset. They applied feature selection methods and classifiers. It proved the high efficiency that ML can provide in Drug Discovery. A larger feature-space can be experimented to produce results that relate more to the real-world as the real-world feature-space is usually large. A. Al. Marouf [14] and H. B. Chakrapani [15] considered domains of social media and SQL. They utilize multiple feature selection methods and help to evaluate their efficiency. PCC and Anova-based feature selection prevail most suitable due to their high robustness and accuracy suggesting their high consistency with present datasets of the world.

Now we summarize the above studies to pinpoint the areas in which our study is based:

The base studies such as H. Shi [10] and S. Redkar [11] of this experiment employ multiple feature selection techniques to determine the best among them. They formed their selection upon a simple criteria of high prediction accuracy and thus chose the one with best individual performance. In this study, collective utilization of multiple feature selection techniques is demonstrated to determine the best set of features, which is discussed more in the definition of Priority method. The results produced prove more robust performance than the base studies. It is noticed that the selected features through the method *WrapperSubetEval* in base studies are not capable of delivering peak performance with every classifier. But in this study a single technique of feature selection capable of delivering peak performance with every classifier is attained.

3   Methodology

This section provides the description about data source, the dataset, and techniques employed followed by the methodological framework.

3.1   Data Used

The dataset is drawn from online repository UCI https://archive.ics.uci.edu/ml/datasets, which is a highly trusted source. This is a drug dataset about chemical compounds and contains thousands of features. The instances are to be classified in one of the two classes as active or inactive. The dataset well resembles the real-world data in terms of its quality and size. Thus, the final outcomes perform equally good with any real-world data.

3.2   Feature Selection Techniques

Pearson Correlation Coefficient: This easy-to-understand method comes under category of Filter Feature selection techniques. In this method, the correlation value between input and target features is calculated through below formula:

$$r = \frac{\sum (x - \bar{x})(y - \bar{y})}{\sqrt{\sum (x - \bar{x})^2 \sum (y - \bar{y})^2}} \tag{1}$$

where x and y denote input and target feature. Some recent studies describe utilization of PCC in different fields [16].

Tree-Based-Select From Model: An embedded method [17] that uses Random forest for feature selection by calculating node impurities. Information Gain is one of the attribute selection measures which can be elaborated as:

$$\text{Gain(S, A)} = \text{Entropy(S)} - \sum_{v \in Values(A)} \frac{|S_v|}{|S|} Entropy(S_v) \tag{2}$$

where Values (A) is the all possible values for attribute A, and Sv is the subset of S for which attribute A has value v.

Lasso-Select From Model: It belongs to same category of Embedded techniques. It includes a regularizer which can drive parameters to zero which is the main reason behind its presence among various domains [18]. This is understood more by the following formula:

$$\propto \sum_{i=1}^{k} |w_i|$$ (3)

Higher the values of alpha, the fewer features have non-zero values. With high dimensionality, this technique becomes a promising choice due to presence of more irrelevant features.

Chi-square Method: It deals with degrees of freedom and observed and calculated values to detrmine scores between features. Its application is visible across different domains [19]. Formula for Chi-square calculation is described as:

$$\sum_{i=1}^{n} \frac{(O_i - E_i)^2}{E_i}$$ (4)

where O_i is number of observations in class i and E_i is no. of expected observations in class i if there was no relation.

Anova-f Method: Anova uses F-test to check if there is any significant difference between groups. It supposes hypothesis to be:-

h0 = All groups have same mean.
h1 = Between groups, there is at least one significant difference.
  It's a relevant option with a dataset having numerical input and categorical output. Its usage and comparisons as a feature selection technique can be noticed in recent studies [20].

Priority Method: It is an interesting method which utilizes the results of all other feature selection techniques. Here, the importance of every feature is determined which depends upon the number of techniques that selected this feature.

Priority ∝ *count*

Priority refers to the importance of a feature and count refers to number of feature selection techniques that selected the feature.
  Lets say, if a feature is selected by all feature seletion techniques, then it is ranked higher. It is performed for every feature to finally obtain a set of ranked features. This ranked set is tested with different classifiers and with different feature-set sizes.

Methodological Approach:

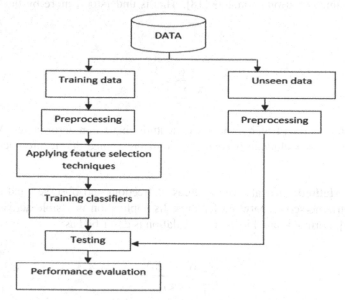

Fig. 2. Methodology

With training and unseen dataset provided, the common machine learning approach was followed as given in Fig. 2. Training and unseen dataset were scanned for erroneous values and preprocessing was performed to clean the dataset. Then, features were selected again and again in different numbers to find the combination with best performance by using feature selection techniques.

All steps after preprocessing were repeated again and again for different amount of features, classifiers and feature selection techniques as described more clearly in next section. This made for many number of combinations and for each combination, observations were noted to derive insights and ultimately figure out the one that gives the best performance.

4   Experimental Results and Analysis

Following observations were noted by applying combinations of type of techniques and amount of features. Performance with training set helps us to know whether the model has learned the training set or not and in what manner did that happen but what helps to relate with real world is unseen dataset performance, hence it is noticed more in following analysis.

4.1   Analysis

The feature set size varied from hundred features as least to all features at most. By increasing the feature set by 100, observations were recorded again and again, starting from 100 features. This continued till 1000 features, after which they were increased by 500. This process promised deeper analysis. The term higher or larger feature sets denotes all feature sets that exceed the length of 700 and lower sets are the ones below. Relative performance evaluation after the analysis of every two techniques is provided based on the performance within the more significant order set. It serves as a checkpoint of performance of feature selection techniques describing local optimum performance. It plots overall accuracy with classifier. As minimum outliers are observed in this study therefore overall accuracy can be trusted to reflect true overview of the performance of techniques with the feature sets. The margins are excluded from the Figs. 3, 4 and 5 as the focus is on the pattern of relative performance. Tables 1, 2 and 3 contain those margins or performance scores. When not specified, assume the documented analysis with unseen set.

The Tables 1, 2 and 3 provide an overview of performance for each feature selection technique by displaying results of different classifiers. Overall accuracy attained among low and high order feature sets on unseen data is shown in the table. They help to understand the performance and contribute in the analysis of the respective classifier and feature selection method. Along every table, detailed analysis that includes both training and unseen dataset is given with respect to every classifier to help acquire useful insights.

Performances of feature selection techniques can be analyzed as:

Pearson Correlation Coefficient (PCC) and Tree-based (TB): Table 2 helps to describe the general performance of PCC and TB method with classifiers on both feature sets which also serves to document its detailed analysis as below:

Low & High-order Sets: The majority of combinations with both PCC and TB display a tendency to yield best performance with low-order sets like BNB, Ad and LR. LR could attain the highest score and outperform all the other combinations.

Table 1. Pearson correlation and tree-based method

Overall Accuracy (Unseen set)				
Classifiers	PCC		TB	
	Low-order	High-order	Low-order	High-order
LR	90.17%	89.46%	89.01%	86.77%
RF	89.27%	89.66%	89.74%	89.85%
BNB	90.3%	90.3%	90.30%	90.3%
Ad	88.81%	87.87%	88.17%	87.42%

In almost every scenario low-order sets outperform high-order ones suggesting more efficiency associated with them than high-orders sets.

Relative Performance: PCC vs TB: As low order sets perform consistently better with all classifiers than high order sets so their behaviour with feature selection techniques is studied more through the following figure to realize any underlying patterns and enhance the performance.

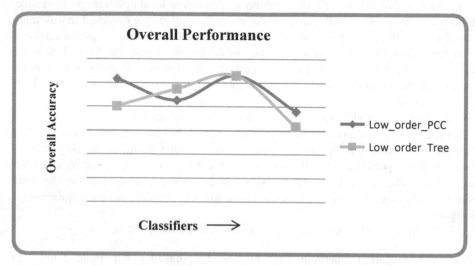

Fig. 3. Relative Performance of PCC and TB

PCC produces more amount of high scores within low order sets as compared to Tree based method with Adaboost and Logistic Regression. Thus, PCC stands as a better choice than TB method.

Lasso and Chi-Square Method: Table 2 describes general performance of these methods and helps to document their analysis below:

Low & High-Order Sets: The prediction model of all classifiers attained better classification accuracy with low-orders sets and the highest was observed from LR. RF and BNB could attain high scores with high-orders sets but not as consistently.

Table 2. Lasso and Chi-square Method

Overall Accuracy (Unseen set)				
Classifiers	Lasso		Chi-sq	
	Low-order	High-order	Low-order	High-order
LR	90.45%	84.44%	89.95%	89.75%
RF	89.30%	89.40%	89.61%	89.82%
BNB	90.3%	90.3%	90.30%	90.30%
Ad	87.63%	88.26%	88.14%	88.48%

Thus, behaviour with the feature sets suggests the presence of necessary features in higher amount with low-order sets.

Relative Performance: Lasso & Chi-square: Following figure is plotted to understand the relative performance of these two methods under low-order sets (Fig. 4):

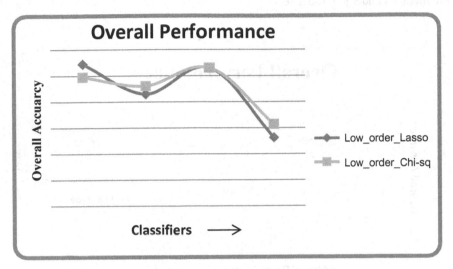

Fig. 4. Relative Performance of Lasso and Chi-sq

Lasso and Chi-square both run closely and display high performance. LR tops the score value with Lasso but Chi-sq excels with two classifiers suggesting equal capability for both the techniques.

Anova-f and Priority Method: Below Table 3 describes general behaviour of these methods:

Table 3. Anova-f and Priority method

Overall Accuracy (Unseen set)				
Classifiers	Lasso		Chi-sq	
	Low-order	High-order	Low-order	High-order
LR	90.45%	84.44%	89.95%	89.75%
RF	89.30%	89.40%	89.61%	89.82%
BNB	90.3%	90.3%	90.30%	90.30%
Ad	87.63%	88.26%	88.14%	88.48%

Low & High-order Sets: The number of samples correctly classified under low-order sets were higher than other section with most classifiers. Though, RF attained best with high-order but it was outperformed by LR. This reflects higher redundancy or impure features among larger feature sets.

Relative Performance: Anova & Priority: Figure 5 reflects the relative performance of these methods under low-order sets:

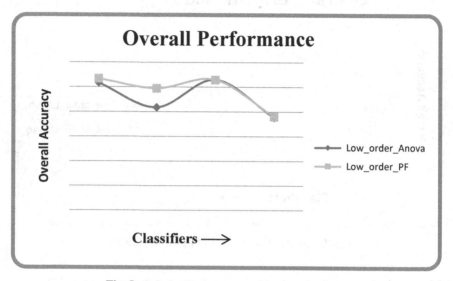

Fig. 5. Relative Performance of Anova nd Priority

Evident from figure, Anova-selected features form decent model but the best is attained with Priority-selected features.

Overall Analysis: The findings of the experiment are summarized below:

Tree-Based method of feature selection indicates high uncertainity in its performance. It fails to deliver high scores with LR on low order sets. Between Lasso and Chi-square the latter responds better to diversity suggesting the higher quality selection of features by this method. It was able to deliver scores within a narrower range than Lasso. But Anova surpasses this narrow range of Chi-square suggesting a more precise feature selection. Thus, Anova emerges more robust than Chi-square.

The sixth method namely Priority technique of feature selection surpasses the performance of all other feature selection techniques. It was able to produce the best results out of all with minimum amount of features. Such performance was expected due to its simple and highly effective mechanism. It utilized the results of all techniques to perform ranking and thus provided best set of features. This work provides useful insights and suggests a robust and secure feature selection method after the analysis study.

5 Conclusion

This research aimed to study the behaviour of different techniques to acquire useful insights and thus form a model with best tools that promises desired performance. It achieves this task through utilization of some smart techniques and by insightful analysis throughout the experiment. Several scenarios of different feature set size were studied. The experiment with feature sets led to the conclusion that a model needs to be tested with different feature sets to arrive at the most efficient solution. Otherwise, big differences having high impact on efficiency can be overlooked. In this study, general behaviour displaying high quality of smaller sets was largely noticed. Best feature set was agreed to be that of 200 features attained through Priority method which is very efficient when compared with original feature set size. This method attained maximum performance with every classifier. Logistic Regression and Priority method of feature selection were concluded to be the most appropriate combination in terms of high accuracy, high reliability and modern-day relevance. Both of these together make up for a good quality prediction model. Quality performance of Priority method also suggests that combining the results of all features selection techniques is very effective method and delivers more reliable and accurate prediction. Evident from the analysis, this study yielded many insights and produced quality performance.

References

1. Poduri, R. (ed.): Drug Discovery and Development. Springer, Singapore (2021). https://doi.org/10.1007/978-981-15-5534-3
2. Hooda, N., Bawa, S., Rana, P.S.: B2FSE framework for high dimensional imbalanced data: a case study for drug toxicity prediction. Neurocomputing **276**, 31–41 (2018)
3. Hooda, N., Bawa, S., Rana, P.S.: Fraudulent firm classification: a case study of an external audit. Appl. Artif. Intell. **32**(1), 48–64 (2018)
4. Hooda, N., Bawa, S., Rana, P.S.: Optimizing fraudulent firm prediction using ensemble machine learning: a case study of an external audit. Appl. Artif. Intell. **34**(1), 20–30 (2020)
5. Bhardwaj, R., Hooda, N.: Prediction of pathological complete response after neoadjuvant chemotherapy for breast cancer using ensemble machine learning. Inform. Med. Unlocked **16**, 100219 (2019)
6. Zelaya, C.: Towards explaining the effects of data preprocessing on machine learning. In: IEEE 35th International Conference on Data Engineering (ICDE), pp. 2086–2090 (2019). https://doi.org/10.1109/ICDE.2019.00245
7. Celik, O., Hasanbasoglu, M., Aktas, M., Kalipsiz, O., Kanli, A.: Implementation of data preprocessing techniques on distributed big data platforms. In: 4th International Conference on Computer Science and Engineering (UBMK) (2019). https://doi.org/10.1109/ubmk.2019.8907230
8. Suto, J., Oniga, S., Sitar, P.P.: Comparison of wrapper and filter feature selection algorithms on human activity recognition'. In: 6th International Conference on Computers Communications and Control (ICCCC), pp. 124–129. https://doi.org/10.1109/ICCCC.2016.7496749, (2016)
9. Dhote, Y., Agarwal, S., Deen, A.J.: A survey on feature selection techniques for internet traffic classification. In: International Conference on Computational Intelligence and Communication, pp. 1375–1380 (2015). https://doi.org/10.1109/CICN.2015.267

10. Shi, H., Liu, S., Chen, J., Li, X., Ma, Q., Yu, B.: Predicting drug-target interactions using Lasso with random forest based on evolutionary information and chemical structure. Genomics **111**(6), 1839–1852 (2019)
11. Redkar, S., Mondal, S., Joseph, A., Hareesha, K.S.: A machine learning approach for drug-target interaction prediction using wrapper feature selection and class balancing. Molecul. Inform. **39** (2020). https://doi.org/10.1002/minf.201900062
12. Clifford, T., Bruce, J., Ajayi, T.O., Matta, J.: Comparative analysis of feature selection methods to identify biomarkers in a stroke-related dataset. In: IEEE Conference on Computational Intelligence in a Stroke-Related Dataset, pp. 1–8 (2019). https://doi.org/10.1109/CIBCB.2019.8791457
13. Zhao, K., So, H.C.: Drug repositioning for schizophrenia and depression/anxiety disorders: a machine learning approach leveraging expression data. IEEE J. Biomed. Health Inform. **23**(3), 1304–1315 (2019)
14. Marouf, A., Hasan, K.Md., Mahmud, H.: Comparative analysis of feature selection algorithms for computational personality prediction from social media. IEEE Trans. Comput. Soc. Syst. (2020). https://doi.org/10.1109/TCSS.2020.2966910
15. Chakrapani, H.B., Chourasia, S., Saha, A., Swathi, J.N.: Predicting performance analysis of system configurations to contrast feature selection methods. In: International Conference on Emerging Trends in Information Technology and Engineering (ic-ETITE), pp. 1–7 (2020). https://doi.org/10.1109/ic-ETITE47903.2020.106
16. Zhi, X., Yuexin, S., Jin, M., Lujie, Z., Zijian, D.: Research on the Pearson correlation coefficient evaluation method of analog signal in the process of unit peak load regulation. In: 13th IEEE International Conference on Electronic Measurement & Instruments (ICEMI), 522–527 (2017). https://doi.org/10.1109/ICEMI.2017.8265997
17. Bachu, V., Anuradha, J.: A review of feature selection and its methods. Cybern. Inf. Technol. **19**(1), 3 (2019)
18. Chen, J., Li, T., Zou, Y., Wang, G., Ye, H., Lv, F.: An ensemble feature selection method for short-term electrical load forecasting. In: IEEE 3rd Conference on Energy Internet and Energy System Integration (EI2) **170**, 22–29 (2019). https://doi.org/10.1016/j.apenergy.2016.02.114
19. Ikram, S.T., Cherukuri, A.K.: Intrusion detection model using fusion of chi-square feature selection and multi class SVM. J. King Saud Univ. Comput. **29** (2017). https://doi.org/10.1016/j.jksuci.2015.12.004
20. Doan, D.M., Jeong, D.H., Ji, S.: Designing a feature selection technique for analyzing mixed data. In: 10th Annual Computing and Communication Workshop and Conference (CCWC) (2020). https://doi.org/10.1109/CCWC47524.2020.9031193

A Survey and Analysis on the Distraction Patterns of the Students in E-Learning and M-Learning Environments

Sri Rama Murthy Karumuri[1](✉), Sreenivasa Rao Meda[2], Pavan Srinivas Narayana[3], and Rajiv K.[4]

[1] St. Peter's Engineering College, Hyderabad, India
sriram.pavani@stpetershyd.com
[2] Jawaharlal Nehru Techological University, Hyderabad, India
[3] Arizona University, Tucson, AZ, USA
[4] Gokaraju Rangaraju Institute of Engineering and Technology, Hyderabad, India

Abstract. The explosive growth of mobile devices helped in adopting Electronic Learning and Mobile Learning. E-Learning using Mobile devices has gone through rapid and unprecedented changes following the profound advances in technology and mobile systems. This paper emphasizes surveying the E-Learning Process among the students and faculty. It helped to identify the possibilities of distraction in the learning process. This research work plans to build algorithms which detect the distraction patterns.

Keywords: E-Learning · Distraction · Students · Faculty · Mobile-Learning

1 Introduction

All over the world, the pandemic is going and the teaching faculty across the world is continuing to get adopted in E-Learning using ubiquitous devices such as desktops, laptops, and mobile phones. This paper focuses on the development of questionnaires disbursed to the student's community and faculty community, obtaining the results and plotting them to evaluate and analyze the possibilities of distraction among the students while teaching and learning happening using mobile devices. The online events and meetings conducted in the industry are also in the scope of development [1].

2 Topics of Discussion

2.1 E-Learning and M-Learning

The process of teaching and learning between a teacher and student with the help of gadgets such as laptops, desktops etc. can be considered as E-Learning or Electronic Learning and if it happens with the help of ubiquitous devices such as smart phones, tablets etc., can be considered as M-Learning or Mobile Learning.

A. K. Luhach et al. (Eds.): ICAICR 2021, CCIS 1575, pp. 55–64, 2022.
https://doi.org/10.1007/978-3-031-09469-9_5

2.2 Types of Students in E-Learning and Mobile-Learning Observed

The subjects of our survey are Post-Graduate and Under-Graduate students who underwent through online learning process. The E-Learning activity with postgraduate students created some flexibility in studying as they were trained to provide resources and they will explore by themselves upon the instruction of their faculty. The groups of Undergraduate students and below level use electronic devices/gadgets to learn and the faculty have to synchronize with all the students listening to him/her.

2.3   Methodology

This research work provided a questionniare to collect responses from the student comunity and faculty community working in Engineering Colleges across Telangana, India. The responses to the questionniare in the form of Categorical Data, binomial data and numerical data helped us to analyze and generate some conclusions.

3   Analysis on the Data Set from the Survey by Students Community

3.1   Analysis on the Online Learning and Types of Gadgets Used

The analysis captured from the questionnaire is shown below: From the survey, 68.8% of the students tend to use Laptops as the mode of online education. In a further development this reserach work could use background algorithms such as Drowsiness and Alertness detection in identifying the attentiveness during the online lecture (Fig. 1).

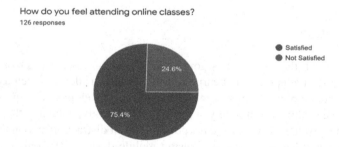

How do you feel attending online classes?
126 responses

- Satisfied
- Not Satisfied

24.6%

75.4%

Fig. 1. Responses on the query to students: How do you feel attending online classes?

As 75% of the students taking part in the survey showed interest in the online mode of education, it would be a great area of improvement to develop new and better algorithms that would benefit the online education platform [4].

As per the survey, 95% observed that there are 2 gadgets at their disposal to attend online classes, and 4.7% of people observed the usage of 4 gadgets. (Availability of Gadgets for domestic usage and personal usage improved when compared to the past decades. There is a drastic decrease in the pricing of the Gadgets).

3.2 Analysis on the Tools, Time Spent by Students Online and Internet Connection Speed

93% of students participating in the survey voted Google Meet and Google Class tools and over 6% informed that Zoom Meetings are helping in their online class work. Google Meet left no room for other tools in conducting online classes. This point helps in understanding that Google is offering Open-Source tools with flexibility of usage.

As noticed from the data that 49.6% of students are attending online classes for more than 4 h per day, it would be better for eyes to take intermediate gaps to maintain eye health(as per the medical guidelines). So this research work would help to develop an algorithm that gives notification periodically to the students after the specified usage limit.

In the past, as cited by Madhusudan Margam in a research paper mentioned If computers are available then the connectivity issue creates hurdles to access the digital resources. Madhusudhan (2007) pointed out that slow internet connection is the highly ranked (72%) obstacle to access online resources. The result also shows that retrieval problems, a slow processor of computers, and lack of time and training are also major issues to connect the internet and to use the resources properly.

As per the survey, only 9.5% of the students agreed that the speed of the Internet is Excellent. 46.8% of members' rated good, 33.3% members rated Average, 6.3% selected below average and 4% rated worst on asking about the speed of the Internet. This showcases that there is a considerable improvement in the speed of the Internet Connection when compared to the past two decades. By the survey, we can understand that the issues such as hurdles to access digital resources due to slow internet connection are rectified. Due to improvements in technology, the processor speed increased making it more convenient for allowing faster internet access (Fig. 2).

3.3 Comparision of Physical Class Room Training and Online Training

Do you feel the Learning environment in the physical classroom is better when compared to the Online Teaching and Gadget Viewing and learning?

125 responses

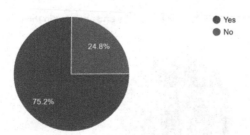

Fig. 2. Responses on the query to student-compare physical class room with online classroom?

75.2% of the candidates who participated in the survey informed that Physical Class-room teaching is better than Gadget Viewing and Learning; this indicates that much more support is needed to train the teachers in offering the Classes Online. As the COVID is prevailing, in the current scenario there is always a need of hybrid teaching constituting both the online and offline teaching methodology.

As per the observation from the query " Are the lectures taught online helping you to learn effectively?" 69.5% of students confirmed that the lectures taught online are helping them to learn effectively, but still, 30% of students aren't happy with the online teaching. This shows that the physical appearance of the faculty/teacher will effectively reach more students compared to online lectures.

When queried about "whether the students are allowed to work in groups?" around 71% reacted that they are working in groups. A mere percentage of 8.7% is not working in groups, 16.5% reacted sometimes they were allowed to work in groups. The observation leads to a state that even in the online learning process, the students (peer) learning in groups may help understand the concepts better and allowing them in groups would result in improvement in the performance of weak learners. (As per the observation, weak learners open up among their peers better than with the faculty who teaches them).

While teaching in a classroom, the teacher may have the flexibility to interact with students, but in the online learning process, there is less chance and very few students react to the teacher's questions, and it is highly difficult for a faculty to observe every student reaction. Instead of narrating with many words, the faculty may show some pictures to convey things to his/her students. In our survey, when posting this query "Did the images used while teaching and explaining the lesson enhance your learning?" 96.8% responded they were able to understand the subject better with the help of images. This conveys the old ideology, "One picture conveys 100 words".

The reaction of students, when queried whether the teacher's presentation (PowerPoint presentation or Prezi or LibreOffice Impress or Beamer or GoogleDoc slides or SLIDEBEAN etc.,) helped them to understand the concepts was answered as 88% positive. Only 11.8% answered vice versa. This is conveying that most of the faculty members are aware of such presentation tools and are delivering the lessons in an organized manner. Moreover above 90% of students conveyed that their faculty also used Multimedia in delivering the course work. This information gives a chance to publish many difficult lessons that can be taught effectively by taking help of Multimedia tools (Fig. 3).

126 responses

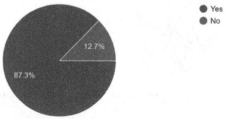

Fig. 3. Response on the query - whether teachers are observing the availability and attention of students in the class?

3.4 Analysis of the Teachers Observation on Students Availability and Attention

When enquired about "Are the teachers observing your availability and attention in the class?" 87.3% of the students replied that they are being observed and 12.7% replied they are not observed properly. This indicates that the student's availability is also a matter of concern and can be use as an area of research. 90.5% of students answered that their teachers are applying spontaneity in clarifying their doubts (Fig. 4).

3.5 Analysis of the Responses of Students About Getting Distracted in the Class

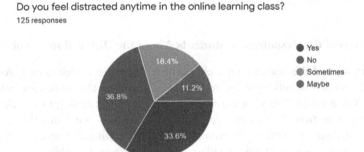

Do you feel distracted anytime in the online learning class?
125 responses

- Yes
- No
- Sometimes
- Maybe

Fig. 4. Responses on query to students: Did you feel distracted anytime in the online learning class?

When students are asked to answer whether they feel distracted when online class is going on, around 37% agreed yes and 35% agreed no. And 18.4% indicated sometimes and 11.4% indicated maybe as their responses. There is a huge scope of research in this area and many automated tools using deep learning/machine learning/AI tools can be implemented to support both faculty and students in automating the process of identifying distraction in students and generate logs of analysis of distracted students.

3.6 Analysis of the Responses of Students About the Tools Utilised by Faculty to Avoid Distraction in Class

There are two ways to teach students online. Lecturing orally or giving a brief overview and providing videos/puzzles/objects with animation (eg. Java Applets) etc,. When a faculty or tutor teaches continuously, there is a chance that the student gets exhausted. Instead, the faculty can generate interest in engaging the students by video lectures. When enquiring students about videos and animations in supporting their effective learning, 90% of the students replied that they are helping to focus and learn effectively whereas about 10% considered that they are distracting. So, still there are some students who get distracted when video based tools are used for teaching (Fig. 5).

Are your classmates continuously listening to the class or they are moving away from the classes?
124 responses

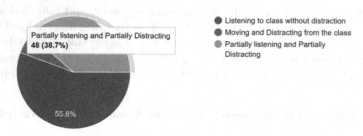

Partially listening and Partially Distracting
48 (38.7%)

● Listening to class without distraction
● Moving and Distracting from the class
● Partially listening and Partially Distracting

55.6%

Fig. 5. Responses on the query to students: Are your classmates continuously listening to the class or they are moving away from the classes?

3.7 Analysis of the Responses of Students About the Distraction of Their Peers

The observation of the students on their peers is one topic of discussion. As per our observation, some students show interest to know how their classmates are behaving in the class. When asked "are your classmates continuously listening to the class or are they moving away from the classes?" responses of around 6% are distracting and around 39% of the students are partially listening and partially getting distracted. There may be certain reasons for lack of interest in a class. A student may not be able to understand the concept or a student may not have an interest in a particular topic or a student dislikes the teacher or a student's health may not support or there may be a chance of discomfort due to the environment around him at his house, etc. All of the above mentioned reasons are assumptions.

Feedback taken from the students on the subjects taught is very essential while teaching. This helps in mirroring a faculty and improving the quality of teaching. The feedback definitely will allow the faculty to refine the quality of online teaching giving the student scope of better attention in the class. Hence it may decrease the level of distraction in students Around 60% agreed that feedback on a faculty is taken for every fortnight and around 40% informed it will be taken on a monthly basis. (This feedback

Does the teacher/faculty create a facility to interact with you and motivate you to continuously listen to her lesson or not?
125 responses

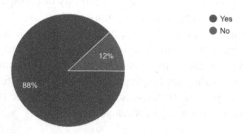

● Yes
● No

12%

88%

Fig. 6. Response on the query to students – About faculty motivation on students.

can help to identify the cause of the students' distraction) Faculty can also better their teaching methodology (Fig. 6).

Motivating a student who is getting distracted is essential in every circumstance. Identifying the root cause of why a student is getting distracted is always an important factor for the faculty. When surveyed "Does the teacher/faculty create a facility to interact with you and motivate you to continuously listen to her lesson or not?" 88% agreed that their faculty is motivating continuously, but this may not be sufficient since there are 34% of students in this group who are observed by their friends while getting distracted.

A faculty can deliver 40% of the content in the class, 20% of the subject a student should apply and learn on his own, 20% from peers, and the remaining 20% from online resources or reference books. The above mentioned is an assumption from us. At certain times the faculty can provide reference books or digital/online references for the students to encourage them to learn more. This may help students to improve performance and also creates interest in the subject. Certain students may show interest in referring to the books suggested by faculty. When queried "are the faculty/teachers supplying any digital material to understand the concepts for reference?" Around 95% of the students agreed "Yes". This conveys that faculty is showing interest in suggesting references to their students for their better performance [5].

If the communication between the teacher and the student goes on one on one basis, at certain times there is a chance that a student (weak learner) will open up and the positivity generated by the teacher interaction may improve the performance of the student. Upon querying that "Are the faculty interacting with you on one on one basis?" Around 17% of the students replied no, which is also a strong point to convey to the faculty and students who are missing the physical mode of education.

As the learning and teaching methodology has become online since the advent of pandemic making the work and study from the home compulsory (going on conti- nuously for many days due to the pandemic situation, the teachers and students are also suggested to work and study from their home. This leads to teaching and learning using Gadgets. Gadget-centered learning and teaching may create eyesight problems and other health issues [6]. When queried "Does the screen resolution and size/fonts affect your eyes?" Around 33% of the students replied yes. This is a serious concern where the administration and teaching staff should look into and give clear instructions to the students on usage the electronic gadgets/devices and minimizing the screentime.

4   Analysis on the Data Set from the Survey by Faculty Community

4.1   Analysis on the Comfortness of Students Observed by Faculty in Online Mode of Education

The survey was conducted during the pandemic when the teaching mode has completely switched over to the E-Learning and M-Learning mode. The responses are plotted and analyzed for the better understanding from the faculty perspective.

When surveyed with the faculty members, "Are the students getting used to the new form of teaching i.e., the online mode?", Around 87% of the teachers agreed that the students are getting used to the new form of teaching whereas still, 13% of the students are yet to get used to it. It was observed that attending online classes with the help of a laptop may increase the performance of the student when compared to attending classes using mobile.

When posted a query to the faculty members, "Have you observed any discomfort in the online way of teaching compared to the offline mode? ", only 55.5% of the faculty members are in their comfort zone in teaching online. There are various types of discomforts in online teaching, like using teaching aids etc,. Observing students physically helps a faculty to know the satisfaction level and level of understanding of the student in an effective way. In online platforms, observing all students at a time may not be possible. There are several views in observing the students, but it is becoming very difficult for the teachers to observe the attention of the students while teaching online. They might be asking to turn on videos, but the thumbnail view will impact the eyes of the teacher if they are very small. This point can also be treated as an input to do some research and to build tools which help the faculty members [7] (Fig. 7).

4.2   Analysis on Categorizing Students and Improving Performance and Reducing Distraction

In offline mode, you have observed various batches so you will be able to categorize students using EGA (Excellent, Good and Average) and you w...ion. Are you able to do the same in online mode?
33 responses

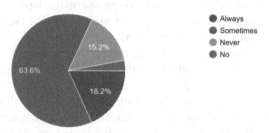

Fig. 7. Responses on the query to faculties – Whether they are categorising students and offering training online.

In offline mode, faculty have observed various batches so faculty will be able to categorize students using EGA (Excellent, Good, and Average) and will be able to train them based on the above observation. "Are you able to do the same in online mode?" to the above query, 18% of the faculty members agreed that they are categorizing on an EGA basis, 63% of the faculty members informed sometimes, 15.2% never, and the remaining none. It would assist the weak learners to learn effectively with peers if they were categorized and trained [8] (Fig. 8).

4.3 Analysis on Whether the Faculty Are Observing the Students Distractions

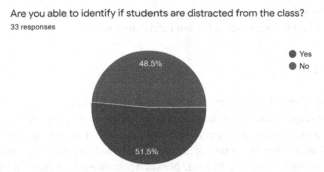

Are you able to identify if students are distracted from the class?
33 responses

48.5%

51.5%

Yes
No

Fig. 8. Responses on the query to faculties – Whether they are able to identify if students are distracted from the class.

When the faculty members are inquired if they can identify if students are distracted from the class? More than 50% of them answered that they observe the student getting distracted from the class. This is relatively a greater task to identify the distracted students and also which is a cumbersome task to manage the class online with this percentage of distracted ones. Our research [9] focuses on helping the teachers to identify the distracted students and generating an automated report of them for each class.

4.4 Analysis on How a Faculty Member is Checking the Understandability of the Students While Taking Online Class

The faculty members are asked "While teaching online, are you continuously teaching or pausing and inquiring the students whether they were able to understand or not?" Around 64% said "Yes" for this one and 30% said "sometimes". This type of pausing and inquiring the students randomly identifies the student's level of understanding and keeps track of the distracted students [10].

When queried faculty "are you nominating any student to reply to your questions such as "are you able to follow or not? In a class", 70% of the faculty agreed that they are nominating students to reply to questions while teaching online. Around 22% said sometimes and 3 to 5% of the faculty said they did not nominate any students. It will be good enough by identifying students with distraction and nominating them for replying to questions while online class is going on.

A categorical answer for the question posted to faculty is: "How many students will respond to your queries such as "are you with me"/"are you able to understand the topic type of questions?" The answers are 0 to 25%, 25 to 50% and More than 50%. The entire faculty answered that students are responding to such questions and each category is ranging from 30 to 35%. This type of questions also helps the faculty members to understand the patterns of distraction of students.

When faculty members were queried that "Are there any students who are over-inquisitive and pausing your lesson?" Around 50% of the faculty responded that there are such students who are Over-Inquisitive. When raised a question to faculty members whether the Over-Iinquisitive nature of such students is distracting the class, the faculty responded that around 45% of the class is getting distracted in such situations. The faculty members should be capable of handling such over-inquisitive-natured students and should hold on to the students for not being distracted.

5   Conclusion

There is a vast scope of development in the field of E-Learning at present. There are a lot of situations and discomforts that needs to be addressed by the developers to make the E-Learning as comfortable as conventional learning. The development of new and comfortable way for the interaction of students and teachers, handling online meetings will be very resourceful to the domain. Newer technologies of machine learning and Application development would make the process easier and resourceful. There is also a need to build some algorithms to identify the distraction of students in online classes and performing experimentaion in building distraction logs of students to teachers.

References

1. Azzi-Huck, K., Shmis, T.: Managing the impact of COVID-19 on education systems around the world: how countries are preparing, coping, and planning for recovery (2020)
2. Kuraishy, S., Bokhari, M.U.: Teaching effectively with e-learning. Int. J. Recent Trends Eng. 1(2), 291 (2009)
3. Hallifax, S., Serna, A., Marty, J.-C., ÉliseLavoué: Adaptive gamifi-cation in education: a literature review of current trends and developments. Trans-Form. Learn. Meaningful Technol. 294–307 (2019)
4. Aljawarneh, S.A.: Reviewing and exploring innovative ubiquitous learning tools in higher education. J. Comput. High. Educ. 32(1), 57–73 (2019). https://doi.org/10.1007/s12528-019-09207-0
5. Gupta, S.B., Gupta, M.: Technology and E-learning in higher education. Technology 29(4), 1320–1325 (2020)
6. Haznedar, Ö., Baran, B.: Development of a General Attitude Scale towards E-Learning for faculty of education students. Educ. Technol. Theory Pract. 2(2), 42–59 (2012)
7. Campbell, J., Gibbs, A.L., Najafi, H., Severinski, C.: A comparison of learner intent and behaviour in live and archived MOOCs. Int. Rev. Res. Open Distrib. Learn. 15(5), 235–262 (2014)
8. Adams, D., Sumintono, B., Mohamed, A., Noor, N.S.M.: E-learning readiness among students of diverse backgrounds in a leading malaysian higher education institution. Malays. J. Learn. Instr. 15(2), 227–256 (2018)
9. Telles-Langdon, D.M.: Transitioning university courses online in response to COVID-19. J. Teach. Learn. 14(1), 108–119 (2020)
10. Palaiologou, I.: Children under five and digital technologies: implications for early years pedagogy. Eur. Early Child Educ. Res. J. 24, 5–24 (2016)

Crop Identification and Disease Detection by Using Convolutional Neural Networks

K. Ravikiran[1(✉)], Ch. Naveen Kumar Reddy[2], P. Gopala Krishna[1],
Mahendar Jinukala[3], and K. Prasanna Lakshmi[1]

[1] Department of Information Technology, Gokaraju Rangaraju Institute of Engineering and
Technology, Hyderabad, Telangana, India
ravi.10541@gmail.com, gopalakrishnaa@griet.ac.in
[2] Department of Information Technology, Vidya Jyothi Institute of Technology, Hyderabad,
Telangana, India
[3] Department of Computer Science and Engineering, Malla Reddy College of Engineering and
Technology, Hyderabad, Telangana, India

Abstract. The main Theme of this work is to implement a crop detector tool which is used to detect the type of crop and disease by taking crop images. The image of crop is given as input to the tool and it gives the name of the crop and disease if it effected with any disease. This work will help people to identify the crops which are not known to them. It is very difficult for the farmers to identify the crop disease with their naked eye to take what type of fertilizers to use on crops. For this work there is a require in depth knowledge to know the types of diseases. So to make it easier this tool also detects if any leaf is infected with any disease. By using the machine learning algorithms such as convolutional neural network and training the dataset with various crop images, if the input matches with any of the trained data, the output is displayed that is the name of the crop and type of disease hence farmers can take immediate remedial to avoid the effect of disease.

Keywords: Crop · Crop diseases · Convolutional neural network · Machine learning · Fertilizers

1 Introduction

A crop is a plant that can be cultivated and harvested for benefit or survival; the majority of crops are harvested as food for humans or animal fodder. People spent most of their time looking for food before agriculture became main stream, hunting wildlife and gathering wild plants. Around 11,500 years ago, people began to learn how to grow cereal and root crops and began to settle into a farming lifestyle. By 2,000 years ago, a substantial part of the Earth's population had become dependent on farming.

Rice or corn was possibly the first domesticated plant [1]. Rice was cultivated by Chinese farmers as early as 7500 BCE.Agriculture allowed people to produce surplus food. If crops failed or traded it for other products they could use this extra food. Food

A. K. Luhach et al. (Eds.): ICAICR 2021, CCIS 1575, pp. 65–77, 2022.
https://doi.org/10.1007/978-3-031-09469-9_6

surpluses allowed people to work at other non-farming tasks. This research work hope that it is extremely beneficial to government agencies and field managers, since they need data on the area of cultivated crops and their spatial distribution for further estimation and planning. It also serves as a reference for younger generations who have never been exposed to farming. While 40 crops contribute 90% of the world's crop, jillion is responsible for the remaining 10%. As a result, human minds find it more difficult to recognise each of them individually. For the situation described above, the algorithm which is built in this work will be an effective solution." It may be a personal question, such as "why can't we use pesticides or fertilizers to solve this?" Here's the solution:

The following reasons make excessive use of fertilisers and chemicals dangerous:

1. Due to use of high pesticides the fertility of the soil will reduce.
2. Excessive use of grains or fruits will make them poisonous.

Importance for identifying crops and detecting plant diseases [2, 3] "Croplands cover 18 million km^2 of land in India, according to the Agriculture Society of India. Plant viruses have infected approximately 30% of the soil, or 5.4 million km^2, Fig. 1 shows the crops infected diseases and impact on farmers. The farmer would have to send crop samples to the agriculture laboratory at regular intervals to ascertain the magnitude of the infection. Orthodox antigen-antibody reactions and microscopic examination are used by the lab technicians there.

1. The following are some of the approach's limitations:
2. Typically costly
3. It takes a few weeks to get the results as well. By this stage, the disease has typically spread across the entire region.
4. As water-soluble nitrogen fertilisers are applied to the soil, a significant portion of the added nutrients is lost to the groundwater by leaching or runoff.
5. Foods grown with chemical fertilisers caused a slew of health problems in both livestock and humans. Pesticide and herbicide residues have an effect on the human central nervous system, respiratory system, and gastrointestinal system, to name a few. When large amounts of pesticides are inhaled, they can cause wheezing and nausea by destroying the lungs. as well as the consequences"

Here is a newspaper attachment showing in the Fig. 2 that effects of fertilizers:

There are farmers who are in financial trouble, and a single crop failure may wipe them out. In 2016, 11,380 farmers committed suicide, according to the National Crime Records Bureau (NCRB). The bad news is that many of them are unable to repay their debts due to crop failures and economic hardship.

(a) . Crop infected with Disease   (b). Crop infected with Disease   (c). Farmer crying

Fig. 1. Crops infected diseases and impact on farmers

So there is an importance for early detection of disease in the crop. "Farmers make up a significant portion of the agriculture sector. Without growers, every state's agricultural system will undoubtedly fail. Agriculture meets the need for food by harvesting and processing crops such as wheat, sugar cane, rice, and many others before they are ready for transportation. Farmers are the backbone of the agricultural system. Given that it is widely accepted that a country's gross domestic product (GDP) must be balanced in order for it to grow, agriculture is one of the most important components. Crops must be cultivated and processed for the agricultural method to function, and this is where farmers come in. A farmer gains experience by spending sufficient time in the field learning what to do in different scenarios. They know what to do if the climate is unpredictable, how to avoid water contamination and salinity, and how to remedy the problem if it arises, among other things." Insect vectors that cause plant damage and create an entry point for pathogens, or that tap into the feeding phloem, transmit most plant viruses. When viruses get inside, their tiny genomes use a handful of genes to control the machinery of plant cells while avoiding the plants' defences. Information on the spatial distribution and area of cultivated crops is required by government agencies and farm managers for planning purposes. Agencies can better plan for the import and export of food products using this knowledge. Although some agriculture and food security ministries hire staff to map different types of crops on an annual basis [4, 5], such field surveys are expensive and only cover a small percentage of farms. Increasing input costs have limited profits and made cultivation unviable. Can easy lending access and better MSPs help?

(a)   (b)

Fig. 2. Paper cutting about farmers

2 Pre-work

The main Objective of the work is "When pests infect plants and crops, it has an impact on the country's agricultural output. Typically, farmers or professionals examine plants with their naked eyes in order to diagnose and treat disease. This method, however, may be time-consuming, costly, and unreliable. Automatic detection employing image processing techniques ensures a quick and accurate result. This study focuses on a novel approach to developing a model for identifying plant disease that is based on the categorization of the leaf image and use deep convolutional networks. The main goal of this work is to identify the type of plant from the leaf, which is an issue of image processing and classification [1, 3, 5]. The secondary goal is to identify the illness that has infected the leaf (if any). To accomplish this, a model that can classify the leaves must be created."

Because there are many species of plants, most people have been unable to recognize them in the past and even now. It's also impossible to tell what disease is afflicting the crop just by looking at the leaf. Our work issue statement is to create a model that can identify the crop/plant from a leaf image while also detecting the disease that has afflicted the leaf [5, 6].

A preliminary investigation is conducted to establish whether the proposed system is feasible, that is, whether it can be created using current technology and whether it is financially viable. The issue statement, as well as the objectives, is assessed, and all this work-related information is gathered from multiple sources. The disadvantages and restrictions on which the model is based are calculated. To develop the system, several datasets relating to the domain are reviewed, and the best matching dataset is collected. The problem statement's input and output limitations, as well as the requirements, are investigated.

3 Methodology

3.1 System Architecture

The design of a CNN is a key factor in its efficiency and efficacy [7, 8]. The speed and precision with which various activities can be completed depends on how the layers are arranged, which components are included in each layer, and how they are designed. One-tier architecture is used in the suggested system. This is also known as Standalone Architecture it is shown as Fig. 3, and it refers to a software package that contains all three layers of an application, namely the Presentation layer, Application layer, and Database layer. The data is saved locally or on a shared drive. The system is entirely client-side and does not require the use of a server to function. All of the components necessary for it to function are housed on the same platform. "The simplest and most direct way to design an application is with one-tier architecture. When compared to multi-tier design, this architecture offers fewer benefits.

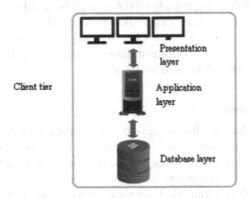

Fig. 3. 3-Tier architecture

If any of the components encounters a difficulty, the complete application will cease to function. Because all of the resources are on the same machine, there is also a security concern. Apart from the downsides, because the proposed system is a single user-based system, one-tier architecture is the best choice for its development because it is quick and does not rely on other systems. The input-output design is implemented in the Presentation Layer. The back-end programme in the application layer performs the necessary actions on the input to generate the appropriate output. The database layer is made up of a list of the dataset's subclasses. The one-tier architectural block diagram is illustrated below." Database architecture is a type of enterprise or organisational software that is built using programming languages. Database architecture is concerned with the design, development, implementation, and management of computer systems that store and organise data for businesses, organisations, and institutions. A database architect creates and implements software that satisfies the requirements of users.

They are as follows: LeNet-5 (1998), AlexNet (2012), GoogleNet (2014), VGGNet (2014) and ResNet (2015).

The Image Net project is a digital database created to aid in the examination of digital object identification programmes. The Image Net project comprises around 14 million photos, the majority of which are set up to train CNN in target recognition, with one million having bounding boxes for usage in networks like YOLO."

3.2 Data Collection Preparation and Training

3.2.1 Data Collection

Data collection is the first and primary thing of any work. Not only that the collected data must be in both large and high in quality. In this research used an open source or licenced dataset to gather the information. The Plant Village dataset, which is open source and available on Kaggle's website [9], was used for this work.

This dataset contains three types of crop leaves i.e. Pepper Bell, Potato & Tomato [10, 11]. These three classes are again divided into 15 sub classes. The sub classes respectively are pepper bell bacterial spot, pepper bell healthy, potato early blight, potato late blight, potato healthy, tomato early blight, tomato bacterial spot, tomato senatorial leaf, tomato spider mites, tomato target spot, tomato yellow leaf curl virus, tomato mosaic virus, tomato healthy. Each subclass has over 1000 photos that describe the many characteristics of the crop and the disease that affects it. This stage usually yields a data representation that will be used for training."

3.2.2 Data Preparation

"After gathering the data, the following step is to prepare the data for training. Many errors, duplicates, missing values, and other issues may exist in the data obtained. This step involves data wrangling or data mugging the results are shown in the Fig. 4 and 5. It is the process of converting and mapping data from one format to another in order to make it more suitable and useful for training. The.jpeg photos are transformed to NumPy arrays that can be used to train the model. Cleaning data entails removing duplicates, dealing with null and missing values, and converting data types (typecasting, for example). To identify the links between variables, data is visualised. Divide the data into two groups: training and testing [12, 13]. A total of 80% of the data is designated as training data,

Fig. 4. Screen shots of data visualization   **Fig. 5.** Screen shots of data wrangling

while the remaining 20% is designated as testing data. The steps of cleaning data and data wrangling are shown in the following images."

4 Implementation

4.1 Training the Model

After the data has been prepared, an algorithm can be used to train it. Because the need is to discover patterns from photos and anticipate future images, Convolutional Neural Networks (CNN) is the best algorithm for our system [7, 8, 11].

A Convolutional Neural Network (CNN/ConvNet) is a Deep Learning algorithm capable of taking an input image, assigning value to various characteristics/objects in the image, and distinguishing between them [13, 14]. The amount of pre-processing required by a ConvNet is far less than that required by other classification techniques. This work can be carried out by gather data that is crop images by using Internet of things using different network models [15]. The design of a ConvNet is comparable to that of Neurons in the human brain, which was influenced by Visual Cortex Structure. Individual neurons only respond to input in the Receptive Zone, a confined area of the visual field. A number of these fields overlap to fill the entire viewable area.

The major steps to implement a CNN are 1. Convolution Operation 2. Rectified Linear Unit (ReLU) 3. Pooling (Average and Max Pooling) 4. Flattening and 5. Fully Connected Layer

1. Convolution Layers the first layer of the ConvNet. In strictly mathematical words, convolution is a function which is derived from two different functions by integration that describes how one's form is changed by the other. "The goal of the Convolution Process is to eliminate high-level features like edges from the input image [13, 16]. There is no requirement for a model to contain only one Convolution Layer. A model can have any number of Convolution Layers. Borders, colour, gradient direction, and other low-level information are typically collected by the first Conv Layer. The design frequently adjusts to the High-Level functionality with extra layers, providing us with a network with a comprehensive understanding of the photos in the dataset. The image serves as the input to this layer, while the convolved feature serves as the output, reducing the input's dimensions."

2. ReLU stands for Rectified Linear Unit Layer. This layer is used to give the model non-linearity. A $y = max$ is the mathematical definition of the function $(0, x)$. Rectified Linear Unit is the name of the node (unit) that implements this activation function (ReLU).For every positive value ReLU is a linear function that returns zero for all negative values [17, 18]. It is showed as in the below Fig. 6.

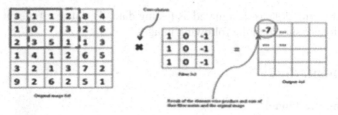

Fig. 6. Rectified linear unit layer convolution

This means that there is no complicated arithmetic involved in calculating. As a result, the model may be trained or operated in less time. It converges at a faster rate. Linearity implies that the slope does not "saturate," or plateau, as x increases. It's a function that's only occasionally used. BecauseReLU is 0 for all negative inputs, it is unlikely to trigger for any particular unit." Because it is linear for half of the variables and non-linear for the other, ReLU is also known as a piecewise linear function or hinge function.

3. Pooling Layer reduces the parameters and helps in retaining only required information. This layer removes any unnecessary parameters. This reduces the amount of time it takes to process the data. It can also be used to choose dominant features that are rotationally and positionally invariant while maintaining the model's efficient training cycle [19]. There are two types of Pooling Like as. 1. Max Pooling and 2. Average Pooling.

   "Max Pooling returns the largest value from the convolved image, whereas Average Pooling returns the average of all values from the convolved image, as the name suggests. As a Noise Suppressant, Max Pooling is used. This completely eliminates disruptive activations and even does de-noise and dimensionality reduction. Average Pooling, on the other hand, uses the reduction in dimensionality as a strategy to remove noise [20, 21]. As a result, it may assume that Max Pooling is significantly more effective than Average Pooling".

4. Flattening: In this layer, it can flattening our entire matrix, which is got from the previous levels, to make it look like a vertical map. As a result, it is passed to the data layer. This is the most crucial phase in the CNN process. Tf.keras.layers is used to latten the image. The Flatten () method is part of the Keras package.

5. Fully Connected Layer: "Adding a Fully-Connected layer is a (typically) low-cost approach to learn non-linear combinations of high-level properties described by the convolution layer's output. The Fully-Connected layer is learning a possibly non- linear job within that space. We're going to flatten our input picture into a column vector now that can be turned it into an appropriate shape for this Multi-Level Perceptron. Each training iteration includes back propagation and the flattened result is input into a neural network feed-forward.

Across a series of epochs, the model can distinguish between dominant and other low- level properties in images, and classify them using certain classification approaches. Soft Max is a classification method. The goal of a fully connected layer is to categorise

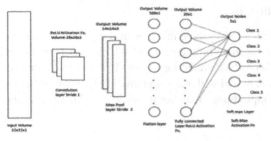

Fig. 7. Fully connected layers

the image into a suitable class using the output of the convolution / pooling phase.it is showed in the Fig. 7.

4.2 Algorithm Implementation

Algorithm 4.1: Algorithm to predict crop and disease

Input: *Initially give non-classified leaf images*
Output: *Crop name and disease name (if it infected)*

Step-I: *Gives input path of the image folder i.*
Step-II: *Performing pre-processing techniques on input data i*
Step-III: *Apply classification and predict the type of Crop o by compare with trained dataset s.*
Step IV: *apply CNN algorithm on o and s   cn*
          Compare with dataset of diseases dataset ds with cn   nd
Step V: *if continue1goto Step-I else 2 to exit.*
Step VI: *stop*

Here input is represented as i, the output of the classification is o. the output of the CNN algorithm is cn(crop name), trained dataset s is the name of the crops and ds is the name of the diseases. The name of the diseases is represented as nd.

5   Results and Dicurtions

5.1   Model Prediction

The model's accuracy is determined using metrics and plotted as a graph using the matplotlib package. The model's classification ability is determined by its accuracy. When the accuracy of the model is higher, the model's capacity to classify images is also higher. This module's major goal is to put the model to the test against new data samples in the actual world. The model's performance through various periods of training is depicted in the Fig. 8.

5.2 Making Predictions

The suggested system's last module involves making predictions using the constructed CNN model. It can estimate how the model will perform in the real world based on these predictions. To produce predictions, provide the model an input image (path of the image).After that, the model will assess the image and provide the needed output based on how closely the input image matches the model's classes. It is shown in the Fig. 9.

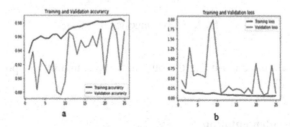

Fig. 8. Accuracy graphs

Fig. 9. Output of tomato leaf

5.3 Input and Output Analysis

Input Analysis: "The user gives the input in the form of string which represents the path of the input image. The image is converted in to the array. This array is predicted with the trained model. This array is matched with the model's classes one by one. The image is classified based on the percentage of matching. The highest percentage match is selected as the class of the image. The model receives input in the form of an array, while the user supplies the image as input in the form of the picture's path." **Output Analysis:** After training the model with proper parameters, the model is analysed for accuracy of the different types of images. The model is trained number of times. Finally, the model with the highest accuracy is chosen for deployment. Figure 8 shows the test Performance Evaluation accuracy. Input and Output Desig: **Input Design:** As input to the model, the user must specify the path to the image (or the image's name). Following the user's input, the image is extracted, transformed to an array, and stored. The input design is as shown in the Fig. 10. It is self-evident that the greater the number of epochs, the greater the model's accuracy. **Output Design:** The model is used to test the stored array, and the class that matches the array with the highest percentage is shown as output. The output design is as shown in the Fig. 10.

a   b

Fig. 10. a. Input design b. Output design

6 Conclusion

Farmers are essential to the existence of a wide range of living creatures, including humans. They use primary resources responsibly and employ both primitive and complex strategies to do so. Because they play such a vital role in society, it is tragic to learn that some of them commit themselves for reasons mentioned in introduction. As responsible citizens, in this research work developed the Crop and Leaf Disease Detector tool. The tool will be beneficial to both younger generations (in terms of recognising the crop and its significance) and farmers (reducing the risk of crop failure thereby maximising the yield). Pattern recognition with transfer learning from the Convolutional Neural Network. Inception v3 is an effective technique for autonomous high precision detection of crops and crop diseases, according to the findings of this study. This method avoids the time- consuming and arduous process of eliminating features from photographs in order to train models, and the model may be trained fast on a desktop and deployed on a mobile device. In this work looked at a number of simulation methodologies to illustrate the CNN's presentation of plant diseases. The results of the experiments show that some simple methods, such as naive visualisation of the hidden layer output, are insufficient for viewing plant illness, while other state-of-the-art methods have potential practical uses. The Model has been successfully deployed. The model is also put to the test with real-world leaves. The model's output is persuasive and suited for application in the field of agriculture. To generate output, the suggested model only requires the crop image and does not rely on sophisticated processes or devices.

Future Enhancement
Deep Learning methodology can be applied to improve the outcomes even more, but this requires a lot of learning data, thus this is the future scope. The image pre-processing and classifier can both benefit from the CNN model. There is a large scope for development or to enhance. The model which is created in this work is missing datasets on cropped photographs and the effect of a virus on a specific day. In the presence of this work for farther it can create a more advanced version that detects herb chronology (plant age) and, with the help of microbiologists, it can even approximate the life of a certain virus, which would be beneficial. The proposed methodology might be integrated with other yet-to-be-developed illness detection and classification systems based on colour and texture analysis in the future to provide a professional framework for early illness alert and administration in which the form of disease can be determined by colour and texture analysis. This method may be used to detect all types of crops and crop illnesses

in everyday life. Device efficiency will be improved in the future by employing advanced approaches for extracting the leaf entity from a dynamic environment in the field. Specific methods can be extended to other plant diseases and early warning systems for corn, cotton seeds, tomatoes, vegetables, and beans, among other things. Certain cataloguing strategies can be applied in the future to improve the system's performance.

References

1. Zhou, Y., et al.: Mapping paddy rice planting area in rice-wetland coexistent areas through analysis of Landsat 8 OLI and MODIS images. Int. J. Appl. Earth Observ. Geoinf. **46**, 1–12 (2016)
2. Khirade, S.D., Patil, A.B.: Plant disease detection using image processing. In: 2015 International Conference on Computing Communication Control and Automation, pp. 768–771 (2015). https://doi.org/10.1109/ICCUBEA.2015.153
3. Yeh, J.-F., Wang, S.-Y., Chen, Y.-P.: Crop disease detection by image processing using modified Alexnet. In: IEEE 3rd Eurasia Conference on Biomedical Engineering, Healthcare and Sustainability (ECBIOS-2021) (2021)
4. Heri Andrianto, S., Faizal, A., Armandika, F.: Smartphone application for deep learning-based rice plant disease detection. In: 2020 International Conference on Information Technology Systems and Innovation (ICITSI), pp. 387–392 (2020)
5. Wu, S., Bao, F., Xu, E., Wang, Y.-X., Chang, Y.-F., Xiang, Q.-L.: A leaf recognition algorithm for plant classification using probabilistic neural network. In: IEEE Symposium on Signal Processing and Information Technology 2007 (2007)
6. Li, L., Zhang, S., Wang, B.: Plant disease detection and classification by deep learning—a review. IEEE Access **9**, 56683–56698 (2021). https://doi.org/10.1109/ACCESS.2021.306 9646
7. Yuan, Y., Xu, Z., Lu, G.: SPEDCCNN: spatial pyramid-oriented encoder-decoder cascade convolution neural network for crop disease leaf segmentation. IEEE Access **9**, 14849–14866 (2021). https://doi.org/10.1109/ACCESS.2021.3052769
8. Rajiv, K., Rajasekhar, N., Prasanna Lakshmi, K., Srinivasa Rao, D., SabithaReddy, P.: Accuracy evaluation of plant leaf disease detection and classification using GLCM and multiclass SVM classifier. In: Sharma, H., Saraswat, M., Kumar, S., Bansal, J.C. (eds.) CIS 2020. LNDECT, vol. 61, pp. 41–54. Springer, Singapore (2021). https://doi.org/10.1007/978-981-33-4582-9_4
9. To obtain data set. https://www.kaggle.com
10. Brahimi, M., Boukhalfa, K., Moussaoui, A.: Deep learning for tomato diseases: classification and symptoms visualization. Appl. Artif. Intell. **31**(4), 299–315 (2017)
11. Hemanth, D.J., Anitha, J., Naaji, A., Geman, O., Popescu, D.E.: Son, L.H.: A modified deep convolutional neural network for abnormal brain image classification. IEEE Access **7**, 4275–4283 (2019). https://doi.org/10.1109/ACCESS.2018.2885639
12. El-Kereamy, A., et al.: Deep learning for image-based cassava disease detection. Front. Plant Sci. **1852** (2017)
13. Huang, J., Wang, H., Dai, Q., Han, D.: Analysis of NDVI data for crop identification and yield estimation. J. Sel. Top. Appl. Earth Observ. Remote Sens. **7**(11), 4374–4384 (2014)
14. Fina, F., Birch, P., Young, R., Obu, J., Faithpraise, B., Chatwin, C.: Automatic plant pest detection and recognition using k-means clustering algorithm and correspondence filters. Int. J. Adv. Biotechnol. Res. **4**(2), 189–199 (2013)
15. Ravikiran, K., Sudhakar Dr., N.: Maximizing throughput in multi hope wireless network by considering intra and inter flow spatial reusability. J. Adv. Res. Dyn. Control Syst. JARDCS, 708–717 (2018). ISSN 1943-023X

16. Cao, J., Mao, D., Cai, Q., et al.: A review of object representation based on local features. J. Zhejiang Univ. Sci. C **14**, 495–504 (2013)
17. Ngugi, L.C., Abelwahab, M., AboZahhad, M.: Recent advances in image processing techniques for automated leaf pest and disease recognition—a review. Inf. Process. Agricult. **180**, 26–50 (2020)
18. Mohanty, S.P., Hughes, D.P., Salathé, M.: Using deep learning for image-based plant disease detection. Front. Plant Sci. **7**, 1419 (2016)
19. Garcia-Ruiz, F., Sankaran, S., Maja, J.M., Lee, W.S., Rasmussen, J., Ehsani, R.: Comparison of two aerial imaging platforms for identification of Huanglongbing-infected citrus trees. In: Computers and Electronics in Agriculture, vol. 91, pp. 106–115 (2013). ISSN 0168-1699
20. Krizhevsky, A., Sutskever, I., Hinton, G.E.: ImageNet classification with deep convolutional neural networks. In: Part of Advances in Neural Information Processing Systems (NIPS 2012), vol. 25 (2012)
21. Kessentini, Y., Besbes, M.D., Ammar, S., Chabbouh, A.: A two stage deep neural network for multi-norm license plate detection and recognition. Expert Syst. Appl. **136**, 159–170 (2019)

Enhanced Service Point Approach for Microservices Based Applications Using Machine Learning Techniques

Vinay Raj[1]([✉])[iD] and Sadam Ravichandra[2][iD]

[1] BVRIT Hyderabad College of Engineering for Women, Telangana, India
vinay.raj@bvrithyderabad.edu.in
[2] National Institute of Technology Warangal, Telangana, India
ravic@nitw.ac.in

Abstract. The migration of service oriented architecture (SOA) based applications to microservices architecture is a current research trend in the domain of software engineering. Estimating the effort required for migration is a challenging task as the traditional methods are not suitable for this new architectural style of microservices. Service Points (SP) is one new approach proposed by us for estimating the effort required for the migration of SOA based applications to microservices architecture. However, the use of machine learning techniques gives promising benefits in software effort estimation. To improve the accuracy of the service points approach, multiple regression analysis with the Leave-N-Out policy is applied. The standard service points approach, service points approach with Karner's ratings and proposed machine learning based approach are considered for comparison with actual efforts of the chosen dataset of applications. The accuracy of the models is evaluated using different measures such as MRE, RMSE, MAE, etc. It is clear that the effort estimation using regression analysis gives higher accuracy. Using machine learning techniques improves the accuracy of the effort estimation and helps software architects in better planning and execution of the migration process.

Keywords: Microservices · Effort estimation · Machine learning · Regression

1 Introduction

To over the challenges in existing software architectures such as monolithic and SOA, microservices emerged as a new design style using cloud-based containers for deployment. It is a style of designing applications where each service is a small, loosely coupled, scalable and reusable service that can be designed and deployed independently [1]. Each service should perform only one task and should have its own database and independent deployment architecture. Microservices uses communication protocols like HTTP/REST and JSON for data exchange

A. K. Luhach et al. (Eds.): ICAICR 2021, CCIS 1575, pp. 78–90, 2022.
https://doi.org/10.1007/978-3-031-09469-9_7

between the services [2]. Unlike SOA, microservices can be deployed independently as there is no centralized governance and no dependency on middleware technologies. It is effortless to scale on-demand microservices with the use of cloud-based containers. Microservices architecture suits well with the DevOps style as every task is to be broken into small units, and complete SDLC is to be done independently [3]. DevOps and agile methodologies require the fast design of applications and deployment to production.

With the various benefits of microservices, software architects have started migrating their existing legacy applications to microservices architecture [4]. Many companies, including Netflix, Amazon, and Twitter, have started building their new applications with this style of architecture [5]. As microservices has emerged recently, there is a huge demand in both industry and academia to explore the tools, technologies, and programming languages used in this architecture. However, some software architects are in chaos, whether to migrate to this new style or not, as they are unaware of the pros and cons of using microservices. The major challenge is estimating the effort required to migrate the existing applications to microservices [6,7].

Effort estimation helps software architects in the proper execution and management of the project. Effective estimation helps in proper scheduling of the software engineering activities. Software effort is given by the formula effort = people * time [8]. It has to be done during the early stage of the application design as it gives insights on the effort and cost required to complete the application. Moreover, estimating the accurate effort required for the migration process is a challenging task. Underestimation and overestimation of the effort required may lead to serious project management issues. Software effort estimation techniques are divided into four types: empirical, regression theory-based, and machine learning techniques based estimation [9]. The empirical way of estimating is very popular as it gives a clear picture of the effort required numerically, and few of the models include function point, use case point, and analogy based techniques. Moreover, these techniques are not suitable for measuring the effort for service-based systems as they are designed for procedural object-oriented systems.

All the traditional approaches available for effort estimation cannot be used directly for service-based systems. Approaches need to be modified and extended to cope with these service-based systems like service oriented architecture and microservices architecture [10,11]. Service points [12] is one such approach proposed by us in our earlier works to estimate the effort required for migration. It is a formal approach recasted from use case points approach in which the service graph [22] is used to calculate the effort instead of use case diagram that is used in use case points.

Machine learning models have been widely applied in software effort estimation and it has given promising benefits [13,14]. In order to validate the efficiency of the service points method, N applications of SOA are chosen which are migrated to microservices and the regression analysis is performed on the chosen datasets. The results of the proposed techniques are compared with the actual efforts, and the accuracy of each technique is also evaluated.

The remaining paper is organized as follows. The technical details of service points approach are presented in Sect. 2. The proposed machine learning based approach is discussed in Sect. 3 and the corresponding experimental results are presented in Sect. 4. Section 5 concludes the paper.

2   Service Points Approach

In this section, the technical details of service points approach are presented. The steps for effort estimation using the service point technique are illustrated in Fig. 1. The brief description of each step is also discussed in this section.

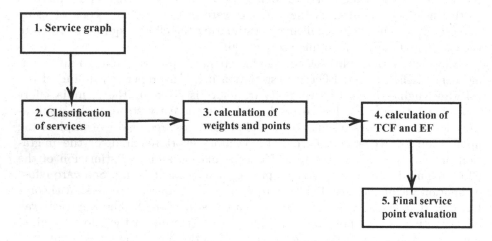

Fig. 1. Service point calculation steps

2.1   Classification of Services

The first step of the service point approach is to classify the services based on the interactions it has with other services. Each service's dependencies on other services are considered and classify them as simple, average, and complex. A service is classified as simple if it interacts with less than four services, average if it interacts with less than eight services, and service is treated as complex if it interacts with more than or equal to eight services [15].

2.2   Calculation of Weights and Points

The next step is to calculate the unadjusted service points based on the weights assigned to each service type. It is calculated by summation of number of services of each type multiplied by weight assigned to corresponding service type.

Unadjusted Service Points (USP) is calculated as shown in Eq. (1).

$$USP = \sum_{i=1}^{3} S_i \times W_i \qquad (1)$$

where S_i is the number of services of type i and W_i is the corresponding weight of the service of type i where i={simple, average, complex}.

2.3   Technical and Environmental Factors

The final value of the service point depends on 21 technical and environmental factors which contribute to the complexity and the efficiency of the system. Each factor has a value assigned between 0 and 5 depending on the importance and impact the factor has on the system. The rating of each factor between 0 and 5 for each factor is collected through online survey.

Calculation of Technical Complexity Factor (TCF). To calculate the TCF, total weight of the factors is calculated which is obtained by multiplying the value assiged to each factor between 0 to 5 and weights assigned to each factor. Calculation of TFactor is given by Eq. (2).

$$TFactor = \sum_{i=1}^{13} TF_i \times W_i \qquad (2)$$

where TF_i is the rating of the technical factor i and W_i is the weight assigned to corresponding factor. Technical Complexity Factor (TCF) is calculated by the below Eq. (3).

$$TCF = 0.6 + (0.01 \times TFactor) \qquad (3)$$

Calculcation of Environmental Factor (EF). Similarly, the impact of environmental factors in the final service point is evaluated by finding the EF score. To calculate the EF value, the weight of each factor is multiplied with the rating assigned to each factor. It is given by Eq. (4).

$$EFactor = \sum_{i=1}^{8} EF_i \times W_i \qquad (4)$$

where EF_i is the rating of the environmental factor i and W_i is the weight assigned to the corresponding factor. Environmental Factor (EF) is calculated by the below Eq. (5).

$$EF = 1.4 + (-0.03 \times EFactor) \qquad (5)$$

2.4   Final Service Point Evaluation

The final Service Points (SP) is calculated by multiplying the unadjusted service point with both technical and environmental factor values. It is given by the below Eq. (6).

$$SP = USP \times TCF \times EF \tag{6}$$

According to Karner, [15], the effort required to implement each use case point is 20 h. Hence, we do consider the same 20 h for each service point. Therefore, to estimate the final man-hours, the calculated service point should be multiplied by 20 to get the effort required for migration.

We define the naming convention for different approaches used for comparison in this paper. The service points approach with the ratings collected through the online survey proposed by Vinay Raj et al. [12] is denoted as *SP-Vinay Approach*; the service points approach with the Karner's default value as *SP-Karner Approach* and the SP-Vinay approach with regression analysis as *SP-Regression Approach*. These notations are used throughout this paper.

3   Proposed Approach

In this section, the regression approach, description of the datasets and the measures to predict the accuracy of the proposed models are discussed.

3.1   Regression Analysis

It is one of the popular analysis methods to study the relationship between dependent and independent variables and present the relationship in the form of a model [16]. If we have more than two variables, then it is referred as multiple regression and it is the most preferred and applied method for cost estimation [17]. Since the proposed service point approach is based on the multiple factors including USP, TCF and EF, we define the multiple regression based effort estimation which is represented based on the below equation.

$$y = \beta_0 + \beta_1 x_1 + \beta_2 x_2 + \epsilon \tag{7}$$

where y represents the effort caculated, x_1 represents the size metric calculated with USP of the chosen application and TCF, x_2 represents the adjustment factor (AF) considered as an independent variable in this multiple regression and the coefficients β_1, β_2, and β_0 represents the contant values. Here the additional ϵ represents the error induced during the calculation of the effort.

$$Size(x_1) = USP \times TCF \tag{8}$$

Adjustment Factor is calculated as the product of environment factor (EF) and the productivity factor (PF). The value of PF can be considered as 20 h as proposed by Karner, if the projects do not have any historical data. We consider only the EF in the calculation of x_2 as TCF is already included in the first variable x_1.

$$AdjustmentFactor(x_2) = {}_pPF \times EF \qquad (9)$$

However, we calculate the productivity factor ${}_pPF$ by dividing the actual effort by the SP as it gives the accurate effort required to implement each service point.

$$_pPF = \frac{ActualEffort}{SP} \qquad (10)$$

3.2 Datasets

The use of microservices architecture has just started and there are very few projects which are migrated from SOA. The authors in [18] state that data collection is more important for validation of effort estimation techniques. Due to the inability to access SOA projects developed in the industry and the unavailability of datasets based on UML artifacts in the industry, the study research investigation is collected from [19]. The dataset is represented a dataframe and the size of the dataset is 7 rows with 5 columns. So, gathering the information such as number of services and coupling/dependencies between the microservices of the real time projects was a difficult task. Out of the 7 applications we gathered, 5 applications were collected from Indian IT organizations and one application from a research centre in UK where a team is working on the best approaches for migration of SOA based applications to microservices. The remaining one application is developed at our university by a team of Post Graduate (PG) students which is related to the online exam portal during the pandemic time. The details of the data collected are presented in Table 1. The Unadjusted Service Points (USP) is also calculated for the applications and is presented in Table 1.

Table 1. Characteristics of 7 applications

Application	Total No. of services			USP
	Simple	Average	Complex	
A1	6	5	2	22
A2	2	2	2	12
A3	6	10	2	32
A4	23	15	4	65
A5	0	7	3	23
A6	3	14	0	31
A7	20	15	21	113

3.3 Evaluation Criteria

To evaluate the accuracy of the estimated approach, several frequently used measures [18, 20] are considered such as magnriture relative error (MRE), mean of MRE (MMRE), root mean square error (RMSE), and prediction within 25% of the actual value. The definitions of the measures are discussed below.

– The magnitude of relative error (MRE) is calculated as given below.

$$MRE = \frac{ActualEffort - EstimatedEffort}{ActualEffort} \qquad (11)$$

– MMRE is the mean of the MREs of all the applications and it is used to evaluate the prediction performance of the model. The Mean of MRE is calculated as

$$MMRE = \frac{1}{n}(\sum_{i=1}^{n} MRE_i) \qquad (12)$$

– The Root Mean Square Error (RMSE) evaluates the difference between actual effort and the estimated effort. It is used to find the standard deviation of the errors which occur after applying the proposed method on the datasets. RMSE is calculated as given below.

$$RMSE = \sqrt{\frac{1}{n}\sum_{i=1}^{n}(ActualEffort - EstimatedEffort)^2} \qquad (13)$$

– To verify whether the predicted values are within m% of the actual values, we use a measure and in software engineering, the value of m is typically set to 25%. The measure PRED(25) is calculated as

$$PRED(25) = \frac{k}{n} \qquad (14)$$

where k is the number of observations for those whose MRE is less than or equal to 0.25 and n is the total number of applications.
– The above discussed measures are criticised and behave differently when evaluating prediction models, hence two other measures are suggested [21]. Mean Absolute Error (MAE) is unbaised and it is calculated as given below.

$$MAE = \frac{1}{n}\sum_{i=1}^{n} |\, ActualEffort_i - EstimatedEffort_i \,| \qquad (15)$$

where n is the number of applications chosen for evaluation of performance.
– Standardized accuracy (SA) is one the recommended measures for comparing the performance of prediction models which is based on MAE. It is defined as follows:

$$SA = 1 - \frac{MAE_{Pj}}{MAE_{guess}} \times 100 \qquad (16)$$

where MAE_{Pj} is the MAE of the proposed approach and MAE_{guess} is the value of MAE of a random guess. The standard accuracy represents the impact of MAE_{Pj} when compared to any random guess. For effort estimation techniques, the value of MAE should be less and SA should be maximum.

4 Experimental Results

The SP-Vinay approach, SP-Karner approach and SP-Regression approach are applied on the 7 applications and the results obtained by comparing these three methods are presented in this section.

4.1 Application of Service Points Method

The service points approach is applied on the 7 applications and the effort is calculated by considering the TCF and EF values. The effort is calculated by considering the collected ratings and also with the Karner's default value. The PF value for calculating the effort is taken as 20 man-hours. The magnitude of relative error (MRE) is also calculated with the help of actual efforts of the applications. The results of the efforts calculated are presented in Table 2.

Table 2. Applying service point approach to applications.

Application	Actual effort [h]	SP-Vinay approach		SP-Karner's approach	
		Estimated effort [h]	MRE	Estimated effort [h]	MRE
A1	396	326	0.176	305	0.229
A2	140	178	−0.271	166	−0.185
A3	587	474	0.192	444	0.243
A4	1205	962	0.201	902	0.251
A5	518	340	0.343	319	0.384
A6	502	459	0.08	430	0.143
A7	2034	1673	0.177	1567	0.229

4.2 Application of Proposed Regression Model

The proposed regression method is applied on the same dataset and the function for effort estimation is obtained. First, the variables x_1 and x_2 are calculated with the Eqs. (8) and (9). The calculated values of the variables are presented in Table 3. These values x_1 and x_2 will be used in the calculation of the effort using the regression model. We consider the TCF value which is calcuated using the ratings collected through online survey in the regression analysis.

Using the calculated values of variables, we applied multiple linear regression on the applications. However, to improve the accuracy we apply Leave-N-Out policy where we train the model only on first 5 applications to calculate the coefficients and test with the remaining two applications. The values of the coefficients calculated are presented in the effort estimation function, given in the below equation.

$$\hat{y} = -274.10 + 15.017x_1 + 17.136x_2 \tag{17}$$

Table 3. Variable values for multiple regression analysis.

Application	Size (x_1)	AF (x_2)
A1	23.43	16.8
A2	12.78	10.9
A3	34.08	17.1
A4	69.22	17.3
A5	24.49	21.1
A6	33.01	15.1
A7	120.34	16.8

Using the calculated coefficient values $\beta_0 = -274.10$, $\beta_1 = 15.017$, and $\beta_2 = 17.136$, we test the remaining two applications. The efforts calculated using the generated coefficients are presented in the Table 4. It is clear from the table that the values are very close to the actual efforts of the applications. The proposed regression model works as recommendation system for estimating the effort required for migration of SOA applications to microservices. The coefficients generated are used to calculate the efforts for all the other applications which are used for training the model as well.

Table 4. Application of regression model to testing data

Application	Actual effort [h]	Estimated effort (Regression) [h]	MRE
A6	502	480.36	0.043
A7	2034	1940.99	0.045

4.3   Comparison

The estimation function is calculated for all the 7 applications by regression analysis on the 6 applications and leaving one application everytime. The values of the coefficients are calculated and the effort by regression analysis are generated for all the applications. The results of the comparison of all the proposed methods are presented in Table 5. For each approach, the estimated effort in hours and estimation success values are given in the table. It is clear that the efforts calculated through the regression analysis give better values closer to the actual efforts required for migration. For application A2, the efforts estimated through SP-Vinay approach and SP-Karner's approach are more than the actual efforts. Hence the estimation success percentage is more than 100 which is marked as *. Generally success percentage more than 100 does not makes sense. So, only the SP-Regression model gives better result for the application A2. The efforts estimated by the standard SP-Vinay approach, SP-Karner approach, SP-Regression approach and the actual efforts are compared and presented as a line graph as shown in Fig. 2. The x-axis represents the 7 applications and the y-axis represents the efforts in man-hours for each application. From the graph, it is clear that the effort estimated with the regression model is close to the actual efforts of all the applications.

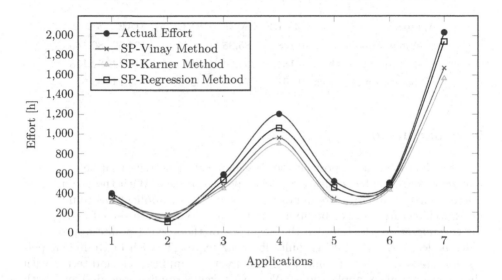

Fig. 2. Comparison of efforts estimated by proposed methods.

The accuracy of the proposed methods are evaluated using the measures discussed in Sect. 3.3 and the values are presented in Table 6. From the results, the MAE value is very less and SA value is also better for effort estimated through regression model. Though the MMRE and PRED values are close to each other, the RMSE value is better only for the regression model.

Table 5. Comparison of proposed effort estimation techniques

Application	Actual effort [h]	SP-Vinay approach		SP-Karner's approach		SP-regression approach	
		Estimated effort [h]	Estimation success (%)	Estimated effort [h]	Estimation success (%)	Estimated effort [h]	Estimation success (%)
A1	396	326	82.32	305	77.02	366	92.42
A2	140	178	127*	166	118*	105	75.0
A3	587	474	80.74	444	75.63	531	90.45
A4	1205	962	79.83	902	74.85	1062	88.13
A5	518	340	65.63	319	61.58	455	87.83
A6	502	459	91.43	430	85.65	480	95.61
A7	2034	1673	82.25	1567	77.04	1941	95.42

Table 6. Accuracy of the proposed methods using different measures.

Approach	MMRE	RMSE	PRED(25)	MAE	SA
SP-Vinay approach	0.128	185.95	0.857	138.57	86.143
SP-Karner approach	0.184	234.24	0.714	178.42	82.158
SP-regression approach	0.107	74.55	0.857	63.24	93.67

5 Conclusion

Effort estimation is an important software engineering activity that helps project managers and architects effectively schedule the project. With the evolution of microservices, companies are migrating existing legacy applications to microservices architecture. Service points is an approach to estimate the effort required for the migration. To improve the accuracy of the service points approach, a machine learning model using multiple linear regression with Leave-N-Out policy is proposed, where the model is trained with N applications and tested with the remaining all-N applications. We have taken 7 applications designed with SOA and migrated to microservices, and the efforts are calculated using the regression function. The accuracy of the proposed models is evaluated using different metrics such as MRE, RMSE, PRED, MAE, and SA. The comparison results show that the efforts estimated using the proposed regression model are close to the actual efforts, and the error rate is very low compared to the SP standard approach and SP-Karner's approach.

References

1. Thönes, J.: Microservices. IEEE Softw. **32**(1), 116 (2015)
2. Raj V, Ravichandra S. Microservices: a perfect SOA based solution for enterprise applications compared to web services. In: 2018 3rd IEEE International Conference on Recent Trends in Electronics, Information & Communication Technology (RTEICT), pp. 1531–1536. IEEE, 18 May 2018

3. Salah, T., Zemerly, M.J., Yeun, C.Y., Al-Qutayri, M., Al-Hammadi, Y.: The evolution of distributed systems towards microservices architecture. In: 2016 11th International Conference for Internet Technology and Secured Transactions (ICITST), pp. 318–325. IEEE, 5 December 2016

4. Raj, V., Sadam, R.: Patterns for migration of SOA based applications to microservices architecture. J. Web Eng. **10**, 1229–46 (2021)

5. Raj, V., Sadam, R.: Evaluation of SOA-based web services and microservices architecture using complexity metrics. SN Comput. Sci. **2**(5), 1–10 (2021). https://doi.org/10.1007/s42979-021-00767-6

6. Taibi, D., Lenarduzzi, V., Pahl, C.: Processes, motivations, and issues for migrating to microservices architectures: an empirical investigation. IEEE Cloud Comput. **4**(5), 22–32 (2017)

7. Soldani, J., Tamburri, D.A., Van Den Heuvel, W.J.: The pains and gains of microservices: a systematic grey literature review. J. Syst. Softw. **1**(146), 215–232 (2018)

8. Pendharkar, P.C., Subramanian, G.H., Rodger, J.A.: A probabilistic model for predicting software development effort. IEEE Trans. Softw. Eng. **31**(7), 615–24 (2005)

9. Subramanian, G.H., Pendharkar, P.C., Wallace, M.: An empirical study of the effect of complexity, platform, and program type on software development effort of business applications. Empirical Softw. Eng. **11**(4), 541–53 (2006)

10. Canfora, G., Fasolino, A.R., Frattolillo, G., Tramontana, P.: A wrapping approach for migrating legacy system interactive functionalities to service oriented architectures. J. Syst. Softw. **81**(4), 463–80 (2008)

11. Siddiqui, Z.A., Tyagi, K.: A critical review on effort estimation techniques for service-oriented-architecture-based applications. Int. J. Comput. Appl. **38**(4), 207–16 (2016)

12. Raj, V., Ravichandra, S.: A novel effort estimation approach for migration of SOA applications to microservices. J. Inf. Syst. Telecommun. (JIST). **3**(36) (2021)

13. Sehra, S.K., Brar, Y.S., Kaur, N., Sehra, S.S.: Research patterns and trends in software effort estimation. Inf. Softw. Technol. **1**(91), 1–21 (2017)

14. Wen, J., Li, S., Lin, Z., Hu, Y., Huang, C.: Systematic literature review of machine learning based software development effort estimation models. Inf. Softw. Technol. **54**(1), 41–59 (2012)

15. Karner, G.: Resource estimation for objectory projects. Objective Syst. SF AB. **17**(17), 1–9 (1993)

16. Montgomery, D.C., Peck, E.A., Vining, G.G.: Introduction to Linear Regression Analysis. Wiley, Hoboken 9 Apr 2012

17. Shepperd, M., Schofield, C.: Estimating software project effort using analogies. IEEE Trans. Softw. Eng. **23**(11), 736–43 (1997)

18. Sarro, F., Petrozziello, A., Harman, M.: Multi-objective software effort estimation. In: 2016 IEEE/ACM 38th International Conference on Software Engineering (ICSE), pp. 619–630. IEEE, 14 May 2016

19. Munialo, S.W., Wanjala, S.: A size metric-based effort estimation method for service oriented architecture systems (Doctoral dissertation, MMUST) (2020)

20. Menzies, T., Yang, Y., Mathew, G., Boehm, B., Hihn, J.: Negative results for software effort estimation. Empirical Softw. Eng. **22**(5), 2658–2683 (2016). https://doi.org/10.1007/s10664-016-9472-2

21. Port, D., Korte, M.: Comparative studies of the model evaluation criterions MMRE and pred in software cost estimation research. In: Proceedings of the Second ACM-IEEE International Symposium on Empirical Software Engineering and Measurement, pp. 51–60, 9 October 2008
22. Raj, V., Sadam, R.: Performance and complexity comparison of service oriented architecture and microservices architecture. Int. J. Commun. Netw. Distrib. Syst. **27**(1), 100–17 (2021)

An Efficient Novel Approach for Detection of Handwritten Numericals Using Machine Learning Paradigms

Pavithra Avvari[✉], Bhavani Ratakonda, K. Sandeep, Y. Jeevan Nagendra Kumar, and T. N. P. Madhuri

Department of IT, Gokaraju Rangaraju Institute of Engineering and Technology, JNTU(H), Hyderabad, India
pavithra.griet@gmail.com, bhavani1592@grietcollege.com

Abstract. The goal of recognizing handwritten numbers on paper is to extract the characteristics of the entered handwritten number. The human visual system is one of the wonders of the world. People can easily find and recognize the numbers as they are used for recognition and identification. Most people easily recognize numbers without effort. Humans are amazing at deciphering what our eyes show. All work is done subconsciously, and no additional training is required to recognize numbers. Generally, we do not need to assess the difficulty of a problem that our visual system solves. However, recognizing numbers for mechanical devices such as computers is not that easy. If we try to develop a computer program to detect numbers, the difficulty of visually recognizing patterns is significant. When it comes to coding, what seems simple when we see it will be quite complicated. Simple intuitions, for example, are for a system that recognizes strokes, circles, curves, straight lines, curves, and more. Example of recognizing a number like 9, you should recognize the loop at the top and a straight vertical bar at the bottom right. This is not easy to express algorithmically. That is why we came up with a prototype for number recognition. Although identification, classification and recognition are simple tasks with the help of machine learning, we are trying to develop a system that recognizes numbers as accurately as possible. The main goal of focusing on handwriting recognition is to learn about neural networks. Images are divided into pixels and recognized in pixel order.

Keywords: K nearest neighbours · Stochastic gradient descent · Support vector machines · Neural networks · Deciphering · Metrics · Dataset hyperplanes · Regression

A. K. Luhach et al. (Eds.): ICAICR 2021, CCIS 1575, pp. 91–101, 2022.
https://doi.org/10.1007/978-3-031-09469-9_8

1 Introduction

Our project aims at an automatic recognition of digits written by hand. The tendency of writing the digits in different forms is much higher as each person writes them differently. In such cases also, the system developed must be able to recognize the digits correctly and give out the accurate results. There exist many classification and pattern recognition algorithms in machine learning such as KNN, SVM, Neural Networks (CNN, ANN, and RNN) [1, 2]. We try to study how each algorithm works while training and testing the dataset. The project focuses on developing an easy methodology of recognizing the images for a plethora of things. The goal of this system is to provide information about the research project "An Efficient Novel approach for detection of handwritten numerical using Machine Learning paradigms" [12]. It includes what we did for the completion of project, requirements, description of modelling of the project, the technologies we have used for the project, implementation of the project and future enhancements [1, 2].

This project explains in detail about how a machine can identify human written digits. For this process, we are considering MNIST ("Modified National Institute of Standards and Technology") dataset which consist of 60000 images of 28*28 sizes in grey scale[15]. However, considering images as a dataset will not make our work easy. These images need to be pre-processed [2, 4]. As well as many other step need to be performed before entering into training the dataset. We are considering few classification and recognition algorithms like KNN, SVM and CNN [3]. We come up with a conclusion that no algorithm can beat up Neural Network in digit recognizer. We try to achieve the highest accuracy and prediction rates by applying best training methodologies [3, 4].

2 Related Works

The application identification of handwritten numerals using machine learning provides the following uses to the user: this application provides a chance for the user to allow their machine to recognize the digits from 0 to 9 written in any format with ease [2, 3]. It is useful for various kinds of future works like usage of this module in number plate recognition, number detection projects, etc. This also helps in performing multiple further operations like calculating attendance percentage, focusing on absentees, sending text messages to parents, etc. [14]. This document furnishes different diagrams for the "An Efficient Novel approach for detection of handwritten numerical using Machine Learning paradigms" using uml that clearly explains the model of building this particular application [3, 4]. The literary survey provides insights into the project in terms of the user experience and functionality of the project [9].

2.1 Feasibility Study

In the software development process, the feasibility study is critical. It provides the developer an opportunity to assess the operational flexibility of the product that is being developed[13]. The operational flexibility, technical support, the output of the project, and many others are treated as various criteria and parameters to analyse the feasibility of the project. Operational Feasibility, Technical Feasibility, as well as Economic Feasibility are the three basic types of feasibility studies.

2.1.1 Operational Feasibility

The application developed must be in such a way that it is feasible for the users to use with ease. How much the user is willing to use the application determines the operational feasibility of the system. Before checking the operational feasibility, the user must be adequately trained with regard to the application [11]. The user must not feel any difficulty in using the system. However, the percentage of the willingness of the user to use the application entirely depends on the way that the system is built with a user-friendly interface and the method that is taken to popularize the user about the system handling and usage. Our project employs a simple yet intuitive interface for the user to navigate through the application and operate it feasibly.

2.1.2 Technical Feasibility

This study is done to find the technical feasibility. This study determines to find out the technical requirements needed to develop the system.. Our project is developed with utmost care such that it is technically feasible [12]. Changes can be easily made and adopted according to the user's requirements. The trending programming language "Python" and its inbuilt libraries made the application development simple and easy.

2.1.3 Economic Feasibility

This study is done to find the economic feasibility of the developing system. The expenditures must be justified. The existing systems have the economy as one main backdrop because they require other specially developed devices [3, 15]. Thus, our project is designed well with a limited budget, and the hidden reason for this would be freely available technologies. The one and only customized product that has been used as an external device is a webcam which is always an economic-friendly device.

3   System Architecture

See Fig. 1.

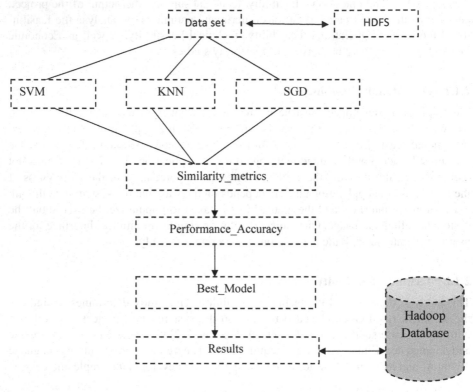

Fig. 1. Model framework

4   Methodology

4.1   Data

Handwritten digits were provided for a total of 70,000 photos from the MNIST (Modified National Institute of Standards and Technology) data set, with 60,000 examples in the training set and 10,000 examples in the test set, both with labeled images of 10 digits (0 to 9). This is a small part of the NIST broad set that was normalized to fit a 20 * 20 pixel frame without changing the aspect ratio [17]. The handwritten digits are images in the form of 28 * 28 grayscale intensities of images that represent an image, with the first column of each image being a label (0 to 9). The same has been decided in the case of the test set, which consists of 10,000 photos with labels ranging from 0 to 9 (Figs. 2, 3 and 4).

Name	Type	Size	Value
X_test	float64	(899, 64)	Min: 0.0 Max: 16.0
X_train	float64	(898, 64)	Min: 0.0 Max: 16.0
data	float64	(1797, 64)	Min: 0.0 Max: 16.0
digits	utils.Bunch	7	Bunch object of sklearn.utils module
n_samples	int	1	1797
y_test	int32	(899,)	Min: 0 Max: 9
y_train	int32	(898,)	Min: 0 Max: 9

Fig. 2. Data

Node	Transferring Address	last contact	configured capacity (GB)	used (GB)	non DFS used (GB)	Remaining (GB)	Used (%)	Remaining (%)	blocks	Block pool used(GB)
DN-1	172.16.9.31:50010	3	9112.91	14.80	71.01	8157.09	0.53	83.99	78.00	5.71
DN-2	172.16.9.32:50010	2	1154.19	14.68	77.66	1421.85	1.03	92.77	76.00	5.98
DN-3	172.16.9.33:50010	1	1450.26	14.84	87.56	1417.88	1.08	89.63	79.00	5.36
DN-4	172.16.9.34:50010	4	1450.26	14.84	87.56	1417.88	1.08	89.63	79.00	5.36
DN-5	172.16.9.35:50010	3	1450.26	14.84	87.56	1417.88	1.08	89.63	79.00	5.36

Fig. 3. Table of memory allocation in hadoop ecosystem

Data set(DS)	Size of the_ fill	Replication®	Block size(BS)	Modification_ Time(MT)	Permissions (P)	Ownr (O)
				12/11/2020 16:24	rwxr-xr-x	IT
1	15.86 MB	6	128 MB	12/11/2020 16:54	rw-r--r--	IT
2	15.86 MB	6	128 MB	12/11/2020 17:24	rw-r--r--	IT
3	146.53 MB	6	128 MB	12/11/2020 17:44	rw-r--r--	IT
4	146.53 MB	6	128 MB	12/11/2020 18:54	rw-r--r--	IT
5	146.53 MB	6	128 MB	12/11/2020 19:24	rw-r--r--	IT

Fig. 4. Table of memory segregation in hadoop environment for file distribution

4.2 Support Vector Machines (SVM)

The ability of a machine with a reference vector to generate the highest level of precision is greater. SVM can be used for classification, which involves drawing a line between two categories or classes to distinguish [6]. Hyperplanes are the lines that connect different classes [8]. However, this distinction is not so clear [11]. In this situation, the dimension of the hyperplane must be changed from 1D to the N-th dimension, which is called the nucleus. Linear nuclei, polynomial nuclei, and functional nuclei with a radial base are the three types of nuclei [8, 9]. In multidimensional space, the created hyperplane divides different classes [17]. SVM iteratively develops an ideal hyperplane that minimizes the error [7, 13]. However, because it takes a long time to train and performs worse with overlapping classes, this classifier is not suitable for large data sets. It is also sensitive to the type of core used [8, 16].

SVM falls into the category of controlled learning and with a bonus for classification and regression problems. In general, SVM draws an optimal hyperplane, which is classified into different categories [18]. In two-dimensional space, we first draw the data points of the independent variable corresponding to the dependent variables. Then begin the classification process by looking at the hyperplane or any linear or nonlinear plane that distinguishes the two classes at their best (Fig. 5).

Algorithm:		
	1.	*Identify the correct hyperplane which segregates the two classes better.*
	2.	*Look for the maximum distance between nearest data point (of either any class) or hyperplane, the distance is measured as margin. So, look for hyperplane with maximum margin both sides equally. Hyperplane with higher margin is more robust, whereas low margin has changed for misclassification.*
	3.	*SVM selects the classifier accurately to maximized margin.*
	4.	*SVM is robust to the classifier and have a feature to ignore outliers and try to look for a hyperplane with maximum margin*

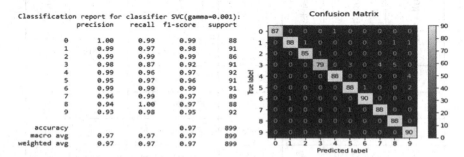

Fig. 5. Support Vector Machines (SVM)

4.3 K Nearest Neighbours (KNN)

This is the most basic classifier for categorizing images. This classifier is effectively explained with a simple expression in plain language: "Tell me your neighbors and I will tell you who you are." This approach is based solely on the distance between two illuminated vectors [7]. Finds the most common data among the closest K samples to distinguish the new data. Euclidean distance can be used as a distance metric [8].

This algorithm gave an accuracy of 92.8%. However, this algorithm has many significant drawbacks in terms of various aspects such as the choice of features [8], dimensionality reduction, etc. KNN is the nonparametric method or classifier used for both classification and regression problems [17]. This is the delayed or late learning classification algorithm, in which all the calculations are done until the last stage of the classification, and these are instance-based learning algorithms where the convergence is done locally. As it is the simplest and easiest to implement, there is no explicit training phase before and the algorithm does not perform training data aggregation (Fig. 6).

Algorithm:		
	1.	*Compute the distance metric between the test data point and all labeled data points.*
	2.	*Order the labeled data points in increasing order of distance metric.*
	3.	*Select the top K labeled data points and look at class labels.*
	4.	*Look for the class labels that majority of these K labeled data points have and assign it to test data points.*

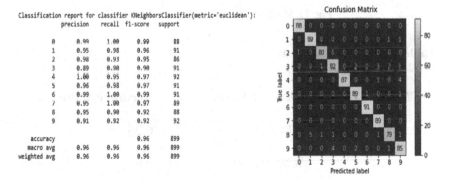

Fig. 6. K Nearest Neighbours (KNN)

4.4 Stochastic Gradient Descent

Stochastic gradient descent is a very popular and common algorithm that is used in various machine learning algorithms; the most important thing is that it forms the basis of neural networks. Gradient descent is an iterative algorithm that starts from an arbitrary point on a function and moves down its slope in steps until it reaches the lowest point of that function [18] (Figs. 7 and 8).

Algorithm:	
1.	Find the slope of the objective function **with respect to each parameter/feature**. In other words, compute the gradient of the function.
2.	Pick a random initial value for the parameters. (To clarify, in the parabola example, differentiate "y" with respect to "x". If we had more features like x1, x2 etc., we take the partial derivative of "y" with respect to each of the features.)
3.	Update the gradient function by plugging in the parameter values.
4.	Calculate the step sizes for each feature as: **step size = gradient * learning rate**.
5.	Calculate the new parameters as: **new params = old params -step size**
6.	Repeat steps 3 to 5 until gradient is almost 0.

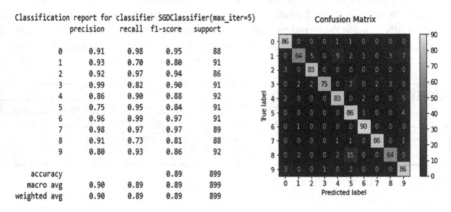

Fig. 7. Stochastic Gradient Descent (SGD).

Table: Comparison Analysis

Name of the Classifiers	F1 Score	Accuracy Score
SVM	0.92	0.96
KNN	0.90	0.95
SGD	0.81	0.89

In this section, the processed images are sent as input to various algorithms. The precision and F1 evaluation values are 0.96, 0.95, 0.89 and 0.92, 0,90, 0.81, respectively. Choosing the correct data set, pre-preparing the data with the right techniques, planning the model, and many other tasks combine to create better performance. The CNN model in our model efficiently organizes all the test photos with the names of the individual classes. This did not happen in any case. Each age group has its own data set [18]. Accuracy seems to increase with each generation. The pass set was tested after the

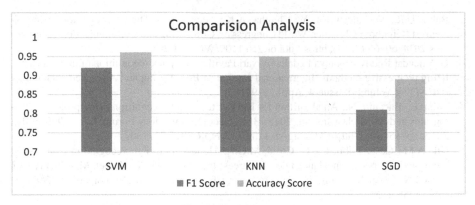

Fig. 8. Model accuracy

model was developed on the preparatory data set and showed a precision of 0.96. Then when the model was obtained with test data as input, the model showed an accuracy of 0.97%.

5   Conclusion

In this section we saw how the different algorithms work in handwriting recognition. There are many classification and recognition algorithms. K-Neighbor and Support Vector Machine are some of the most famous and widely used. All these algorithms consider various factors during training and testing. Also considered is the MNIST handwritten digit dataset used, consisting of approximately 60,000 images with sizes 28 * 28 grayscale images of handwritten digits 0 to 9. All images should be pre-processed using appropriate techniques. In the study, the main characteristics are extracted from each image for further processing for training. The processed images are sent as input to various algorithms. The precision and F1 evaluation values are 0.96, 0.95, 0.89 and 0.92, 0,90, 0.81, respectively. Choosing the correct data set, pre-preparing the data with the right techniques, planning the model, and many other tasks combine to create better performance. The CNN model in our model efficiently organizes all the test photos with the names of the individual classes. This did not happen in any case. Each age group has its own data set. Accuracy seems to increase with each generation. The pass set was tested after the model was developed on the preparatory data set and showed a precision of 0.96. Then when the model was obtained with test data as input, the model showed an accuracy of 0.97%. The excellent performance of the model is a direct result of the inclusion and structure of the authentic image of the model.

References

1. Abu Ghosh, M.M., Maghari, A.Y.: A comparative study on handwriting digit recognition using neural networks. In: 2017 International Conference on Promising Electronic Technologies (ICPET), 2017, pp. 77–81 (2017). https://doi.org/10.1109/ICPET.2017.20

2. Babu, U.R., Venkateswarlu, Y., Chintha, A.K.: Handwritten Digit Recognition Using K-Nearest Neighbour Classifier. World Congress on Computing and Communication Technologies **2014**, 60–65 (2014). https://doi.org/10.1109/WCCCT.2014.7
3. G. Vijendar Reddy, Sukanya Ledalla ,Avvari Pavithra: A quick recognition of duplicates utilizing progressive methods 'International Journal of Engineering and Advanced Technology (IJEAT)' at Volume-8 Issue-4, April 2019
4. Tuba, E., Bacanin, N.: An algorithm for handwritten digit recognition using projection histograms and SVM classifier. In: 2015 23rd Telecommunications Forum Telfor (TELFOR), 2015, pp. 464–467. https://doi.org/10.1109/TELFOR.2015.7377507
5. Gil, A.M., Costa Filho, C.F.F., Costa, M.G.F.: Handwritten digit recognition using SVM binary classifiers and unbalanced decision trees. In: Campilho, A., Kamel, M. (eds.) ICIAR 2014. LNCS, vol. 8814, pp. 246–255. Springer, Cham (2014). https://doi.org/10.1007/978-3-319-11758-4_27
6. Ahamed, Hafiz &Alam, Ishraq& Islam, Md. (2019): SVM Based Real Time Hand-Written Digit Recognition System
7. Al-Wzwazy, Haider. (2016): Handwritten Digit Recognition Using Convolutional Neural Networks. International Journal of Innovative Research in Computer and Communication Engineering
8. Ratakonda, B., Avvari, P., Rajarao, B., Sreevani, V., Ganapathi Raju, N.V.: Smart Parking for Smart Cities using IoT in 3rd International conference on Design and manufacturing aspects for sustainable energy(ICMED-2021) (2021). https://doi.org/10.1051/e3sconf/202 130901128
9. Jeevan Nagendra Kumar, Y., Spandana, V., Vaishnavi, V.S., Neha, K., Devi, V.G.R.R.: Supervised machine learning approach for crop prediction in agriculture sector. In: IEEE - 5th International Conference on Communication and Electronics Systems (ICCES), pp. 736–741. ISBN: 978-1-7281-5370-4
10. Prasanna Lakshmi, K., et al.: Video genre classification using convolutional recurrent neural networks. Int. J. Adv. Comput. Sci. Appl. **11**, 170–176 (2020). ISSN: 2156-5570 (Online) ISSN: 2158-107X (Print))
11. Shailaja, V., Lohitha, R., Musunuru, S., Deepthi Reddy, K., Padma Priya, J.: Predictive analytics of performance bof india in the olympics using machine learning algorithms. Int. J. Emerging Trends Eng. Res. **8**(5), May 2020. ISSN 23473983
12. Zaguia, A., Raju, V., Jeevan Nagendra Kumar, Y., Rawat, U.: Secure Vertical Handover to NEMO using Hybrid Cryptosystem. Hindawi, Article ID 6751423, Hindawi
13. Jeevan Nagendra Kumar, Y., Rajini Kanth, T.V.: GIS-MAP based spatial analysis of rainfall data of Andhra Pradesh and telangana states using R. Int. J. Electr. Comput. Eng. (IJECE) **7**(1), February 2017, Scopus Indexed Journal, ISSN: 2088-8708
14. Ratakonda, B., Therala, A., Hanumanthu, C.K.: Driving license detection using QR code. In: International Conference on Design and Manufacturing Aspects for Sustainable Energy, 19 August 2020, ICMED (2020). https://doi.org/10.1051/e3sconf/202018401010
15. Prasanna Lakshmi, K., et al.: Efficient mining of data streams using associative classification approach. Int. J. Softw. Eng. Knowl. Eng. **25**(3), 605–631 (2015). ISSN (Online): 1793-6403. ISSN (Print) :0218-1940
16. Ledalla, S., Mahalakshmi, T.S.: Sentiment analysis using legion kernel convolutional neural network with LSTM. Int. J. Innov. Technol. Exploring Eng. **8**, 226–229 (2019)
17. Subbarayudu, Y., Sureshbabu, A.: Distributed multimodal aspective on topic model using sentiment analysis for recognition of public health surveillance. Expert Clouds and Applications, 16 July 2021, doi.https://doi.org/10.1007/978-981-16-2126-0_38 Springer, Singapore. Print ISBN978-981-16-2125-3 Online ISBN978-981-16-2126-0.

18. Rajiv, K., Rajasekhar, N., Prasanna Lakshmi, K., Srinivasa Rao, D., Sabitha Reddy, P.: Accuracy evaluation of plant leaf disease detection and classification using GLCM and multiclass SVM classifier. In: Sharma, H., Saraswat, M., Kumar, S., Bansal, J.C. (eds.) CIS 2020. LNDECT, vol. 61, pp. 41–54. Springer, Singapore (2021). https://doi.org/10.1007/978-981-33-4582-9_4

Multiclass Classification in Machine Learning Algorithms for Disease Prediction

Pallavi Tiwari[✉], Deepak Upadhyay, Bhaskar Pant, and Noor Mohd

Department of Computer Science and Engineering, Graphic Era Deemed to be University,
Dehradun, India
{Pallavitiwari_20061041.cse,deepakupadhyay.ece}@geu.ac.in

Abstract. This paper proposes multiclass classification using different symptoms of patients into 40 different classes. This paper also represents the comparative study of the performance of four different Machine Learning models on the test symptoms data of the patients and suggests the most effient model to classify into 40 classes. Random Forest, Support Vector Machine (SVM), Naive Bayes and Decision tree are used for building the model. The performance of the algorithms is being analyzed on the parameter like accuracy, precision, and F1-score. The results reveal that Random Forest and Decision Tree are more accurate than other machine learning algorithms.

Keywords: Machine learning · Support Vector Machine · Decision Tree · Multiclass classification

1 Introduction

Education and healthcare are two sectors where machine learning is being employed. Machine learning has become more popular as a result of advances in processing power and the availability of datasets on open-source repositories. In healthcare, machine learning is utilized in a wide range of settings. There is a lot of data in the healthcare business that can assist uncover patterns and forecast future outcomes. In healthcare, machine learning is utilized to tackle a variety of issues [1–3]. There is no one-size-fits-all approach to determining the severity of cardiac disease [4]. Machine learning models may be built using the dataset and individual patient data to predict outcomes. As a consequence of the data entered, the forecast result will be unique to that individual. Type-2 diabetes can be avoid-ed by controlling one's weight, diet, and other lifestyle factors [5]. There is no specific therapy for coronavirus. This year's coronavirus came from China. This disease is being treated with a variety of methods, but there aren't any clearly defined measures to follow. Human cognition is the goal of artificial intelligence (AI). A paradigm change in healthcare is being brought about by the rising availability of healthcare data and the rapid advancement of analytics tools [1]. In recent years, several models for automated detection of illnesses such as cancer, COVID-19, and diabetes [2] have been established as of late, researchers have been building smartphone applications that use machine learning models to diagnose diseases in real time. It's even possible to

© Springer Nature Switzerland AG 2022
A. K. Luhach et al. (Eds.): ICAICR 2021, CCIS 1575, pp. 102–111, 2022.
https://doi.org/10.1007/978-3-031-09469-9_9

create smartphone applications that can assess a person's likelihood of contracting an illness and then suggest a diagnosis based on their current health status [6]. In spite of this, early diagnosis remains an ill- posed challenge Many academics have recently begun employing deep-learning models to get much better results than machine learning models [2, 3]. Using machine learning algorithms, this study predicts an individual's risk of coronavirus, heart disease, and type 2 diabetes. People are required to enter their personal in- formation into a mobile application and then submit the information. The danger is forecasted within a few seconds of real-time analysis. Firebase is a cloud-based mobile application that serves as a real-time database. A database stores the model's training parameters, allowing for real-time prediction. Furthermore, the user is informed of the model's accuracy. An additional feature is real-time sharing of news articles from reputable sources. The app also includes a link to the source of the news. One of the most pressing concerns of human civilization is healthcare, which affects the quality of life for everyone.

It is a key component of the system [7]. The healthcare industry, on the other hand, is incredibly diverse, widely distributed, and disjointed. Providing optimal medical care necessitates access to relevant patient information, which is rarely available when it is needed [8]. In addition, the wide variation in the order of diagnostic tests suggests the necessity of a sufficient and appropriate collection of tests [14] expanded this claim by suggesting that the significant differences found in the request for general practice pathology arise primarily from individual variations in clinical practice and are therefore likely to improve through more transparent and better-informed decision-making for physicians [8]. Many heterogeneous factors, such as demographics, medical history, drug allergies, biomarkers or genetic markers may be found in medical data. Each one provides a distinct perspective on the patient's state. In addition, as previously indicated, statistical features varied significantly among the sources. When evaluating such data, researchers and practitioners confront two major challenges: the curse of dimensionality (the number of dimensions as well as the number of samples rises exponentially in the space of features) and the heterogeneity of function sources and statistical attributes. As a result of these factors, individuals have been unable to receive the care they need due to delays and errors in their disease diagnosis. This necessitates the development of methods that can diagnose the disease in its earliest stages as well as assist physicians in determining treatment decisions [14]. To deal with all of this information in the medical, computer, and statistical domains, it is imperative that new methodologies be developed to model illness prediction and diagnosis [12]. Modern machine learning (ML) provides a wealth of useful tools for analysing large amounts of data. Because of this, its technology may already be used to analyse medical data. Furthermore, a wide range of medical diagnostic work has been done on small-specialized diagnostic issues [9] where the early ML applications have been identified. Stable people and those with Parkinson's disease may be distinguished using ML classifiers, making it an important tool in clinical diagnosis.

2 Methodology

The Methodology diagram as shown in Fig. 1 consists of a dataset which is the Disease Symptom Prediction dataset. It involves the next step of data preprocessing, following

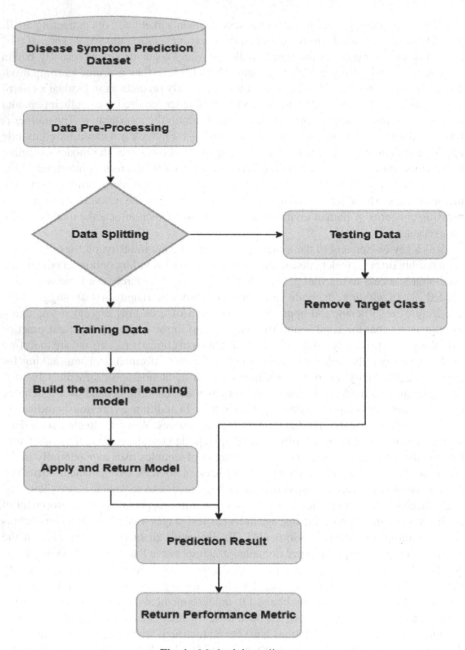

Fig. 1. Methodology diagram

this step the preprocessed dataset is then divided into two parts which are training data and testing data. In the case of training data, the next step is to build different machine learning models and then apply the training data to train the data from these models and return to the step of the prediction result. On the other hand, from testing data, the next step is to remove the target class and test the output and return to the prediction result. From prediction results, this paper analyzes the performance of each model. Discussion of these steps is done in the following steps.

2.1 Data Collection

The Disease Symptom Prediction Dataset has been used which was available online on the Kaggle. The sample image of the dataset used is shown in Tables 1 and 2.

So, there are 4920 instances in total, containing 40 unique disease and 17 symptoms columns that have been used to predict the disease in this research work.

The dataset used has missing values too, as some of the diseases can be detected using few symptoms and some require a greater number of symptoms to be accurately detected. These missing values are handled through data preprocessing using python.

Table 1. Dataset 1 sample: predicting disease.

	Disease	Symptom_1	...	Symptom_16	Symptom_17
0	Fungal infection	itching	...	NaN	NaN
1	Fungal infection	skin_rash	...	NaN	NaN
2	Fungal infection	itching	...	NaN	NaN
3	Fungal infection	itching	...	NaN	NaN
4	Fungal infection	itching	...	NaN	NaN

Table 2. Dataset 2 sample: symptom severity

	Symptom	Weight
0	itching	1
1	skin_rash	3
2	nodal_skin_eruptions	4
3	continuous_sneezing	4
4	shivering	5

2.2 Data Preprocessing

The missing data in this case comes under MNAR (Missing Not At Random), this means when data are missing, not at random, the missingness is specifically related to what is missing, e.g. a person does not attend a drug test because the person took drugs the night before [16]. In this case, symptoms are missing because there exists only that number of symptoms for that disease. These are handled carefully in this model using python. Table 3 shows the missing values in the Dataset 1.

With the help of dataset 1 and dataset 2, preprocessing of data through python library is being used and final resultant dataset Table 4 which is clean and preprocessed is used in building the model.

The resultant dataset has been then splitted into training and testing data in where mostly about 80% considered to be training data and remaining 20% to be testing data. For dividing the dataset python inbuild library scikit-learn and function train_test_split() is used.

Table 3. Sum of missing values of each attribute

Disease	0
Symptom_1	0
Symptom_2	0
Symptom_3	0
Symptom_4	348
Symptom_5	1206
Symptom_6	1986
Symptom_7	2652
Symptom_8	2976
Symptom_9	3228
Symptom_10	3408
Symptom_11	3726
Symptom_12	4176
Symptom_13	4416
Symptom_14	4614
Symptom_15	4680
Symptom_16	4728
Symptom_17	4848

Table 4. Dataset after preprocessing

	Symptom_1	Symptom_2	Symptom_3	...	Symptom_17	Disease
0	1	3	4	...	0	Fungal infection

(*continued*)

Table 4. (*continued*)

	Symptom_1	Symptom_2	Symptom_3	...	Symptom_17	Disease
1	3	4	0	...	0	Fungal infection
2	1	4	0	...	0	Fungal infection
3	1	3	0	...	0	Fungal infection
4	1	3	4	...	0	Fungal infection
...	...	...	...	...	...	...
4915	5	3	5	...	4	(vertigo) Paroymsal Positional Verigo
4916	3	2	2	...	0	Acne
4917	6	4	0	...	0	Urinary tract infection
4918	3	3	3	...	2	Psoriasis
4919	3	7	4	...	3	Impetigo

2.3 Building the Model

The model is built using Python.Scikit-learn library to implement the four machine learning algorithm. Scikit-learn is a Python module that integrates a wide range of cutting-edge machine learning methods for supervised and unsupervised issues on a medium-scale[18]. The library imported to build the models are as follows:

1. **from sklearn.naive_bayes import GaussianNB:**
   This Library is used to build the Gaussian Naïve Bayes model and to implement and train this model GaussianNB().fit(x_train, y_train) function is used.
2. **from sklearn import svm:**
   This Library is used to build the Support Vector machine model and to implement and train this model svm.SVC(kernel = 'rbf', gamma = 0.5, C = 0.1).fit(x_train, y_train) function is used.
3. **from sklearn.ensemble import RandomForestClassifier:**
   This Library is used to build the Random Forest model and to implement and train this model RandomForestClassifier().fit(x_train, y_train) function is used.
4. **from sklearn.tree import DecisionTreeClassifier:**
   This Library is used to build the Support Vector machine model and to implement and train this model DecisionTreeClassifier().fit(x_train, y_train) function is used.

2.4 Performance Metric of Model

Following performance metric of the four models have been considered for the analysis and comparison. Table 5 shows the comparison and analysis of the four machine learning algorithms in the tabular form.

1. **Accuracy**
   Accuracy of model is defined as total prediction that are predicted correctly divided by the total predictions done by the model.

$$\text{Accuracy} = \frac{True\ Positive + True\ Negative}{True\ Positive + True\ Negative + False\ Positive + False\ negative}$$

2. **Precision**
   Precision is defined as positive predictions that are predicted correctly divided by the total positive prediction.

$$\text{Precision} = \frac{True\ Positive}{True\ Positive + False\ Positive}$$

3. **Recall**
   Recall is defined as how many of the returned predictions that predicted that it belongs to certain class were actually predicted that they belong to that class.

$$\text{Recall} = \frac{True\ Positive}{True\ Positive + False\ Negative}$$

4. **F1-Score**
   F1-Score is defined as the harmonic mean of Precision and Recall.

$$\text{F1-Score} = 2 * \left(\frac{Precision * Recall}{Precision + Recall}\right)$$

The performance metric of the models are calculated using the library sklearn.metrics. Since multiclass classification is where there exist more than two classes and they are solved by further diving the problem into series of binary classes. And since the many binary classes so will be that many values of precision, recall and f1_score and here comes the method of averaging which will output one precision value of that model. There are three types of averaging that can be done macro, micro and weighted. In this paper the metric is calculated using the average type "weighted" as the classes are imbalanced and it is best technique to used it for.

3 Result Analysis as Per Given Algorithms

In this paper, four machine learning models are used, SVM, Random Forest, Decision Tree and Gaussian Naïve Bayes for the prediction of disease based on the symptoms using disease symptom prediction, Kaggle Dataset. The performance of all models was evaluated based on four parameters, accuracy, precision, F1_score and recall. The performance result of the models is shown in Table 5 and Fig. 2 respectively.

Table 5. Performance metric of models

Model	Accuracy	Recall	Precision	F1_score
Multiclass SVM	0.92	0.99	0.99	0.92
Random Forest	0.99	0.99	0.99	0.99
Decision Tree	0.99	0.99	0.99	0.99
Naïve Bayes	0.86	0.86	0.87	0.85

Decision tree and Random Forest performed well in comparison to Gaussian Naive Bayes and SVM. Model. Most accurate algorithm is Decision tree and Random Forest with accuracy 99%, followed by SVM with 92% and then Naive Bayes that has the least accuracy of 86%. When it comes to Precision all algorithm has Precision 99% except Naïve bayes which has Precision 87%.

This study demonstrates how ML Predictive models can be created, verified, and used to diagnose various diseases quickly. The study also demonstrates the critical significance of supervised machine learning algorithms in the prediction and diagnosis of diseases, which can help alleviate the enormous load on healthcare systems in most countries throughout the world.

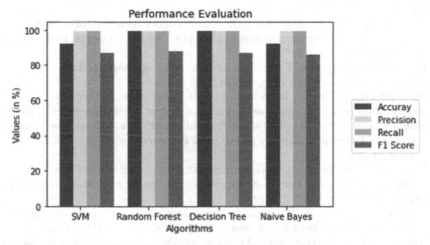

Fig. 2. Performance evaluation of algorithms

4 Conclusion

In this paper attempt has been made to analyze and compare various machine learning models based on multiclass classification of various diseases based on their symptoms. The goal of this study was to see how well algorithms perform when dealing with multiclass data. For disease symptom prediction dataset used from the Kaggle, which comprises 4920 instances, and used a test_train split to divide the data into two halves, training and testing datasets. To test the performance, 17 different symptoms are analyzed to predict various diseases using four different algorithms. Finally, after the implementation phase, it was determined that Random Forest and Decision Tree provide the highest level of accuracy in the dataset used, at 99%, while Naive Bayes provides the lowest level of accuracy, at 86%.

References

1. Ali, F., et al.: A smart healthcare monitoring system for heart disease prediction based on ensemble deep learning and feature fusion. J. Inf. Fusion **63**, 208–222 (2020)
2. Bakator, M., Radosav, D.: Deep learning and medical diagnosis: a review of literature. J. Multimodal Technol. Interact. **2**, 47 (2018)
3. Ebrahimighahnavieh, M.A., Luo, S., Chiong, R.: Deep learning to detect Alzheimer's disease from neuroimaging: a systematic literature review. J. Comput. Methods Progr. Biomed. **187**, 105242 (2020)
4. Goel, S., Deep, A., Srivastava, S., Tripathi, A.: Comparative analysis of various techniques for heart disease prediction. In: 4th International Conference on Information Systems and Computer Networks, pp. 88–94. IEEE, Mathura (2019)
5. Hong, S., Zhou, Y., Shang, J., Xiao, C., Sun, J.: Opportunities and challenges of deep learning methods for electrocardiogram data: a systematic review. J. Comput. Biol. Med. **122**, 103801 (2020)
6. Hossain, M.E., Khan, A., Moni, M.A., Uddin, S.: Use of electronic health data for disease prediction: a comprehensive literature review. In. IEEE/ACM Trans. Comput. Biol. Bioinform. **18**(2), 745–758 (2021). IEEE
7. Ibrahim, I., Abdulazeez, A.: The role of machine learning algorithms for diagnosing diseases. J. Appl. Sci. Technol. Trends **2**(01), 10–19 (2021)
8. Jo, T., Nho, K., Saykin, A.J.: Deep learning in Alzheimer's disease: diagnostic classification and prognostic prediction using neuroimaging data. J. Front. Aging Neurosci. **11**, 220 (2019)
9. Khalid, H., et al.: A comparative systematic literature review on knee bone reports from MRI, x-rays and CT scans using deep learning and machine learning methodologies. J. Diagn. **10**, 518 (2020)
10. Liu, X., et al.: A comparison of deep learning performance against health-care professionals in detecting diseases from medical imaging: a systematic review and meta-analysis. J. Lancet Digit. Health **1**(6), e271–e297 (2019)
11. Nagaraju, M., Chawla, P.: Systematic review of deep learning techniques in plant disease detection. Int. J. Syst. Assur. Eng. Manag. J. PeerJ. Comput. Sci. **7**, e432 (2020)
12. Shafaf, N., Malek, H.: Applications of machine learning approaches in emergency medicine; a review article. J. Arch. Acad. Emerg. Med. **7**(1), 34 (2019)
13. Mohd, N., Singh, A., Bhadauria, H.S.: A novel SVM based IDS for distributed denial of sleep strike in wireless sensor networks. Wirel. Pers. Commun. **111**(3), 1999–2022 (2019). https://doi.org/10.1007/s11277-019-06969-9
14. Solares, J.R.A., et al.: Deep learning for electronic health records: a comparative review of multiple deep neural architectures. J. Biomed. Inform. **101**, 103337 (2020)
15. Kumar, I., Mohd, N., Bhatt, C., Sharma, S.K.: Development of IDS using supervised machine learning. In: Pant, M., Kumar Sharma, T., Arya, R., Sahana, B.C., Zolfagharinia, H. (eds.) Soft Computing: Theories and Applications. AISC, vol. 1154, pp. 565–577. Springer, Singapore (2020). https://doi.org/10.1007/978-981-15-4032-5_52

16. All About Missing Data Handling. https://towardsdatascience.com/
17. Mohd, N., Singh, A., Bhadauria, H.S.: Intrusion detection system based on hybrid hierarchical classifiers. Wirel. Pers. Commun. **121**(1), 659–686 (2021). https://doi.org/10.1007/s11277-021-08655-1
18. Scikit-learn: Machine Learning in Python. http://jmlr.org/
19. Sharma, V., Yadav, S., Gupta, M.: Heart disease prediction using machine learning techniques. In: 2nd International Conference on Advances in Computing, Communication Control and Networking, pp. 177–181 (2020)

An Improved JAYA Algorithm Based Test Suite Generation for Object Oriented Programs: A Model Based Testing Method

Madhumita Panda[1] and Sujata Dash[2(✉)]

[1] Maharaja Sriram Chandra Bhanja Deo University, Mayurbhanj, India
[2] Maharaja Sriram Chandra Bhanja Deo University, Baripada, India
sujata238dash@gmail.com

Abstract. The model based testing approaches are not always capable of suggesting exact optimized and prioritize test cases, like conventional approaches, therefore some popular metaheuristic algorithms are gradually fabricated with model based testing methodologies for generating optimized test data. The metaheuristic algorithms are complex in terms of their algorithm specific parameter settings; they cannot provide good results without proper parameter settings. In accordance with the above-described issues, here in this work a novel methodology is proposed for test suite generation, using an improved metaheuristic Jaya algorithm along with UML state machine model. Experimenting with the benchmark triangle classification problem, the results prove, the performance as well as exploitation capability of the improved JAYA algorithm is quite good; over the widely popular Differential Evolution algorithm.

Keywords: Model based testing · Improved Jaya algorithm · Metaheuristic algorithms

1 Introduction

The object-oriented program testing is quite complex and still remains a critical research area since decades [1, 2]. The traditional testing approaches are unsuitable for object-oriented testing, thus a different testing practice, model-based testing is followed for deriving test cases [3, 4]. Gradually the Nature inspired algorithms proved their efficiency in proving sub-optimal solutions in various fields of engineering [11], thus researchers started fabricating those nature inspired metaheuristics with the software testing process [5–7]. The popular and widely accepted nature inspired metaheuristics mainly includes the evolutionary and swarm based algorithms, starting from the Genetics algorithm to recently popular [19, 20, 22], Bacteria foraging algorithm (BFO), Grey wolf algorithm and the list goes on [11]. Every metaheuristic algorithm has its own specific set of parameters and without proper knowledge of those parameters the algorithms are unable to provide their best results [11]. Keeping in mind those problems arising in metaheuristics due to improper parameters settings, a parameter free algorithm known as teacher learning based algorithm (TLBO) was proposed [12]. The Teacher learning based algorithm

© Springer Nature Switzerland AG 2022
A. K. Luhach et al. (Eds.): ICAICR 2021, CCIS 1575, pp. 112–122, 2022.
https://doi.org/10.1007/978-3-031-09469-9_10

includes two stages and it has only two parameters, the size of the population and iteration numbers. Very recently keeping in mind the popularity of the TLBO algorithm, a parameter free algorithm, the JAYA algorithm was introduced, this algorithm is even simpler than the TLBO algorithm, having one stage only [12]. The JAYA algorithm is gradually getting popular, efficiently handling the engineering optimization problems [12], in facial emotion recognition [13], Dimensional optimization [14], economic optimization [15] etc. Thus, keeping in track with the above research findings, this paper proposes a novel improved JAYA algorithm as well as the framework for testing object-oriented programs. The metaheuristic Improved JAYA algorithm is employed in the proposed framework to automatically select a set of test suites to test the object-oriented triangle classification program. Results indicate that the JAYA algorithm provides good exploitation feature to generate test suits. The proposed work targets the following modules for fulfilling the above mentioned objectives,

- Generation of test suites for testing the feasible test sequences of triangle classification problem using a novel Improved JAYA algorithm.
- Generation of test suites for testing the feasible test sequences of triangle classification problem using Differential Evolution algorithm.
- A set of experiments were carried out using the standard triangle classification problem followed by an exhaustive comparison between the metaheuristics i.e. JAYA, Differential Evolution and improved JAYA algorithms.

The remaining sections of this work are systematized as follows, the Sect. 2 conveys a detailed explanation of the classical JAYA algorithm, the novel improved JAYA algorithm and their specific set of parameters; Sect. 3 explains the suggested framework for the generation of feasible test suits, Sect. 4 includes the extensive experimental set up Sect. 5 provides experimental results and discussions with the detailed statistical analysis. Lastly, the conclusions and prospective future directions are projected in Sect. 6.

2 Proposed Algorithm

The metaheuristic Jaya algorithm [16] was introduced by Venkata Rao [14], it's a very simple and parameter free algorithm that has been already used for numerous optimization problems in diverse domains of continuous space. In this paper an improved Jaya algorithm with improved exploration and convergence speed is proposed by adding an efficient mutation scheme the conventional JAYA algorithm. This improved Jaya algorithm was applied in one research work for automatic ear image enhancement of the ear biometric system [18]. It was noticed that the improved JAYA algorithm show better performance for image enhancement in comparison to other two metaheuristics i.e. PSO and Differential Evolution based image enhancement techniques. Therefore, this paper used the Improved JAYA algorithm as well as the Conventional JAYA algorithm and compared the performance of the respective algorithms with widely popular Differential evolution algorithm, in terms of test data generation and computational speed, for the first time in the field of object-oriented testing.

2.1 JAYA Algorithm

The metaheuristic JAYA algorithm is a parameter free optimization algorithm The principle of the algorithm is to obtain good solutions avoiding bad solutions. Iteration-wise updating each solution is mathematically expressed in [18] as follows:

$$
X_{i,j}(g+1) = X_{i,j}(g) + r_{1,i,j} * \left(X_{i,best}(g) - |X_{i,j}(g)| \right) - r_{2,i,j} \\
* \left(X_{i,worst}(g) - |X_{i,j}(g)| \right)
\tag{1}
$$

where $X_{i,j}(g)$ is the jth parameter value for i^{th} solution at g iteration. $X_{i,best}(g)$ is the value of the best solution for i^{th} parameter at g^{th} iteration and $X_{i,worst}(g)$ is the value of the ith parameter for the worst solution at the same g^{th} iteration. Two random numbers $r_{1,i,j}$ are $r_{2,i,j}$ generated in the range of [0, 1] at iteration g, $X_{i,j}(g+1)$ hold the updated values of the jth parameter for i^{th} candidate solution in $(g+1)$. The neighborhood positions are exploited and candidate solutions are continuously upgraded in subsequent iteration using Eq. (1) to lead the convergence towards global solution. The two random numbers $r_{1,i,j}$ and $r_{2,i,j}$ help in improving the searching capability of Jaya algorithm. Initially the candidate solutions are updated at current iteration n, then based on fitness values the best individual solutions are updated after comparing the current solution $X_j(g)$ and updated solution $X_j(g+1)$ for the next iteration $(g+1)$ as described in [22]:

$$
X_j(g+1) = \begin{cases} X_j(g), & \text{iff } \left(X_j(g) \right) > f \left(X_j(g+1) \right) \\ X_j(g+1), & Otherwise \end{cases}
\tag{2}
$$

Thus the solutions of subsequent iteration are better than the corresponding solutions of current iteration. The modified fitness values of the candidate solutions are the inputs for next iteration. In this manner the algorithm always converges towards best solution.

2.2 Improved JAYA Algorithm

In order to improve convergence rate, a mutation operator has been introduced with Jaya algorithm and the proposed technique is known as an improved version of Jaya algorithm (IJA). It is revealed in [18], that the Differential evolution metaheuristic algorithm shows better performance than the Particle Swarm Optimization algorithm in robust performance and faster convergence towards global optima. Therefore the mutation operator of the Differential Evolution algorithm has been used in the JAYA algorithm to add diversification. In order to establish balance between the exploitation and exploration strategies an adaptive mutation operator is introduced. Mathematically the mutation operator is defined in the following Eq. (3),

$$
X_j(g+1) = X_{r_1}(g) + F * \left(X_{r_2}(g) - X_{r_3}(g) \right)
\tag{3}
$$

here $j \in \{1, \ldots, K\}$, j^{th} candidate solution of the population of size K. Correspondingly, r_1, r_2, and r_3 are the indices of the candidate solutions $\{1, \ldots, K\}$. Here, F is the scaling factor used to avoid the population stagnation and to control the difference vector in the mutation operation, it is in the range of [0, 1]. The an adaptive scaling factor has been used here is described as in Eq. (4).

$$
F = 0.8 + rand * ((G_{max} - g)/G_{max})
\tag{4}
$$

where g and G_{max} are the current iteration and maximum number of iterations respectively. The rate of mutation in Eq. (3) can also be evaluated adaptively, and when in this manner a random real number, greater than the rate of mutation. is generated then the mutation operation will be performed.

$$rand \geq \left(1 - \frac{g}{G_{max}}\right) \tag{5}$$

The rate of mutation fluctuates between 1 to 0, through initial iteration to a maximum number of iterations.

3   Projected Framework

This work proposes a framework; Fig. 1 for testing object oriented programs using the UML state machine model of the triangle classification problem and a novel improved JAYA algorithm. Initially the UML state machine model; Fig. 2 is developed and then it is converted to state chart graph. After that the nodes and edges are assigned weights [1, 2]. Then the SCG graph is traversed using the DFS algorithm in order to find out the total path cost and the feasible paths. The fitness function of the feasible paths is the total path weight [1, 2]. The JAYA, improved JAYA and DE metaheuristic algorithms are applied to generate test suits, fulfilling the transition coverage criteria.

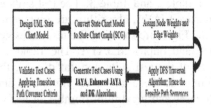

Fig. 1. Projected framework for model based testing

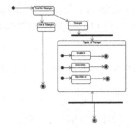

Fig. 2. The UML state machine model

4 Experiments

First of all, a UML state machine model was generated using ArgoUML, for the example problem, i.e., classification of triangles. After that metaheuristic JAYA, improved JAYA and DE algorithms, are used to generate test suits automatically using Matlab R2016b.

The fitness function of the problem is the total path weights of respective feasible paths, it is a maximization problem. The range of data variation is −10000 to 10000. To verify the exploitation and exploration capabilities of the metaheuristic algorithms, i.e. JAYA, Improved JAYA and DE a number of experiments were conducted with varying populations (10, 20, 30) and fixed generation (10), and then with varying generations (20, 30, 50) and fixed populations (10). After that again the different combination of generation, 20, 30 and population 50, 100 were taken to thoroughly test the time complexity and exploration capabilities of the algorithms.

Case study

Triangle classification problem is the benchmark problem in software testing domain [1, 2], specifically test data generation [3, 9]. The distinctive attribute of the problem is, it needs separate groups of test data to test first the triangle properties and then the types of triangles like scalene, equilateral and isosceles. [1]. This problem is selected as the case study to automatically generate test suites using Improved JAYA, DE and JAYA algorithms. This example problem has four feasible path sequences and six states (S1, S2, S3, S4, S5, S6). The statistical results after using JAYA, DE, and improved JAYA algorithms are depicted in Table 2 and Table 3. The test suits generated for respective path sequences using improved JAYA, algorithm are represented in Fig. 3 and Fig. 4 respectively. The Fig. 5 and Fig. 6 are showing the test suites generated by all the three algorithms i.e., JAYA, DE and Improved JAYA. The Table 2 and Table 3, show the detailed statistical analysis of the test suits generated using the proposed framework and metaheuristic algorithms. In these tables the minimum and maximum point outs the lower number of test cases and maximum number of test cases generation for the individual path. The maximum point outs the upper bound in test cases generation for a particular path. The table shows a minimum value to be zero when in at least one of the executions no data is available for covering a path, in the same way if the maximum value provided is zero then it signifies no data is generated at all for testing that path. Lastly the Table 4 shows the execution time of the three algorithms (Table 1).

Table 1. Test sequences of the triangle classification problem

Test sequence1	S1–S3	Not a triangle
Test sequence 2	S1–S2–S4	Scalene-triangle
Test sequence3	S1–S2–S5	Isosceles-triangle
Test sequence4	S1–S2–S6	Equilateral triangle

5   Results and Discussions

The aim of conducting the experiments with varying generations and populations was to figure out the exploration and exploitation capabilities of the algorithms. The detailed statistical analysis of the results like max, min, and average performance of the algorithms along with standard deviations were recorded in Table 2 and Table 3. The worst-case analysis of the algorithms shows that for path sequence 3, the critical path of the problem only improved JAYA achieved the best results, with large population size. The same trend is observed in average case analysis too. In most of the iterations the JAYA, improved JAYA, DE algorithms generated no data for path sequence2 and 3 whereas the Improved JAYA generated test data uniformly for every path sequence in case of maximum. The Fig. 3(a, b, c) depicts the test cases generated by improved JAYA with generation 10 and population variation 10, 20, 30, similarly Fig. 4(a, b, c) shows the test cases generated by improved JAYA with generation 20, 30,50 and population variation 10. In the next experiment the results of all the three algorithms for generating all four paths are recorded in Table 3 by varying the population to 10, 20, 50 and keeping the number of generations fixed at 10. The best, worst, and average case analysis of the results along with statistical analysis is provided in Table 3. Here it is observed that for path sequence 3, all of the three algorithms are providing almost zero results for best case in population 10 and 20, the DE is giving best result for only path sequence1 and JAYA for path sequence4 in all the three generations. The worst-case analysis shows that DE is giving best results for path sequence1, JAYA for path sequence 4, Improved JAYA for path sequence2 and 3. The average case analysis shows the same results. The Fig. 5(a, b, c) depicts the test cases generated by all the three algorithms at generation fixed at 10 and population size (30, 50,100). The Fig. 6(a, b, c) show the generated test cases, at generation fixed at 20 and population size (30, 50,100). When the results of Table 2, and Table 3 were compared, it was clear that the JAYA, DE and Improved JAYA, are not able to provide adequate number of test suits, when the population size and generations are small. The improved JAYA algorithm generated stable and uniform test suits, only when the population size is large.

Table 2. The statistics for test suite generation using Jaya, De, Improved Jaya with population size (30) & generation number (10, 20, 30)

Generation/ population		Model-based algorithm	Sequence1	Sequence2	Sequence3	sequence4
Gen = 10 Pop = 30	Minimum	JA	2	0	0	1
		DE	4	0	0	8
		EJA	1	1	0	1

(continued)

Table 2. (*continued*)

Generation/population		Model-based algorithm	Sequence1	Sequence2	Sequence3	sequence4
	Maximum	JA	17	19	19	20
		DE	13	12	14	18
		EJA	16	17	17	20
	Mean	JA	8.62	8.91	2.36	10.11
		DE	8.81	7.76	1.76	7.76
		EJA	7.57	9.51	4.97	7.91
	Standard deviation	JA	2.6285	3.398	1.879	3.349
		DE	3.06	4.87	7.86	9.05
		EJA	3.104	3.206	2.623	3.338
Gen = 20 Pop = 30	Minimum	JA	0	0	0	3
		DE	0	3	0	4
		EJA	1	1	0	1
	Maximum	JA	17	18	7	20
		DE	13	15	9	16
		EJA	19	19	15	17
	Mean	JA	8.33	9.025	2.19	10.405
		DE	5.19	15.26	5.7	12.03
		EJA	6.33	10.2	5.395	7.075
	Standard deviation	JA	2.767	3.14	1.403	3.071
		DE	2.81	4.44	5.06	5.3
		EJA	2.841	2.953	2.566	2.991
Gen = 30 Pop = 30	Minimum	JA	0	1	0	1
		DE	1	0	0	4
		EJA	1	2	0	2
	Maximum	JA	19	21	18	17
		DE	18	12	13	19
		EJA	18	17	19	21
	Mean	JA	6.037	11.784	6.041	6.125
		DE	5.53	18.9	5.03	10.53
		EJA	6.99	10.75	5.896	6.352
	Standard deviation	JA	2.81	3.096	2.438	2.562
		DE	3.34	5.36	3.99	4.35
		EJA	2.534	2.076	2.904	2.072

Table 3. The statistics for test suite generation using Jaya, De, Improved Jaya with population size (10, 20, 50) & generation number (10)

Generation/ population	Metaheuristic optimization algorithms		Sequence1	Sequence2	Sequence3	Sequence4
Gen = 10 Pop = 10	Minimum	JA	0	0	0	1
		DE	1	0	0	0
		EJA	1	0	0	1
	Maximum	JA	7	7	5	8
		DE	5	6	4	6
		EJA	7	7	9	6
	Mean	JA	2.4	3.7	2.3	4.3
		DE	2.3	1.8	1.5	2.7
		EJA	3.28	2.68	2.5	3.16
	Standard deviation	JA	1.56	1.67	1.04	1.67
		DE	1.45	2.28	2.43	3.84
		EJA	1.06	1.28	1.77	1.29
Gen = 10 Pop = 20	Minimum	JA	2	1	0	2
		DE	11	2	0	0
		EJA	1	1	0	2
	Maximum	JA	11	11	8	11
		DE	5	18	0	0
		EJA	12	12	10	11
	Mean	JA	5.74	5.68	2.34	6.24
		DE	3.25	1.57	2.7	4.5
		EJA	5.16	6.72	2.52	5.6
	Standard deviation	JA	2.036	2.42	1.47	2.43
		DE	3.07	14.05	2.71	3.4
		EJA	2.67	2.138	1.665	2.014
Gen = 10 Pop = 50	Minimum	JA	7	2	0	6
		DE	5	3	0	6
		EJA	6	3	1	4
	Maximum	JA	26	25	12	31

(continued)

Table 3. (*continued*)

Generation/population		Metaheuristic optimization algorithms	Sequence1	Sequence2	Sequence3	Sequence4
		DE	25	18	17	28
		EJA	22	23	21	30
	Mean	JA	12.52	14.28	3	18.2
		DE	11.5	13.8	10.2	14.9
		EJA	13.5	15.2	16.82	14.48
	Standard deviation	JA	4.33	5.55	2.26	4.24
		DE	2.94	4.45	4.46	6.29
		EJA	4.3	4.85	4.32	4.4

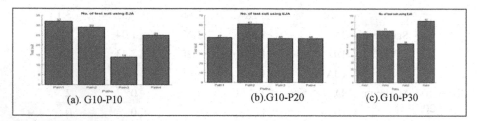

(a). G10-P10   (b).G10-P20   (c).G10-P30

Fig. 3. Test suites using Improved Jaya (A, B, C), with generations (10) and population size 10, 20, 30

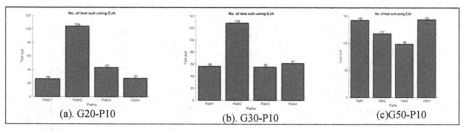

(a). G20-P10   (b). G30-P10   (c)G50-P10

Fig. 4. Test suite using Improved Jaya (A, B, C), with fixed population 10 and variations in generations 20, 30, 50

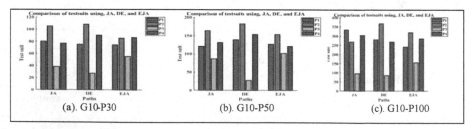

(a). G10-P30   (b). G10-P50   (c). G10-P100

Fig. 5. Test suites generation using Jaya, De and Improved Jaya (A, B, C), with generations **10** and population size **30, 50, 100**

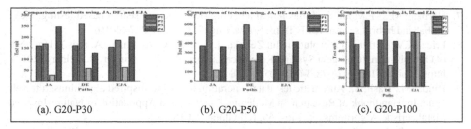

Fig. 6. Test suite generation using Jaya, De and Improved Jaya (A, B, C), with fixed number of generations (20) and variations in population size (30, 50, 100)

Table 4. Average run time (in seconds) for generation of test suits based on JAYA, DE, and Improved JAYA with generation 10 and population size 50.

JAYA	DE	Improved JAYA
0.004	0.025	0.018

6 Conclusions

The testing of object-oriented programs, particularly the test suite generation from design artifacts is a very difficult task. This work provided a novel Improved JAYA algorithm-based framework to generate optimized test suits. The optimal test suites were generated using the proposed framework and UML behavioral model. The proposed framework efficiently generated uniform test suits for all the feasible paths. The obtained simulation results ensured the efficiency of the improved JAYA algorithm over the performances of the individual JAYA and DE algorithm in terms of the exploration and exploitation capabilities. The framework can be further improved by using the hybrid version of this metaheuristic JAYA algorithm along with different UML diagrams.

References

1. Panda, M., Dash, S.: Test-case generation for model-based testing of object-oriented programs. In: Jena, A.K., Das, H., Mohapatra, D.P. (eds.) ICDCIT 2019. SBPR, pp. 53–77. Springer, Singapore (2020). https://doi.org/10.1007/978-981-15-2455-4_3
2. Panda, M., Dash, S.: Test suit generation for object oriented programs: a hybrid firefly and differential evolution approach. IEEE Access **8**, 179167–179188 (2020)
3. Shirole, M., Kumar, R.: UML behavioral model-based test case generation: a survey. ACM SIGSOFT Softw. Eng. Notes **4**(38), 1–13 (2013)
4. Utting, M., Pretschner, A., Legeard, B.: Taxonomy of model-based testing approaches. Softw. Test. Verif. Reliab. **5**(22), 297–312 (2012)
5. Saeed, A.S., AbHamid, H., Mustafa, M.B.: The experimental applications of search-based techniques for model-based testing: taxonomy and systematic literature review. J. Appl. Soft Comput. **49**, 1094–1117 (2016)
6. Harman, M., Jones, B.F.: The seminal workshop: reformulating software engineering as a metaheuristic search problem. ACM SIGSOFT Softw. Eng. Notes **6**(26), 62–66 (2001)

7. Harman, M., McMinn, P.: A theoretical and empirical study of search-based testing: local, global and hybrid search. IEEE Trans. Softw. Eng. **2**(36), 226–247 (2010)

8. Price, K.V.: Differential evolution. In: Zelinka, I., Snášel, V., Abraham, A. (eds.) Handbook of Optimization. Intelligent Systems Reference Library, vol. 38. Springer, Heidelberg (2013). https://doi.org/10.1007/978-3-642-30504-7_8

9. Panda, M., Dash, S.: Automatic test data generation using bio-inspired algorithms: a travelogue. In: Handbook of Research on Modeling, Analysis and Application of Nature-Inspired Metaheuristic Algorithms, pp.140–159. IGI Global (2018)

10. Samual, P., Mall, R., Bothra, A.K.: Automatic test case generation using unified modeling language (UML) state diagrams. IET J. Softw. **2**(2), 79–93 (2008)

11. Molina, D., et al.: Comprehensive Taxonomies of Nature and Bio-inspired Optimization: Inspiration versus Algorithmic Behavior, Critical Analysis and Recommendations. arxivpreprint arXiv:2002.08136 (2020)

12. Rao, R.V.: A self-adaptive multi-population based Jaya algorithm for engineering optimization. Swarm Evol. Comput. **37**, 1–26 (2017). https://doi.org/10.1016/j.swevo.2017.04.008

13. Wang, S.H., et al.: Intelligent facial emotion recognition based on stationary wavelet entropy and Jaya algorithm. Neurocomputing **272**, 668–676 (2017). https://doi.org/10.1016/j.neucom.2017.08.015

14. Rao, R.V., et al.: Dimensional optimization of a micro-channel heat sink using Jaya Algorithm. J. Appl. Therm. Eng. **103**, 572–582 (2016). ISSN: 1359-4311

15. Rao, R.V., et al.: Economic optimization of shell-and-tube heat exchanger using Jaya algorithm with maintenance consideration. Appl. Therm. Eng. **116**, 473–487 (2017)

16. Rao, R.: Jaya: a simple and new optimization algorithm for solving constrained and unconstrained optimization problems. Int. J. Ind. Eng. Comput. **7**(1), 19–34 (2016)

17. Cohen, B.: The Maturation of Search-Based Software Testing: Successes and Challenges. In: 12th International workshop on SBST (2019). ISBN: 978-1-7281-2233-5

18. Sarangi, P.P., et al.: An evaluation of ear biometric system based on improved Jaya algorithm and SURF descriptors. J. Evol. Intell. **13**, 443–461 (2019)

Analysing Sentiments of People Over Vaccines in Reddit Posts Using Natural Language Processing

J. Srinivas[1]([✉]), K. Venkata Subba Reddy[2], N. Rajasekhar[3], and N. V. Ganapathi Raju[3]

[1] SR University, Warangal, India
jagirdar.srinivas@gmail.com
[2] Kallam Haranadhareddy Institute of Technology, Guntur, India
[3] Gokaraju Rangaraju Institute of Engineering and Technology, Hyderabad, India

Abstract. Misinformation on vaccines is deeply rooted in many major societies of the world which according to the World Health Organization is one of the main threats for public health globally in 2019. One of the main reasons for rapid spread of such misinformation on vaccines is social media posts. With proper analysis of social media posts, the main factors contributing for such misinformation can be identified. This paper performs sentiment analysis on Reddit posts related to vaccines using Natural Language Processing (NLP) techniques like stopwords, spacytextblob, wordcloud, subjectivity and polarity. The research found out that out of the total 1487 reddits 9.21% of them were positive reddits 83.86% of were neutral reddits 6.92% of them were negative reddits.

Keywords: Vaccine hesitancy · Sentiment analysis · Natural Language Processing · Machine learning

1 Introduction

Over the years confusion over taking vaccines is largely prevalent in the society and therefore marked as one of the significant contributors of global sickness by World Health Organisation in 2019 [1]. According to the Strategic Advisory Group of Experts (SAGE) Working on Vaccine confusion defines confusion in vaccines as the "delay in acceptance or refusal of vaccination despite the availability of vaccination services. Vaccine hesitancy is complex and context-specific, varying across time, place, and vaccines. It is influenced by factors such as complacency, convenience, and confidence" [2]. Moreover the internet is a main factor for rapid dissemination of vaccine hesitancy as such myths and information can spread like wild fire [3]. Social media influences the decisions of the society to take, reject or postpone the vaccination. [4, 5] and could be a reason for the spread of avoidable diseases. One way to cope up with this hesitancy of accepting vaccines is to monitor social media posts related to vaccination. It is very significant to gauge the opinions and the social behaviour of people who have certain inclinations towards anti vaccinations. Opinion research or sentiment analysis of vaccination related

© Springer Nature Switzerland AG 2022
A. K. Luhach et al. (Eds.): ICAICR 2021, CCIS 1575, pp. 123–131, 2022.
https://doi.org/10.1007/978-3-031-09469-9_11

posts on social media can be performed to find out the reasons behind the vaccination hesitancy. In social media people are allowed to post their views on a certain topic freely. These posts if carefully analyzed may give some insights to the medical agencies to cope up with the existing problem of vaccine hesitancy. Social media can be effectively used to track people with vaccine hesitancy, communicable diseases and also for circulating health guidelines rapidly [6]. Text mining techniques can be used to detect vaccine hesitancy in social media posts [7]. Researchers also performed Sentiment Analysis (SA) [8] for finding out the stances of people on vaccines. The social posts can be analyzed and classified according to their polarity viz. positive, neutral and negative [9, 10]. In the literature there exists three methods of SA namely document-level SA, Sentencelevel SA and aspect-level SA [11]. Anti Vaccination campaigns also contribute to the hesitancy of public from taking vaccines. And mostly all the information is about such campaigns is circulated through social media. Investigating a persons' overt behavior towards vaccination on social media stages is a proved technique for finding the sources of such misinformation. On these platforms the main point of discussions will be vaccines. A study performed by some researchers showed that people are influenced over the internet against vaccination of children [12]. This research examines the individual's attitude towards vaccination on reddit posts. By using years of longitudinal data extracted from reddit posts, this research tries to identify individuals who are pro vaccine, individuals who are anti vaccine and finally neutral towards vaccination. This research hopes that this classification will later help health officials to encourage the neutral class of people to take vaccinations. Similarly the anti vaccination class of individuals can be convinced to take vaccines by properly counseling them. As the problem statement of this research clearly introduced now, in the coming sections of the paper related work, system architecture, experiments conducted and results obtained will be discussed. Finally, the paper will be concluded and insights into future work of this research will be discussed.

2 Related Work

A study in the past identified the confusions and apprehensions of individuals on multiple social media forums for solving the health issues of people globally [13]. One more set of investigators tried to understand the attitudes of twitter users on vaccinations by capturing four years of tweets. They applied NLP techniques for identifying the sentiments of individuals by analyzing user tweets [14]. A group of researchers tried to find the facts for refusing vaccinations by some individuals by analyzing their behavior on social media especially twitter [15]. They classified the tweets related to vaccination as positive and negative by using NLP techniques.

An alternate research explored the perspectives and experiences of advertisers of vaccination while they promote vaccines on the social media [16, 17]. They used qualitative methods to sample participants who were involved in promotion of vaccinations on social media. The work applied risk communication principles, framework analysis for analyzing the data generated by these participants. A survey performed by researchers found out that how people with infants were flooded with anti vaccination messages [18] over social media. One more study tried to investigate how social media influences the circulation of health related misinformation globally [19]. They investigate the vaccine autism controversy. For this they collected data from Twitter, Reddit and also online news for around two years in the United States, the United Kingdom and Canada. One more study analyzed and later tried to address the health related misinformation on social media [20]. A group of analysts performed [21] investigations on twitter and concluded that sentiment analysis plays an important role in detecting the attitude of the public towards vaccination. In order to gauge the opinion of public towards COVID-19 vaccine a group of researchers performed sentiment analysis on twitter posts [22].Time series forecasting was performed on the current scenario of vaccination in USA. A group of investigators from Philippines [23] analyzed the sentiments of public over twitter using Naïve Bayes algorithm and attained an accuracy of 81.77%. A similar kind of research was performed by a group of researchers from Indonesia [24] on twitter data using Naïve Bayes algorithm. Their investigations revealed that in a total of 58,301 tweets 34 thousand were negative, 24 thousand were positive and three hundred and one tweets were neutral during a week. A group of researchers [25] analysed twitter data related to covid-19 tweets using three ML algorithms namely Multinomial Naïve Bayes (MNB), Support Vector Machine (SVM), and Logistic Regression (LR). LR gave an accuracy of 97.3% where as SVM gave an accuracy of 96.26% and finally MNB achieved an accuracy of 88%. The next section of this paper explains the system design that is followed for performing this research. NLP techniques were also used to identify the writers of text in social media by a group of researchers [26]. NLP techniques were applied on social media posts for determining whether they were fake or real [27]. Supervised text classification, an important aspect in NLP can be also performed using Artificial Neural Networks [28]. Before performing textual analysis some researchers created clusters of text streams in social media applications using tree based approaches and ternary features [29].

3 Work Flow and Results

The current section gives details of the various stages like data collection, pre-processing, word cloud representation and finally sentiment analysis. Figure 1 depicts the work flow model used by this research to perform sentiment analysis.

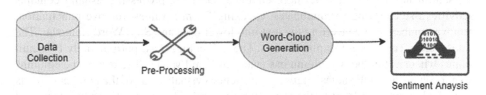

Fig. 1. Work flow of the system

3.1 Data Collection and Pre-processing

For this research the paper considered "reddit_vm.csv" dataset which is publicly available on Kaggle Dataset [30]. It has 1487 posts related to vaccination with eight columns.

Table 1 illustrates the column names and their type. Out of the eight column names, three belong to integer type and five belong to object type. Figure 2 represents the sample of the data set considered for this research. Out of the eight columns title, id, url, body and time stamp are categorical whereas scores, comms_num and created are non-categorical.

Table 1. Table captions should be placed above the tables

S. no	Column	Datatype
1.	title	object
2.	score	int64
3.	id	object
4.	url	object
5.	comms_num	int64
6.	created	int64
7.	body	object
8.	timestamp	object

	title	score	id	url	comms_num	created	body	timestamp
0	Health Canada approves AstraZeneca COVID-19 va...	7	lt74vw	https://www.canadaforums.ca/2021/02/health-can...	0	1614400425	NaN	27-02-2021 06:33
1	COVID-19 in Canada: 'Vaccination passports' a ...	2	lsh0ij	https://www.canadaforums.ca/2021/02/covid-19-i...	1	1614316267	NaN	26-02-2021 07:11
2	Coronavirus variants could fuel Canada's third...	6	lohlle	https://www.canadaforums.ca/2021/02/coronaviru...	0	1613886608	NaN	21-02-2021 07:50
3	Canadian government to extend COVID-19 emergen...	1	lnptv8	https://www.canadaforums.ca/2021/02/canadian-g...	0	1613795713	NaN	20-02-2021 06:35
4	Canada: Pfizer is 'extremely committed' to mee...	6	lkslm6	https://www.canadaforums.ca/2021/02/canada-pfi...	0	1613468188	NaN	16-02-2021 11:36

Fig. 2. Sample records of the reddit dataset

The next step is to perform data pre-processing so that the NLP techniques applied for sentiment analysis become more effective. Data Pre-processing usually contains activities like checking for duplicates, checking for null values, remove punctuation, remove numbers and converting the text into lower case and Stop Word Removal. The dataset did not contain any duplicate rows. The 'url' column has approximately 1036 null values where as the 'body' column has nearly 366 null values. The rest of the columns do not contain any null values. Figure 3 represents a visualization of the number of posts published on reddit related to the topic 'vaccination'. This research used seaborn and matplotlib package of the python programming language for generating visualizations of the data. Figure 4 represents the heat map generated for 'score','coms_num' and 'created' columns that are non-categorical in nature. A heatmap is generated to see the correlation between non-categorical features. This research used Pearson Correlation. The next is to remove stop words from the data set. Frequently occurring words in the posts are identified and removed as they increase the processing overhead. Articles, pronouns found in the posts are identified and then removed. This research uses the "stopwords" list already present in the nltk library of python programming language to remove the stopwords present in the dataset.

3.2 Word Cloud Generation and Statistical Analysis

The next step is to generate word clouds from the data present in the pre-processed dataset. The words that frequently appear in the posts will have bigger size in the cloud when compared to the words that have less frequency. In this paper, two word clouds are generated on the data present in the dataset. Figure 5 represents a word cloud where the column "title" was focussed and Fig. 6 represents a word cloud where "body" was the focussed column name. One can observe that words like "Vaccine", "Vaccination", "Vaccinate", "Vaccinated", "Anti", "Vaxxer", "covid", "measles", "children", "cause" e.t.c appear with large fonts in Fig. 5. Similar results are found in Fig. 6.

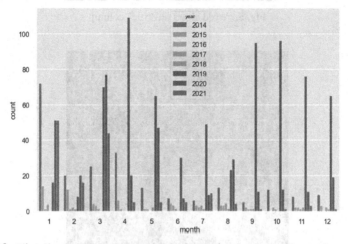

Fig. 3. Visualization of monthly published posts in a year related to topic vaccine

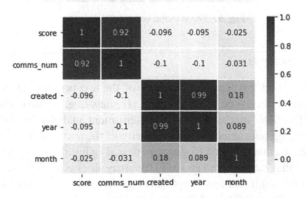

Fig. 4. Heat map of correlation between categorical values

Fig. 5. Word cloud on 'title' column

Fig. 6. Word cloud on 'body' column

3.3 Sentiment Analysis

The next step is to perform sentiment analysis of the text present in the dataset. Traditionally there exists three type of sentiments, viz. negative, positive and neutral. This research uses "TextBlob" package to perform sentiment analysis. Sentiment analysis is performed by finding out subjectivity and polarity of the text. Traditionally subjectivity refers to the metrics that are used to gauge personal opinions, emotions or judgments. It is a float value that ranges between [0, 1]. Polarity lies between [−1, 1] where in −1 represents negative sentiment and 1 represents positive statement. 0 represents neutral. The following results are obtained from the sentiment analysis performed. Out of the total reddit posts 9.21% were positive posts on vaccinations, 6.92% of the posts carried negative sentiment and 83.86% were neutral. Figure 7 graphically represents the sentiment analysis performed on the vaccine data set. The analysis found that a majority of posts were neutral. Government authorities can target the people who have posted these neutral posts and convince them towards vaccination. This will contribute to the betterment of the global health.

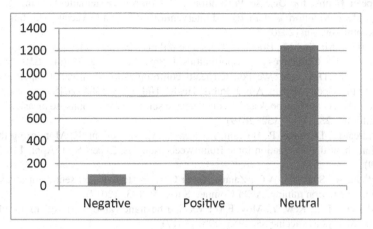

Fig. 7. Sentiment analysis on vaccine related reddit posts

4   Conclusions and Future Work

After performing this research the following conclusions related to vaccines are drawn out. It is observed that there is a lot of information and misinformation about vaccines on social networking sites like reddit, twitter, facebook and watsapp. This makes it absolutely necessary for authorities to monitor social media posts for effective implementation of vaccination strategies. An automatic system that effectively extracts and analyses the text related to vaccination on social media platforms is to be developed. Machine Learning based sentiment analysers are effective while dealing with current challenges. Due to induction of artificial intelligence, detection of sentiment polarity towards vaccination on social media posts has become easy and cost effective. This research analysed the sentiments of reddit users with respect to vaccines using NLP techniques and found out that a majority of users have a neutral attitude towards vaccination and they can be influenced by using concepts like target marketing. In a total of 1487, 83.86% were neutral reddits and 6.92% of them were negative reddits. As a future scope, the sentiment analyser can be equipped with tools to detect the origins of negative & neutral posts. Once location of such posts is detected health care professionals can plan vaccination drives more effectively in such areas. In future this research intends to analyse posts from twitter, facebook and watsapp.

References

1. World Health Organization: Ten Threats to Global Health in 2019 (2019). https://www.who.int/news-room/spotlight/ten-threats-to-global-health-in-2019. Accessed 27 May 2021
2. MacDonald, N.E.: Vaccine hesitancy: definition, scope and determinants. Vaccine **33**, 4161–4164 (2015)
3. European Centre for Disease Prevention and Control: Systematic Scoping Review on Social Media Monitoring Methods and Interventions Relating to Vaccine Hesitancy; ECDC: Stockholm, Sweden (2020)
4. Rosselli, R., Martini, M., Bragazzi, N.L.: The old and the new: Vaccine hesitancy in the era of the Web 2.0. Challenges and opportunities. J. Prev. Med. Hyg. **57**, E47–E50 (2016)
5. Broniatowski, D.A., et al.: Weaponized health communication: Twitter bots and Russian trolls amplify the vaccine debate. Am. J. Public Health **108**, 1378–1384 (2018)
6. Deiner, M.S., et al.: Facebook and Twitter vaccine sentiment in response to measles outbreaks. J. Health Inf. **25**, 1116–1132 (2019)
7. D'Andrea, E., Ducange, P., Bechini, A., Renda, A., Marcelloni, F.: Monitoring the public opinion about the vaccination topic from tweets analysis. Expert Syst. Appl. **116**, 209–226 (2019)
8. Yadollahi, A., Shahraki, A.G., Zaiane, O.R.: Current state of text sentiment analysis from opinion to emotion mining. ACM Comput. Surv. **50**, 1–33 (2017)
9. Mohd Azizi, F.S., Kew, Y., Moy, F.M.: Vaccine hesitancy among parents in a multi-ethnic country Malaysia. Vaccine **35**, 2955–2961 (2017)
10. Chou, W.S., Oh, A., Klein, W.M.P.: Addressing health-related misinformation on social media. JAMA **320**(23), 2417–2418 (2018)
11. Henriquez Miranda, C., Pla Santamaría, F., Hurtado Oliver, L.F., Guzmán, J.: Análisis de sentimientos a nivel de aspecto usando ontologías y aprendizaje automático. Proces. Leng. Nat. **59**, 49–56 (2017)
12. Salmon, D.A., Moulton, L.H., Omer, S.B., DeHart, M.P., Stokley, S., Halsey, N.A.: Factors associated with refusal of childhood vaccines among parents of school-aged children: a case-control study. Arch. Pediatr. Adolesc. Med. **159**(5), 470–476 (2005)
13. Suarez-Lledo, V., Alvarez-Galvez, J.: Prevalence of health misinformation on social media: systematic review. J. Med. Internet Res. **23**(1), e17187 (2021)
14. Mitra, T., Counts, S., Pennebaker, J.: Understanding anti-vaccination attitudes in social media. In: Proceedings of the International AAAI Conference on Web and Social Media, vol. 10, no. 1 (March 2016)
15. Dredze, M., Broniatowski, D.A., Smith, M.C., Hilyard, K.M.: Understanding vaccine refusal: why we need social media now. Am. J. Prev. Med. **50**(4), 550–552 (2016)
16. Steffens, M.S., Dunn, A.G., Wiley, K.E., Leask, J.: How organisations promoting vaccination respond to misinformation on social media: a qualitative investigation. BMC Public Health **19**(1), 1–12 (2019)
17. Royal Society for Public Health: Moving the needle: promoting vaccination uptake across the life course: Royal Society for Public Health (2018). https://www.rsph.org.uk/uploads/assets/uploaded/f8cf580a-57b5-41f4-8e21de333af20f32.pdf. Accessed 15 Jan 2019
18. Wolfe, R.M.: Vaccine safety activists on the Internet. Expert Rev. Vaccines **1**(3), 249 (2002)
19. Jang, S.M., Mckeever, B.W., Mckeever, R., Kim, J.K.: From social media to mainstream news: the information flow of the vaccine-autism controversy in the US, Canada, and the UK. Health Commun. **34**(1), 110–117 (2019)
20. Chou, W.Y.S., Oh, A., Klein, W.M.: Addressing health-related misinformation on social media. JAMA **320**(23), 2417–2418 (2018)

21. Yousefinaghani, S., Dara, R., Mubareka, S., Papadopoulos, A., Sharif, S.: An analysis of COVID-19 vaccine sentiments and opinions on Twitter. Int. J. Infect. Dis. **108**, 256–262 (2021)
22. Sattar, N.S., Shaikh, A.: COVID-19 vaccination awareness and aftermath: public sentiment analysis on Twitter data and vaccinated population prediction in the USA. Appl. Sci. **11**(13), 6128 (2021)
23. Villavicencio, C., Macrohon, J.J., Inbaraj, X.A., Jeng, J.H., Hsieh, J.G.: Twitter sentiment analysis towards COVID-19 vaccines in the Philippines using Naïve Bayes. Information **12**(5), 204 (2021)
24. Ritonga, M., Al Ihsan, M.A., Anjar, A., Rambe, F.H.: Sentiment analysis of COVID-19 vaccine in Indonesia using Naïve Bayes algorithm. In: IOP Conference Series: Materials Science and Engineering, vol. 1088, no. 1, p. 012045. IOP Publishing (2021)
25. Khakharia, A., Shah, V., Gupta, P.: Sentiment analysis of COVID-19 vaccine tweets using machine learning. SSRN 3869531 (2021)
26. Sheshikala, M., Kothandaraman, D., Roopa, G.: Natural language processing and machine learning classifier used for detecting the author of the sentence. Int. J. Recent Technol. Eng. **8**(3), 936–939 (2019)
27. Srinivas, J., Venkata Subba Reddy, K., Sunny Deol, G.J., VaraPrasada Rao, P.: Automatic fake news detector in social media using machine learning and natural language processing approaches. In: Satapathy, S.C., Bhateja, V., Favorskaya, M.N., Adilakshmi, T. (eds.) Smart Computing Techniques and Applications. SIST, vol. 224, pp. 295–305. Springer, Singapore (2021). https://doi.org/10.1007/978-981-16-1502-3_30
28. Kumar Ravi, R., Reddy, M.B., Praveen, P.: Text classification performance analysis on machine learning. Int. J. Adv. Sci. Technol. **28**, 691–697 (2020)
29. Raj, P., Srinivas, C., GuruRao, C.V.: Clustering text data streams – a tree based approach with ternary function and ternary feature vector. Procedia Comput. Sci. **31**, 976–984 (2014)
30. https://www.kaggle.com/khsamaha/reddit-vaccine-myths-eda-and-text-analysis.   Accessed 10 July 2021

CREA-Components Reusability Evaluation and Assessment: An Algorithmic Perspective

N. Md Jubair Basha[1]([✉]), Gopinath Ganapathy[1], and Mohammed Moulana[2]

[1] Department of Computer Science, Bharathidasan University, Tiruchirappalli,
Tamil Nadu, India
jubairbasha@gmail.com
[2] CSE Department, Koneru Lakshmaiah Education Foundation, Guntur,
Andhra Pradesh, India

Abstract. Component identification is an important task in evaluating and assessing the reusability of software components. Earlier various approaches were proposed for the component identification process. An exhaustive literature review is conducted and identified the relevant respective research gap on the evaluation and assessment of reusability of software components. In order to fill the identified gap, CREA-Component Reusability Evaluation Assessment with an algorithmic perspective is proposed to overcome the identified limitations and realized the proposed approach and metrics by evaluating and assessing the reusability of software components. Experimental results were presented with the desired dataset consisting of 24 mobile applications to prove the proposed work by analyzing the component reusability score and summarizing the components assigned with the highest score that will need less effort to reuse.

Keywords: Component reusability score · Method invocation · Component interaction · Method direct call · Static methods

1 Introduction

Software Reuse has been extensively deliberated more than the past four decades. This must be the clue to authorize the software industry to attain remarkable enhancements in productivity and quality that is essential to convince expected increasing challenges [1, 2]. Failure to take up appropriate reuse approach may lead to cost, schedule and assets overrun and may build running uncertainly but not willing to attempt it repeatedly [3]. In other words, if a certain organization does not accept software reuse before its competitors, it will probably be out of the market. Frakes et al. [4] have analyzed that enough advancements has existed on software reuse and domain engineering numerous notable issues stay afterwards. One of the main issues is scalability, which is the issue of applying reuse and domain engineering. One main concern is how to construct finest use of reusable components for systems of software. At any moment, the latest projects are taken ahead, afterwards the appropriate components must be required for the development process. The project proposals need to be evaluated by a batch comprising of

A. K. Luhach et al. (Eds.): ICAICR 2021, CCIS 1575, pp. 132–142, 2022.
https://doi.org/10.1007/978-3-031-09469-9_12

skilled analysts and further individual from component department organizing a software component board. Everybody must be required to determine either the suggested components are existed and essential to be evolved or not. If it is opted to build the component, it is redirected to component building with a time limit. When prepared, it is enumerated to the component repository, whichever next grabs an updated variety situation as showed in the Fig. 1. As component is utilized, the software component batch must examine its desirability. Which component is extremely utilized? Which are not utilized atmost? How ample you acquire across the existing legacy components? This examination assists to develop the component system [5]. This research leads to the problem of Component Identification from the repository. This research problem scopes to the identification of components from the existing components in a repository as per the customer's requirements rather than the developing of components from the scratch.

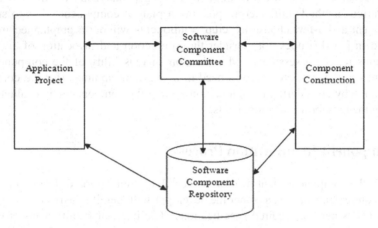

Fig. 1. Component management representation

The rest of the paper presents the literature review on component identification and evaluation in Sect. 2. In Sect. 3, an elaborative process of component identification with its structure and flow of the process is presented. Section 4 explains the algorithmic approach and various metrics for evaluation and assessment of reusable components. An experimental setup with desired data set is presented for evaluating the proposed approach and identifying the respective easily reusable components in Sect. 5 is discussed with its preliminary results. In Sect. 6, the conclusion and further work is presented with clear directions.

2   Research Review on Component Identification and Evaluation

Cai, Zhen-gong, et al. [6] had stated that the Component Identification as a NP-Complete problem. Many addressed frequently constructing over a matrix study, mainly addressed depend on graph-based [7], clustering analyses [8–10], evolutionary approach [11–13] to identify components and [14, 15] have evaluated the software components only by considering the coupling and cohesion factors. Ani et al. [16] presented the evaluation of Use Case Points (UCP) based framework to evaluate the reusability representation. But this structure consists of QMOOD metrics for analyzing the levels of reusability. In [17] presents architecture from software execution by identifying a group of components but fails to identify the interaction between classes. Aggarwal Jyothi et al. [18] presented to identify aggregate the main reusability factors for component based systems but could not able to identify the mainly reusable software for generating a latest software system. After the exhaustive literature review, the research gap analyzed from the above works is that various methods utilize corresponding a plan of component kinds to structure a component and a-few choose to setup components without a preplanned form. As presented in [14–17] does not consider the interaction and invocation of among the components for the assessment and evaluation of reusability of the components. To fill this research gap, there is a dire need to propose an approach for the component identification by considering the interaction among the components by evaluating and assessing the reusability of components.

3   Component Identification Process

In Fig. 2, the component identification process has been explored. In this process, as per the requirements of the customer the developer will identify the respective software components as per the required specifications. The input of requirements is given to the repository so that the components interaction information may be gathered. From this component interaction information, the component reusability score may be generated by the proposed algorithm for component reusability evaluation. This algorithm evaluates the reusability of components by considering the static methods and pair-wise similarity method with class correlate, method direct call and method indirect call. With the generated reusability score of components helps in the reusable component formation. From this step, it is easy to identify the components as per the requirements of the customer. A Requirements based evaluation will be carried out after the identification of the components in conjunction with the needs of the requirements of the customer.

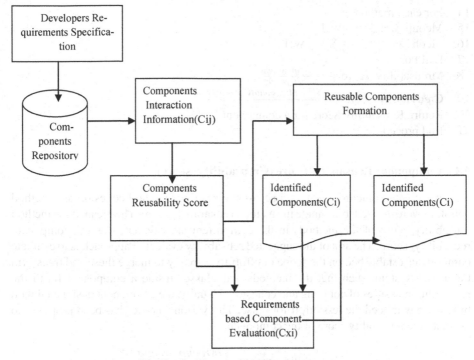

Fig. 2. Component identification process

4   Component Reusability Evaluation Algorithm (CREA)

The proposed algorithm fills the identified research gap of considering the interaction of components for evaluating the component reusability score. The Component Reusability evaluation algorithm (CREA) is as follows:

//Procedure Component_Reusability_Rating_(MI, CC, MDC, MIC)

1. Input: MI (x,x) ← methods with similarity matrix and 'x' is the number of methods in a class of a component
2. CC (j.m) ← similarity of 'j' classes of for each method in a component
3. MDC (p,p) ← similarity of 'p' static methods of each component
4. MIC (q,q) ← similarity of 'q' final methods through a component
5. Output: Reusability Score of a component
6. For each method do
7. Wt1 ← MethodInvocation(MI)
8. End for
9. For each method do
10. Wt2 = ClassCorrelate(CC)
11. Wt3 = MethodDirectCall(MDC)
12. Wt4 = MethodIndirectCall(MIC)
13. End for

14. For each method do
15. Mcoup_weight ← Wt1
16. Mcoh_weight ← $\frac{1}{3} \sum_{I=0}^{n}$ Wt1
17. End For
18. Mreusability_score ← $\frac{Mcoup\_weight}{Mcoh\_weight}$
19. Creusability_score ← $\frac{\sum_{i=1}^{n} Mreusability\_score(i)}{n}$
20. Return Reusability Score for a component
21. End procedure

4.1 Component Reusability Score (Creusability_score)

The investigated outcomes acquired across the result of method cohesion and method coupling were utilized to compute the method reusability_score. The mean of the method reusability_score of the methods in the component are calculated as the component reusability_score. The aim of the suggested reusability evaluated approach is to estimate components established on the scope of effort to be ready to merge these and transform them as a system, such that the methods and classes inside a component fulfill the reusability measures of coupling and cohesion. Usually, the component designated with best score will need the less effort for reuse. The various metrics has been proposed to evaluate the reusability score of the components.

$$Mreusability\_score \leftarrow \frac{Mcoup\_weight}{Mcoh\_weight}$$

$$Creusability\_score \leftarrow \frac{\sum_{i=1}^{n} Mreusability\_score(i)}{n}$$

The method level reusability score is analyazed by the Mreusability_score metric and the component level reusability score is analyzed by the Creusability_score metric. But the Mresubility score is purely depending on the invocation of methods as per the method calls which includes the direct call and indirect calls of methods.

5 Results Discussion

The experimental work is carried by collecting the samples of mobile applications includes the data set of software components. The evaluation was performed on 24 popular mobile applications are drawn out from the repository. The particulars of the mobile applications are listed in the Table 1. The number of classes are calculated as number of methods in the component. Similarly, the number of static methods and final methods in the various components of the available mobile applications are listed below. But the final methods are not considered for the reusability evaluation as they are not applicable to re-implement and inherit the classes and methods for import purpose. Only static methods are applicable for the considering the reusability evaluation aspects. The direct method calls and indirect method calls will also helps in invocation and interaction of components.

Table 1. List of mobile applications with their static and final methods

Application name	Total number of methods	Number of static methods	Number of final methods
HR portal application	1193	345	121
E-post office system	956	123	78
Library management system	1284	476	295
E-travel system	1956	1322	445
Payroll system	682	245	93
Hotel management system	1354	962	324
E-voting system	1894	1157	422
Budget approval systems	2234	1325	388
Product master maintenance system	1542	922	295
Recipe management system	895	223	94
Defect tracking system	1473	922	425
E-separation system	928	344	181
Effort tracker system	1233	844	235
Appraisal tracker system	1879	1160	322
Knowledge management system	1723	993	422
Lost articles reconcillation system	1825	1123	388
Online auctioning system	1456	822	292
Online course coordination system	1535	985	184
Point of sale system	1276	732	221
Resource management system	1342	921	384
Resume builder system	1856	1118	456
Speed cash system	1922	1393	298
Secure banking system	2184	1548	842
Online testing system	1154	642	191

5.1 Method Interaction

Methods Interaction (MI) is a relationship between methods in a component which acts for method imports. The pair-wise relationship between methods is calculated as follows:

$$MI(Mi, Mj) = \begin{cases} 1, & \text{if method } Mi \text{ imports } Mj, \\ 0, & \text{Otherwise}, \end{cases} \quad (1)$$

where *Mi, Mj* are methods within a component.

Table 2 presents the interaction among the methods and designated the matrix with the above computation.

Table 2. Methods interaction matrix

Methods	m1	m2	m3	m4	m5
m1	0	0	1	1	1
m2	1	0	0	1	1
m3	1	1	0	1	0
m4	1	1	0	0	1
m5	1	0	1	1	0

Relativity Property is put in to MI Matrix, since module imports persuade relative relationship as both are related so importing the properties of the methods. The representation is in Table 3.

Table 3. Method interaction after applying the relativity property

Methods	m1	m2	m3	m4	m5
m1	0	0	1	1	1
m2	1	0	0	1	1
m3	1	1	0	1	0
m4	1	1	0	0	1
m5	1	0	1	1	0

The slanting part in the import matrix are filled with 1, because every method imports itself. The relative property is put in to the MI matrix, such that the method m1 imports method m2 and module m2 imports m3, then it is indirected that the module m1 imports module m3 exclusively. Succeedingly putting in the relative property, MI matrix is shown in Table 3. The MI is standardized so that the count of the calculated entries in each row is 1. Figure 3 shows the number of invocations of methods i.e. direct calls, indirect calls and components interaction. Table 4 shows the Reusability Score of a

Component (Creusability_score) by considering the parameters of a mobile application such as total number of components, number of method invocations, i.e. method coupling weight, method cohesion weight and Method Reusability Score (Mreusability_score). Usually, the component assigned with highest score will need the less effort to reuse. It has been identified that out of 24 applications considered for the reusability evaluation only application components has the highest score on a scale of 5.These application components will takes less effort to reuse in other applications.

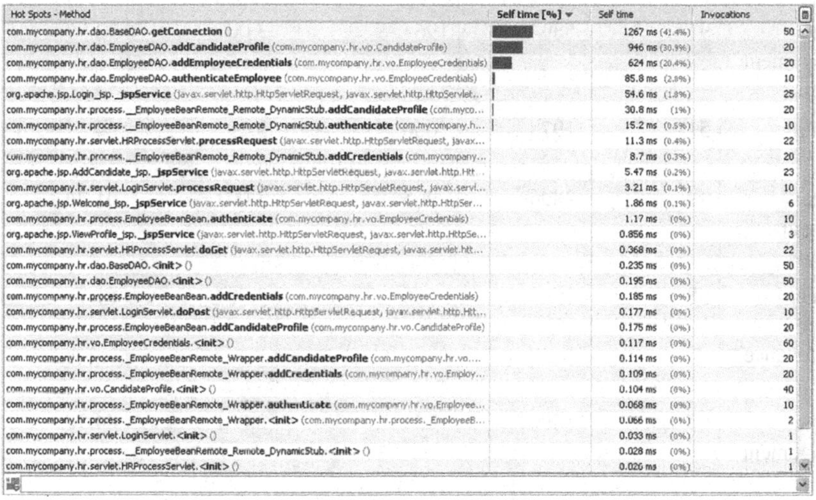

Hot Spots - Method	Self time [%]	Self time	Invocations
com.mycompany.hr.dao.BaseDAO.**getConnection** ()		1267 ms (41.4%)	50
com.mycompany.hr.dao.EmployeeDAO.**addCandidateProfile** (com.mycompany.hr.vo.CandidateProfile)		946 ms (30.9%)	20
com.mycompany.hr.dao.EmployeeDAO.**addEmployeeCredentials** (com.mycompany.hr.vo.EmployeeCredentials)		624 ms (20.4%)	20
com.mycompany.hr.dao.EmployeeDAO.**authenticateEmployee** (com.mycompany.hr.vo.EmployeeCredentials)		85.8 ms (2.8%)	10
org.apache.jsp.Login_jsp.**_jspService** (javax.servlet.http.HttpServletRequest, javax.servlet.http.HttpServlet...		54.6 ms (1.8%)	25
com.mycompany.hr.process.__EmployeeBeanRemote_Remote_DynamicStub.**addCandidateProfile** (com.myco...		30.8 ms (1%)	20
com.mycompany.hr.process.__EmployeeBeanRemote_Remote_DynamicStub.**authenticate** (com.mycompany.h...		15.2 ms (0.5%)	10
com.mycompany.hr.servlet.HRProcessServlet.**processRequest** (javax.servlet.http.HttpServletRequest, javax...		11.3 ms (0.4%)	22
com.mycompany.hr.process.__EmployeeBeanRemote_Remote_DynamicStub.**addCredentials** (com.mycompany...		8.7 ms (0.3%)	20
org.apache.jsp.AddCandidate_jsp.**_jspService** (javax.servlet.http.HttpServletRequest, javax.servlet.http.Htt...		5.47 ms (0.2%)	23
com.mycompany.hr.servlet.LoginServlet.**processRequest** (javax.servlet.http.HttpServletRequest, javax.servl...		3.21 ms (0.1%)	10
org.apache.jsp.Welcome_jsp.**_jspService** (javax.servlet.http.HttpServletRequest, javax.servlet.http.HttpSer...		1.86 ms (0.1%)	6
com.mycompany.hr.process.EmployeeBeanBean.**authenticate** (com.mycompany.hr.vo.EmployeeCredentials)		1.17 ms (0%)	10
org.apache.jsp.ViewProfile_jsp.**_jspService** (javax.servlet.http.HttpServletRequest, javax.servlet.http.HttpSe...		0.856 ms (0%)	3
com.mycompany.hr.servlet.HRProcessServlet.**doGet** (javax.servlet.http.HttpServletRequest, javax.servlet.htt...		0.368 ms (0%)	22
com.mycompany.hr.dao.BaseDAO.**<init>** ()		0.235 ms (0%)	50
com.mycompany.hr.dao.EmployeeDAO.**<init>** ()		0.195 ms (0%)	50
com.mycompany.hr.process.EmployeeBeanBean.**addCredentials** (com.mycompany.hr.vo.EmployeeCredentials)		0.185 ms (0%)	20
com.mycompany.hr.servlet.LoginServlet.**doPost** (javax.servlet.http.HttpServletRequest, javax.servlet.http.Htt...		0.177 ms (0%)	10
com.mycompany.hr.process.EmployeeBeanBean.**addCandidateProfile** (com.mycompany.hr.vo.CandidateProfile)		0.175 ms (0%)	20
com.mycompany.hr.vo.EmployeeCredentials.**<init>** ()		0.117 ms (0%)	60
com.mycompany.hr.process._EmployeeBeanRemote_Wrapper.**addCandidateProfile** (com.mycompany.hr.vo....		0.114 ms (0%)	20
com.mycompany.hr.process._EmployeeBeanRemote_Wrapper.**addCredentials** (com.mycompany.hr.vo.Employ...		0.109 ms (0%)	20
com.mycompany.hr.vo.CandidateProfile.**<init>** ()		0.104 ms (0%)	40
com.mycompany.hr.process._EmployeeBeanRemote_Wrapper.**authenticate** (com.mycompany.hr.vo.Employee...		0.068 ms (0%)	10
com.mycompany.hr.process._EmployeeBeanRemote_Wrapper.**<init>** (com.mycompany.hr.process._EmployeeB...		0.066 ms (0%)	2
com.mycompany.hr.servlet.LoginServlet.**<init>** ()		0.033 ms (0%)	1
com.mycompany.hr.process.__EmployeeBeanRemote_Remote_DynamicStub.**<init>** ()		0.028 ms (0%)	1
com.mycompany.hr.servlet.HRProcessServlet.**<init>** ()		0.026 ms (0%)	1

Fig. 3. Components interaction and method invocations

Table 4. List mobile applications with the component reusability scores

Application name	Total number of components	Number of method invocations	Method cohesion weight (Mcohe_weight)	Method reusability score (Mreusability Score)	Component resuability score (Creusability_score)
HR portal application	84	4985	1661	3.001	35.72
E-post office system	56	3278	1093	2.99	53.39
Library management system	48	2783	928	3.09	64.37
E-travel system	37	1189	397	2.99	64.3

(continued)

Table 4. (*continued*)

Application name	Total number of components	Number of method invocations	Method cohesion weight (Mcohe_weight)	Method reusability score (Mreusability Score)	Component resuability score (Creusability_score)
Payroll system	63	2897	966	2.99	47.4
Hotel management system	91	5894	1964	3.001	32.97
E-voting system	51	1978	660	3.29	64.5
Budget approval systems	49	2896	965	3.001	61.24
Product master maintenance system	58	1998	666	3.00	51.7
Recipe management system	67	1894	631	3.001	44.79
Defect tracking system	45	1987	662	3.001	66.6
E-separation system	73	4589	1530	2.99	40.9
Effort tracker system	67	3428	1142	3.00	44.7
Appraisal tracker system	81	3891	1297	3.00	37.03
Knowledge management system	78	3722	1240	3.001	38.47
Lost articles reconcillation system	56	2893	964	3.001	53.58
Online auctioning system	45	2112	704	3.00	66.66

(*continued*)

Table 4. (*continued*)

Application name	Total number of components	Number of method invocations	Method cohesion weight (Mcohe_weight)	Method reusability score (Mreusability Score)	Component resuability score (Creusability_score)
Online course coordination system	61	3879	1293	3.00	49.18
Point of sale system	77	4009	1336	3.0007	38.96
Resource management system	81	5018	1673	2.999	36.91
Resume builder system	89	6091	2030	3.000	33.70
Speed cash system	75	4319	1440	3.000	40.00
Secure banking system	69	3142	1047	3.000	43.47
Online testing system	63	3890	1297	2.999	47.46

6 Conclusion

The purpose of this proposed work is to present a technique to evaluate and assess the reusability of the mobile applications. This has been achieved by the proposed component reusability evaluation algorithm. Here, the Method Interaction matrix is designated by considering the relative property among the methods. CREA Component Reusability Evaluation and Assessment has been proposed in an algorithmic perspective which leads towards identification of software components as per the requirements of the customer. The proposed algorithmic approach and respective metrics are validated by generating the component reusability scores for about 24 mobile applications. It has been identified that highest score of component reusability will leads towards the less effort to reuse components.

References

1. Basili, V.R., Rombach, H.D.: Support for comprehensive reuse. IEEE Softw. Eng. J. **06**(05), 303–316 (1991)
2. Mohagheghi, P., Conradi, R.: Quality, productivity and economic benefits of software reuse: a review of industrial studies. Empir. Softw. Eng. **12**(05), 471–516 (2007)

3. Frakes, W.B., Isoda, S.: Success factors of systematic reuse. IEEE Softw. **11**(05), 15–19 (1994)
4. Frakes, W.B., Kang, K.C.: Software reuse research: status and future. IEEE Trans. Softw. Eng. **31**, 529–536 (2005)
5. Basha, N., Mohan, C.: A methodology to identify the level of reuse using template factors. arXiv preprint arXiv:1406.3727 (2014)
6. Cai, Z., et al.: A fuzzy formal concept analysis based approach for business component identification. J. Zhejiang Univ. Sci. **12**(9), 707–720 (2011)
7. Khan, M.A., Sajjad, M.: A graph based requirements clustering approach for component selection. Adv. Eng. Softw. **54**, 1–16 (2012)
8. Hasheminejad, S.M.H., Jalili, S.: CCIC: clustering analysis classes to identify software components. Inf. Softw. Technol. **57**, 329–351 (2015)
9. Cui, J.F., Chae, H.S.: Applying agglomerative hierarchical clustering algorithms to component identification for legacy systems. Inf. Softw. Technol. **53**(6), 601–614 (2011)
10. Shahmohammadi, G., Jalili, S., Hasheminejad, S.M.H.: Identification of system software components using clustering approach. J. Object Technol. **9**(6), 77–98 (2010)
11. Hasheminejad, S.M.H., Jalili, S.: SCI-GA: software component identification using genetic algorithm. J. Object Technol. **12**(2), 3–1 (2013)
12. Hasheminejad, S.M.H., Jalili, S.: An evolutionary approach to identify logical components. J. Syst. Softw. **96**, 24–50 (2014)
13. Padhy, N., Singh, R.P., Satapathy, S.C.: Software reusability metrics estimation: algorithms, models and optimization techniques. Comput. Electr. Eng. **69**, 653–668 (2018)
14. Priyalakshmi, G., Latha, R.: Evaluation of software reusability based on coupling and cohesion. Int. J. Softw. Eng. Knowl. Eng. **28**(10), 1455–1485 (2018)
15. Kaur, G.: Component reusability of a software system based on cohesion and coupling. Indian J. Sci. Technol. **9**(27), 1–6 (2016)
16. Ani, Z.C., Basri, S., Sarlan, A.: A reusability assessment of UCP-based effort estimation framework using object-oriented approach. J. Telecommun. Electron. Comput. Eng. (JTEC) **9**(3–5), 111–114 (2017)
17. Liu, C., et al.: A general framework to identify software components from execution data. In: ENASE (2019)
18. Aggarwal, J., Kumar, M.: Software metrics for reusability of component based software system: a review. Int. Arab J. Inf. Technol. **18**(3), 319–325 (2021)

High Utility Itemset Mining Using Genetic Approach

Tracy Almeida e Aguiar[1(✉)], Salman Khan[1], and Shankar B. Naik[2]

[1] Rosary College of Commerce and Arts, Navelim, Salcete, Goa, India
tracyaleida@gmail.com
[2] Directorate of Higher Education, Government of Goa, Penha de França, India
xekhar@rediffmail.com

Abstract. Frequent Itemset Mining(FIM) aims to generate itemsets having their frequency of occurrence not lesser than minimum support specified by the user. FIM does not consider the itemset utility which is the it's profit value. High-utility itemset mining(HUIM) mines high-utility itemsets(HUI) from data. HUIM is a combinatorial optimization. With HUIM algorithms, the time required to search increases exponentially with an increasing number of transactions and database items. To address this issue an efficient algorithm to mine HUIs is proposed.

The proposed algorithm uses a compact form of chromosome encoding by eliminating the itemsets with low transactional utilities. The algorithm employs methodology of self mutation to reduce generation of unwanted chromosomes.

Experimental results have shown that the proposed algorithm finds HUIs for a given threshold value. The proposed algorithm consumes less time as compared to another HUIM algorithm HUIM-IGA.

Keywords: High utility itemset mining · Frequent Itemset Mining · Data mining · Genetic Algorithm · Algorithm

1 Introduction

Quick and accurate information is always a necessity to make efficient decisions [2]. The knowledge discovery process(KDD) aims to discover hidden patterns of knowledge from data [1]. One major step of the KDD process is data mining. FIM is an important task in data mining for finding the most occurring itemsets from transactional databases [3]. In FIM itemsets are mined based upon the frequency of occurrence of itemsets in the database only [4,5]. The information about the quantity of the items and profit values associated with the items are not considered [6,7].

HUIM mines itemsets based upon their utilities. Itemset utility is the profit that it offers [8,9]. In this study, the itemset utility is a function of the quantity and profit of the items contained in the itemsets.

The process of HUIM generates a large number of itemsets in the intermediate stages. The itemsets are searched to generate the HUIs. HUIM is a combinatorial

© Springer Nature Switzerland AG 2022
A. K. Luhach et al. (Eds.): ICAICR 2021, CCIS 1575, pp. 143–150, 2022.
https://doi.org/10.1007/978-3-031-09469-9_13

optimization problem. The time required to generate HUIs is proportional to the number of items [10,11]. Genetic Algorithms(GA) have the potential to address this issue.

GAs avoid generation of all the candidate itemsets in the intermediate stages. GAs encode itemsets as chromosomes. They generate a set(population) of itemsets, evaluate them for their fitness and perform operations to generate fit itemsets from the weaker ones. The efficiency of GAs in searching new HUIs is low and can be enhanced.

Hence, we propose an efficient version GA to generate HUIs from transactional database, which encodes itemsets as chromosomes where in the genes are identified based upon the utilities of the corresponding item in the database.

2   Related Work and Motivation

2.1   Genetic Algorithm

GAs are used to solve NP-Hard problems [12]. GAs encode itemsets in the form of chromosomes, also called as individuals, which are made up of genes. Each gene represents an itemset. In the initial step GA generates a set of individuals whose fitness(utility) are evaluated to identify the HUIs. In case the required number of individuals are not generated then it performs three types of operations on the generated population. The operations are selection, crossover and mutation. The selection operator selects fit individuals. The crossover operator recombines two of the selected individuals with each other by exchanging their bits of pre-identified genes. The mutation operator alters bits of a single individual to generate a fit individual from it.

2.2   High Utility Itemset Mining(HUIM)

The process of HUIM mines itemsets from transactional datasets which have high utility. The utility is a profit value associated with the it. HUIM was proposed in [14]. The algorithm proposed in [15] is a two phased algorithm which, in the intermediate stages, generates a huge set candidate itemsets. This issue was addressed in [16] which avoided generation of candidate itemsets. The major issue with most of the algorithms in HUIM is huge set of candidate itemsets generated in the intermediate phases. This led to the introduction of GAs in HUIM.

The first GA to mine HUIs was proposed in [10]. Several algorithms thereafter were proposed. The algorithm HUIM-IGA discovered HUIs by using the strategy to improve population diversity [13].

The proposed algorithm stores the HUIs in the form of binary tree which increases the efficiency of searching for an existing HUI. It also maintains bit-vectors of each item which stores information about the ids of the transaction containing the item. This bit-vector enable quick identification of the transactions containing all the items of the itemset and calculation of the itemset utility.

3 Problem Definition

3.1 Preliminaries

Let $I = x_1, x_2, ..., x_m$ be the set of literals, called items. $D = \{T_1, T_2, , ...T_n\}$ represents the database containing n transactions, where T_j represents itemset in transaction j. i is the unique identifier of the transaction and $T_j \subseteq I$.

The external utility of item $x_k \in I$ is the profit value denoted as $\mu(x_k)$. The internal utility denoted as $\nu_j(x_k)$, of item in a transaction is the purchase quantity of the item in that transaction, where $x_k \in I$ is the item in transaction j.

Utility of $x_k \in I$ in T_j is

$$u_{Tj}(x_k) = \mu(x_k) * \nu_j(x_k) \tag{1}$$

Utility $x_k \in I$ in D is

$$u_D(x_k) = \sum_{j=i}^{n} u_{Tj}(x_k), n = |D| \tag{2}$$

Utility T_j in D is

$$u_{Tj} = \sum_{x_k \in T_j} u_{Tj}(x_k) \tag{3}$$

The transactional utility x_k in D is

$$u(x_k) = \sum_{x_k \in T_j} u_{Tj} \tag{4}$$

Utility of X in T_j is

$$u_{Tj}(X) = \sum_{x_k \in T_j \cap X} u_{Tj}(x_k) \tag{5}$$

The utility of itemset X in database D is defined as

$$u(X) = \sum_{X \subseteq T_j} u_{Tj}(X) \tag{6}$$

X is HUI if $u(X) \geq s_0$, where s_0 is minimum utility value given by the user.

3.2 Problem Statement

Generate high utility itemsets for a database D of transactions, given the minimum utility, s_0, and external utilities of items.

4 Proposed Algorithm

The proposed algorithm works in the following steps.

4.1 Database Pruning

The algorithm generates an new database D_{bit} from the transactional database D. The transactions in D_{bit} are bit representations of transactions in D. The columns in D_{bit} represent each item in I. If the item is in a transaction in D then the bit for the corresponding item in the transaction in D_{bit} is set to 1 otherwise is set to 0. The algorithm then identifies the items with their utilities less than s_0. The columns pertaining to these items are deleted from D_{bit}. This reduces the number of comparisons required to generate and search for itemsets in the database. Each column in D_{bit} is a vector of bits containing the transaction ids, in D, to which the item pertaining to the column belongs.

4.2 Initial Population Generation

Each itemset is encoded as a chromosome of length l same as the column count of D_{bit} i.e. the count of items with their utilities not less than s_0.

Let N_p be the size of the population. The algorithm generates the a set of N_p chromosomes in the following way. While generating an individual, all the genes are randomly assigned values 0 or 1. The operator AND is performed between the vectors of columns on each item corresponding to the genes which are set to 1. The position of the 1 valued bits in resultant bit-vector contains the ids of the transaction in D_{bit} containing all the items of the itemset encoded as the new individual (chromosome). The utility of the newly generated itemset is the total of the utilities of all these transactions. If the utility of the itemset is not less than s_0 then the generated individual is added to $HUIS$ as an HUI.

After repeating the process for all the individuals, $HUIS$ contains high utility itemsets.

There are two challenges involved in this step. The first challenge is the generation of duplicate HUIs. In this case, the newly generated itemset will have to be searched for in the existing set $HUIS$. In order to make this search efficient, the set $HUIS$ is maintained as a binary tree of length $l + 2$. The root node is empty. Each branch represents an HUI(individual). The other nodes store bits representing the genes of the individual. When a new HUI is inserted into the tree, the first bit is inserted as a root node child. If gene value is 0 then the node is created as a left child. If value of the gene is 1 then node is created as a right child. If the corresponding child node already existed then nothing is done. If the value of the gene is 0 then the algorithm considers the left child node for the second gene node creation. Otherwise the right child node is considered.

Similarly, for the second gene, the child node is created at level 3 in the binary tree base on the value of the second gene in the same way as done for the first gene. The process is repeated till all the genes are processed and a new branch of nodes of depth $l + 1$ is added to the tree. If a new branch is not created and there already existed a branch for the itemset then it implies that the HUI has already been created before. Thus there is no extra step required to check whether an HUI has been already created. This tree structure also avoids comparison with individual HUIs in the set $HUIS$ while searching for an itemset.

The second challenge is that not all the individuals generated during this process will qualify to be high utility itemset. If this happens then the number of HUIs in the set $HUIS$ will be less than N_p.

In both the cases, i.e. if the generated itemset is already existing in set $HUIS$ or the itemset is not an HUI, then itemset is made to undergo mutation and a new itemset is created by exchanging values of randomly selected two genes such that both the genes have different values. The new itemset is evaluated for its fitness and checked whether it has been already included before in set $HUIS$. If not, then it also undergoes mutation.

4.3   Time Complexity

The algorithm has the time complexity of $N_p * l + N_p^2 * l$, where N_p is the size of population and l is the length of the chromosome.

5   Experiments

The performance of the proposed algorithm was compared with HUIM-IGA. The algorithm proposed in this paper was implemented using C++. The experiments were conducted on a 64-bit Intel Core-i5 processor system having 8 GB RAM and Windows 10 operating system.

The dataset used is a synthetic dataset which as generated using the IBM synthetic generator. Size of the population is 20. The number of fitness calculations is 30K. The value of s_0 was set to 40%.

Figure 1 shows the convergence of both the proposed and HUI-IGA algorithms with respect to the count of HUIs generated.

The convergence of the proposed algorithm is faster than the convergence of HUIM-IGA. The number of HUIs with lesser fitness evaluation calculations in the proposed algorithm are more as compared to that in HUIM-IGA. This is due to the intersections of the item bit-vectors at the time of generation of a new individual.

Figure 2 shows the execution time of both, the proposed and HUI-IGA algorithms with respect to the minimum utility threshold s_0.

For lower values of s_0 the proposed algorithm requires more time than HUIM-IGA. The proposed algorithm is better in terms of time efficiency as compared to the HUIM-IGA for higher values of s_0. Since the proposed algorithm stores the HUIs in the form of a tree which avoid unnecessary comparisons required for searching HUIs, the execution time is lower than that of HUIM-IGA.

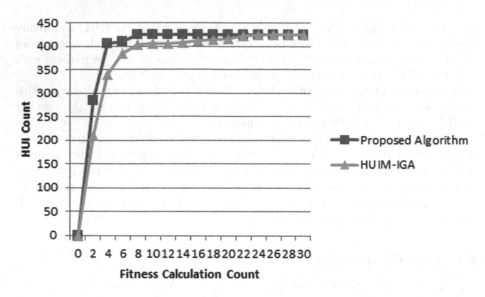

Fig. 1. Convergence with $s_0 = 40\%$

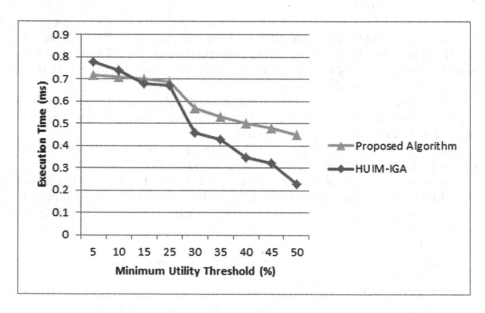

Fig. 2. Execution time vs s_0

6   Limitation of the Study

The proposed algorithm has been experimented on one and only synthetic data. Experiments on multiple dataset and real datasets will enhance the experimental study.

There are possibilities that the proposed algorithm may enter infinite loop while generating a new individual out of duplicate HUI or an unfit individual in the initial population generation stage. A control strategy to avoid repetitive generating of new individuals forever is needed.

Only one algorithm has been considered for comparison. The performance has not been compared with other algorithms. Also, the observations are true for the current dataset used. Whether the same trends will or will not be followed for other datasets has to analysed.

7   Conclusion

HUIM aims to discover itemsets having high utility. HUIM algorithms generate large no of itemsets out of which the HUIs are discovered. This issue has been addressed by Genetic Algorithms. GAs generate a set of individuals and evaluates their fitness. In case of an unfit individual, operations such as mutations and crossover are performed to either convert a weak individual into a fit one or generate a new individual from two parents. In case of high utility itemset mining the individuals represent the itemsets. GAs also have to maintain and search large number of itemsets in their intermediate steps.

A GA which stores HUIs in the form of a tree has been proposed in this paper. This reduces the unnecessary comparisons thereby improving the search efficiency and reducing the overall execution time. The algorithms also maintains the bit image of the transactional database which enables quick calculations of utilities of itemset by performing AND operations between the bi-vectors of items.

The proposed algorithm was implemented in C++ to perform experiments to compare its performance with the state-of-art GA algorithm HUIM-IGA. As per the experiments the proposed algorithm is efficient in mining HUIs for high s_0 values.

A limitation of the proposed algorithm is that the process of generating a new HUI from a duplicate HUI or low utility itemset may enter an infinite loop. The strategy to prevent it from entering an infinite loop is required. Only synthetic data were used in the experiment. A better insight about the performance of the algorithm would be possible using real datasets. Our future work will focus on these issues.

References

1. Han, J., Kamber, M., Pei, J.: Data Mining: Concepts and Techniques, 3rd edn. Morgan Kauffman, Burlington (2011)

2. Barretto, H.M., Dessai, P.S.: Challenges faced by Academic Libraries due to resource sharing and networking models. Libr. Philos. Pract. 1–14 (2021)
3. Zaki, M.J., Meira, W., Jr., Meira, W.: Data Mining and Analysis: Fundamental Concepts and Algorithms. Cambridge University Press, Cambridge (2014)
4. Naik, S.B., Pawar, J.D.: An efficient incremental algorithm to mine closed frequent itemsets over data streams. In: Proceedings of the 19th International Conference on Management of Data, pp. 117–120, December 2013
5. Naik, S.B., Pawar, J.D.: A quick algorithm for incremental mining closed frequent itemsets over data streams. In: Proceedings of the Second ACM IKDD Conference on Data Sciences, pp. 126–127, March 2015
6. Naik, S.B., Khan, S.: Application of Association Rule Mining-Based Attribute Value Generation in Music Composition. In: Bhateja, V., Satapathy, S.C., Travieso-González, C.M., Aradhya, V.N.M. (eds.) Data Engineering and Intelligent Computing. AISC, vol. 1407, pp. 381–386. Springer, Singapore (2021). https://doi.org/10.1007/978-981-16-0171-2_36
7. Amballoor, R.G., Naik, S.B.: Utility-based frequent itemsets in data streams using sliding window. In: 2021 International Conference on Computing, Communication, and Intelligent Systems (ICCCIS), pp. 108–112. IEEE, February 2021
8. Chan, R., Yang, Q., Shen, Y.D.: Mining high utility itemsets. In: Third IEEE International Conference on Data Mining, pp. 19–19. IEEE Computer Society, November 2003
9. Lin, J.C.W., et al.: Mining high-utility itemsets based on particle swarm optimization. Eng. Appl. Artif. Intell. **55**, 320–330 (2016)
10. Kannimuthu, S., Premalatha, K.: Discovery of high utility itemsets using genetic algorithm with ranked mutation. Appl. Artif. Intell. **28**(4), 337–359 (2014)
11. Pattern Mining with Evolutionary Algorithms. Advances in Intelligent Systems and Computing, Springer, Cham (2016). https://doi.org/10.1007/978-3-319-33858-3
12. Karakatič, S., Podgorelec, V.: A survey of genetic algorithms for solving multi depot vehicle routing problem. Appl. Soft Comput. **27**, 519–532 (2015)
13. Zhang, Q., Fang, W., Sun, J., Wang, Q.: Improved genetic algorithm for high-utility itemset mining. IEEE Access **7**, 176799–176813 (2019)
14. Yao, H., Hamilton, H.J., Butz, C.J.: A foundational approach to mining itemset utilities from databases. In: Proceedings of the 2004 SIAM International Conference on Data Mining, pp. 482–486. Society for Industrial and Applied Mathematics, April 2004
15. Liu, Y., Liao, W., Choudhary, A.: A Two-Phase Algorithm for Fast Discovery of High Utility Itemsets. In: Ho, T.B., Cheung, D., Liu, H. (eds.) PAKDD 2005. LNCS (LNAI), vol. 3518, pp. 689–695. Springer, Heidelberg (2005). https://doi.org/10.1007/11430919_79
16. Li, Y.C., Yeh, J.S., Chang, C.C.: Isolated items discarding strategy for discovering high utility itemsets. Data & Knowledge Engineering **64**(1), 198–217 (2008)

Relationships Among Human Genome Graph Elements Using Clusters Detection

Arun Kumar[(✉)] and Vishal Verma

Chaudhary Ranbir Singh University, Jind, Haryana, India
aarunbhardwaj@gmail.com

Abstract. Advancements in genome sequencing technologies have generated massive amount of biological data. Data driven research leads to better understanding and interpretation of complex dimensional data. Objective of a data driven approach in research is to explore approaches for hypothesis generation. To understand complex genomic data, it is important to understand organization of genomes. The organization and interactions among elements of genomes form some kind of patterns and behavior. For example, gene regulation (process to turn gene ON/OFF) is caused by some proteins which is also a pattern. Using these patterns, complex genome data can be understood. Genomic data visualization tools provide insights in understanding building blocks of life and relationships among them. This paper first discusses importance of hypothesis generation using visualization tools for genomic data. Paper discusses graph's hierarchical data representation and clusters of similar nodes or community in a graph mathematically. Also then proposes a technique of detection of clusters or communities of similar genome elements based on sequences shared by them using graph data structure. This helps in understanding organization of genome's structure and relationships among genome elements.

Keywords: Genome visualization · Human genome visualization model · Relationships among genome elements

1 Introduction

Genomic visualization provides patterns among distribution of its elements. Interpretation of this data leads to hypothesis generation for new research [1]. Genome comprises of different building blocks which can be categorized in several entities. Analyzing genome gives insights about the sub-blocks and their interactions. Genomic data visualization tools can be categorized into several formats - Linear and Circular layouts which implement different arrangements like parallel, serial and orthogonal arrangements. Linear layout technique emphasizes on exploration of a part of genome at a time while circular layout has focus on whole genome at once. Having a number of dimensions (genome elements) in genomic data, circular representation [2] gives brief insights about the data.. Multivariate data representation [3, 4] (Higher dimensional data) is a concept This paper explores ways to represent genomic data in hierarchical format. This also leads to finding patterns among the data elements which eventually leads to hypothesis generation for new research.

© Springer Nature Switzerland AG 2022
A. K. Luhach et al. (Eds.): ICAICR 2021, CCIS 1575, pp. 151–161, 2022.
https://doi.org/10.1007/978-3-031-09469-9_14

2 Literature Review

2.1 Linear Layout Based Tools

In such layouts, multiple parallel tracks showcase a section of genome at a time. These tools are often known as Genome Browsers which usually have 3 elements to show - a reference genome, annotations and tracks. These tools enable comparing sequencing data to reference genome or comparison of a sequence to reference genome. These genome browsers have their own limitations such as some show a single chromosome at a time while others predefine some zoom levels. UCSC Genome Browser [5], NCBI Genome Data Viewer [6], Savant Genome Browser [7], MochiView [8] and XENA [9] are such tools.

2.2 Circular Layout Based Tools

For multi-dimensional data, such an arrangement provides an overview of entire genome. These showcase all the elements and their interconnections at a global scale. Following are the tools implementing circular layouts for whole genome visualization.

1. Circos [10] creates plots for visualization of genome. It's written in perl language. This can be accessed at https://circos.ca. It showcases relationships among genomic data elements. Genomic data visualization and similarities among 2 or more genomic sequences can be explored using this tool.

2. JCircos [11] - is a JavaScript based implementation of CIRCOS. It uses circos for visualization. It has several rings where outermost ring represents chromosomes while gene expression and fene fusion can also be seen.

3. Interactive Protein Sequence Visualization [12] - It enables sequence conservation, amino-acid properties and mutational profiles. This tool uses JCircos for error checking, duplicates and matched sequences.

4. CircosVCF [13] - Genome-wide variant data is described in vcf files using circos plots.It showcases Genomic relations among genomes and identification of specific meaningful SNPs regions.

5. BioCircos.js [14] - Ya Cui et al. presented this tool which implements web based applications for biological data visualization and interactions among various subparts of the data.

6. BioNetComp [15] - One of the ways which can represent biological data is using networks. This means explanation of how nodes are connected using edges of a certain graph. This tool compares interactomes using different metrics and data visualization with the help of command line interface.

Apart from these tools, Community detection is a way to identify group of vertices of graphs into small parts of graph called as community or clusters. Communities are categorized into two types - Non Overlapping Community and Overlapping Community.

A Non Overlapping community is a community where each node is present into only one community. There exist various algorithms to detect such communities like Louvain algorithm [16, 17], Random neighbor Louvain (RNL) algorithm [18], Random self-adaptive neighbor Louvain (RSNL) algorithm [19], Parallel Louvain algorithm [20].

Overlapping Community is one where one node is shared by more than one community. There exist many algorithms for detecting these as well like LinkLPA algorithm [21], DEMON algorithm [22] and CoreExp algorithm [23].

Graph: A graph is a mathematical term used to represent relationships among structures/objects.

A graph representation has nodes at the center of the application. These are the places where objects are placed. Edges are connections between these nodes. A graph can be represented using various formations as per the relationships among nodes. To find relationships among them that how these are connected, there are graph theory algorithms and concepts. A cluster is similar type of nodes connected with other nodes having common properties. Clustering is also termed as community. The objective is to divide the data in sub parts with each having some common properties or connected in some predefined manner.

Hierarchical Community Detection in Graph:

Given a graph $G = (V, E)$ where V is set of vertices and E is set of edges. Hierarchy and Community are two problems to analyze.

i) a hierarchy of communities H such that

$$H = \left\{ C^1, C^2, \ldots\ldots\ldots\ldots\ldots\ldots, C^L \right\} \text{ where}$$

$C^t = \{C^t_1, C^t_2, \ldots\ldots, C^t_k\}$ are clusters at level t in hierarchy

$$V_t = \bigcup_k C^t_k \quad \text{and} \quad |c^1| < \ldots\ldots |c^t| \ldots\ldots |c^L| \tag{1}$$

ii) A hierarchy of clusters in this graph form super graphs $G_1,\ldots, G_t, \ldots G_L$ where $G_t = (V_t, E_t)$ represents the relationships among the clusters (nodes in G_t) at t-1 level in hierarchy. This defines the interaction at each level of graph among clusters/communities.

Above two statements when implemented on Human Genome graph data set, this needs to design the hierarchy.

Genomic Structure and Its Elements

Human genome has 4 bases A, T, C, G which form sequences in some specific arrangements. These specific arrangements are named as per their composition and role. These also play important role in genome organization. These are chromosome, biological_region, pseudogene, lnc_RNA, exon, pseudogenic_transcript, ncRNA_gene, miRNA, gene, mRNA, five_prime_UTR, CDS, three_prime_UTR, snRNA, ncRNA, unconfirmed_transcript, snoRNA, scRNA, rRNA, V_gene_segment, D_gene_segment, J_gene_segment, C_gene_segment, scaffold and tRNA. These elements form are connected with each other in some format. Human genome has a total of 24 chromosomes. Genome is also categorized into coding and non-coding regions. In current paper, discussion is focused on how these are connected and their formation with each other using some graph methods.

3 Dataset Tools and Method

3.1 Dataset

Genome Research Consortium is an institute which has released various species genomes sequences and keeps updating them as per the latest developments in research. This paper used annotations file of human genome version GRCh104 in gff3 format.

3.2 Tools

For this analysis, Tools used are python, pandas, numpy, matplotlib, plotly, scipy and net-workx libraries along with Anaconda environment supported jupyter notebooks Dataset. Use Foxit pdf reader to zoom output generated in exploring the data graph. For data anal-ysis, explored on various exploratory data analysis techniques based on statistics. Code files are attached and github link is also given. The resultant graphs are quite dense so to view the results, a tool is needed which can zoom at large scale. Results are analyzed with Foxit Reader which has zoom functionality upto 6400%.

3.3 Methods

For this analysis, Data in genome is comprised of several columns. Origin/Source of all the sequences in genome is also mentioned here as

array(['GRCh38', '.', 'havana', 'mirbase', 'ensembl_havana', 'ensembl', 'havana_tagene', 'ensembl_havana_tagene', 'insdc'], dtype=object)

One can easily see along with other sequence ids, chromosomes are also present (Fig. 1).

```
df.type.unique()

array(['chromosome', 'biological_region', 'pseudogene', 'lnc_RNA', 'exon',
       'pseudogenic_transcript', 'ncRNA_gene', 'miRNA', 'gene', 'mRNA',
       'five_prime_UTR', 'CDS', 'three_prime_UTR', 'snRNA', 'ncRNA',
       'unconfirmed_transcript', 'snoRNA', 'scRNA', 'rRNA',
       'V_gene_segment', 'D_gene_segment', 'J_gene_segment',
       'C_gene_segment', 'scaffold', 'tRNA'], dtype=object)
```

Fig. 1. Above figure represents unique sequences present in dataset.

All these are present among these sequences. To use this data as per our requirements, this dataset is converted into dictionary format (Fig. 2).

```
●  df.seqid.unique()

⊏→  array(['1', '10', '11', '12', '13', '14', '15', '16', '17', '18', '
            '2', '20', '21', '22', '3', '4', '5', '6', '7', '8', '9',
            'GL000008.2', 'GL000009.2', 'GL000194.1', 'GL000195.1',
            'GL000205.2', 'GL000208.1', 'GL000213.1', 'GL000214.1',
            'GL000216.2', 'GL000218.1', 'GL000219.1', 'GL000220.1',
            'GL000221.1', 'GL000224.1', 'GL000225.1', 'GL000226.1',
            'KI270302.1', 'KI270303.1', 'KI270304.1', 'KI270305.1',
            'KI270310.1', 'KI270311.1', 'KI270312.1', 'KI270315.1',
            'KI270316.1', 'KI270317.1', 'KI270320.1', 'KI270322.1',
            'KI270329.1', 'KI270330.1', 'KI270333.1', 'KI270334.1',
            'KI270335.1', 'KI270336.1', 'KI270337.1', 'KI270338.1',
            'KI270340.1', 'KI270362.1', 'KI270363.1', 'KI270364.1',
            'KI270366.1', 'KI270371.1', 'KI270372.1', 'KI270373.1',
            'KI270374.1', 'KI270375.1', 'KI270376.1', 'KI270378.1',
            'KI270379.1', 'KI270381.1', 'KI270382.1', 'KI270383.1',
            'KI270384.1', 'KI270385.1', 'KI270386.1', 'KI270387.1',
            'KI270388.1', 'KI270389.1', 'KI270390.1', 'KI270391.1',
            'KI270392.1', 'KI270393.1', 'KI270394.1', 'KI270395.1',
            'KI270396.1', 'KI270411.1', 'KI270412.1', 'KI270414.1',
            'KI270417.1', 'KI270418.1', 'KI270419.1', 'KI270420.1',
            'KI270422.1', 'KI270423.1', 'KI270424.1', 'KI270425.1',
            'KI270429.1', 'KI270435.1', 'KI270438.1', 'KI270442.1',
            'KI270448.1', 'KI270465.1', 'KI270466.1', 'KI270467.1',
            'KI270468.1', 'KI270507.1', 'KI270508.1', 'KI270509.1',
            'KI270510.1', 'KI270511.1', 'KI270512.1', 'KI270515.1',
            'KI270516.1', 'KI270517.1', 'KI270518.1', 'KI270519.1',
            'KI270521.1', 'KI270522.1', 'KI270528.1', 'KI270529.1',
            'KI270530.1', 'KI270538.1', 'KI270539.1', 'KI270544.1',
            'KI270548.1', 'KI270579.1', 'KI270580.1', 'KI270581.1',
            'KI270582.1', 'KI270583.1', 'KI270584.1', 'KI270587.1',
            'KI270588.1', 'KI270589.1', 'KI270590.1', 'KI270591.1',
            'KI270593.1', 'KI270706.1', 'KI270707.1', 'KI270708.1',
            'KI270709.1', 'KI270710.1', 'KI270711.1', 'KI270712.1',
            'KI270713.1', 'KI270714.1', 'KI270715.1', 'KI270716.1',
            'KI270717.1', 'KI270718.1', 'KI270719.1', 'KI270720.1',
            'KI270721.1', 'KI270722.1', 'KI270723.1', 'KI270724.1',
            'KI270725.1', 'KI270726.1', 'KI270727.1', 'KI270728.1',
            'KI270729.1', 'KI270730.1', 'KI270731.1', 'KI270732.1',
            'KI270733.1', 'KI270734.1', 'KI270735.1', 'KI270736.1',
            'KI270737.1', 'KI270738.1', 'KI270739.1', 'KI270740.1',
            'KI270741.1', 'KI270742.1', 'KI270743.1', 'KI270744.1',
            'KI270745.1', 'KI270746.1', 'KI270747.1', 'KI270748.1',
            'KI270749.1', 'KI270750.1', 'KI270751.1', 'KI270752.1',
            'KI270753.1', 'KI270754.1', 'KI270755.1', 'KI270756.1',
            'KI270757.1', 'MT', 'X', 'Y'], dtype=object)
```

Fig. 2. Above figure represents unique sequence ids present in dataset.

```
1.  seqids = df.seqid.unique()

        ids = []

        for i in seqids:

        ids.append(i)

2.              chr = {}

                t={}

                sub=[]

                for k in ids:

                        k1 = df[df.seqid == k]

                chr[k] =k1.type.unique()

3.

        genome={}

                for k,v in chr.items():

                        temp2 ={}

                                for i in v:

                                        temp2[i] = 'leaf'

                                        genome[k] = temp2

        genome
```

This creates the dataset in hierarchical format where each sequence id has respective type of genome elements.

3.4 Representation Logic

To analyze relationships of elements inside a genome, first dataset is converted into graph implementation of genome structure. For converting the data into a hierarchical dataset, here using columns, all the unique sequence ids are extracted to place them as nodes. Next all the unique elements of the **TYPES** column inside those sequence ids are placed. The data structure used here is nested dictionary so that proper hierarchy order can be managed. NetworkX is a python library for graph exploration. Several types of graph formation are created using NetworkX.

Graph: It is most basic type of graph. It is undirected graph which supports self-loops but does not allow parallel edges. Relationship between Human Genome sequences types are shown in the below image.

```
1. Create the graph template
networkx as nx

G = nx.Graph()

g3=nx.from_dict_of_dicts(genome,       create_using=G)

2. import matplotlib.pyplot as plt

  import matplotlib.cm as cm

  import numpy as np

  f = plt.figure()

  f.set_figwidth(60)

  f.set_figheight(50)

  x = np.arange(219)

  ys = [i+x+(i*x)**2 for i in range(219)]

  colors = cm.rainbow(np.linspace(0, 1, len(ys)))

  nx.draw(g3,node_color=colors, with_labels = True)

  plt.savefig("r1.pdf")
```

In the code above, first libraries needed are imported. Then initialized the graph with data dictionary created before. Next using matplotlib, the graph images are created.

4   Output and Results

Graph: Using above code, generated graph shows some clusters of genome elements and sequence types (Fig. 3).

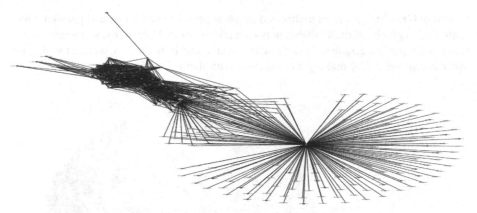

Fig. 3. Graph representation of human genome annotations dataset using dictionary.

Scaffold sequences are clustered on top of the image as a kind of flower. Just below this, overlapping communities can be noticed. Here biological region and scaffolds share sequence types. tRNA is only connected with MT (Mitochondria) chromosome. ncRNA-Gene has also shared multiple connections with chromosomes, biological regions and scaffolds. D_gene_segment, C_gene_segment, J_gene_segment and V_gene_segment are also seen with some connections purely with chromosomes.

MultiDiGraph: These are directed graphs with self-loops and parallel edges. This graph has more enhanced views on relationships among elements of genome and sequence types. All genome elements are shown on edges and sequence types are shown as nodes connected with genome elements. Cluster of scaffolds is clearly visible along with biological regions as well. Both share some sequences (Fig. 4).

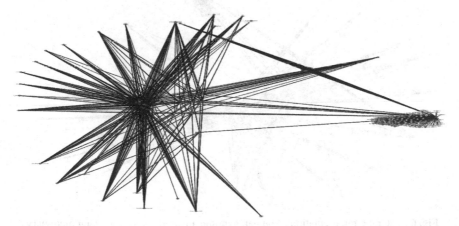

Fig. 4. MultiDiGraph representation of human genome annotations dataset using dictionary.

Circular Graph: This is an undirected graph supporting self loops and parallel edges both. In this graph, all the available items are put in circle. Here all the sequence ids and sequence types are arranged in a circular manner and how do they connect with each other is represented by making a connection with them (Fig. 5).

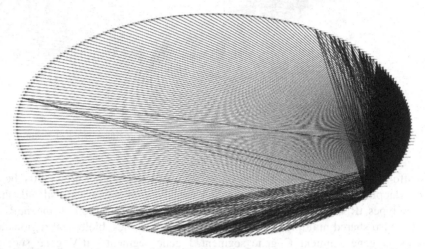

Fig. 5. Circular Graph representation of human genome annotations dataset using dictionary.

Digraph: This type of graph is directed graph. Here also self loops are allowed but parallel edges are not allowed (Fig. 6).

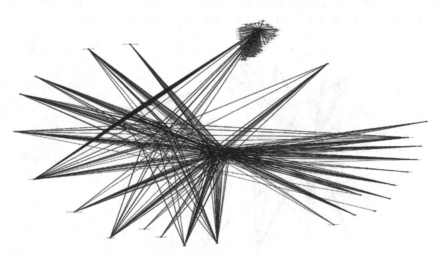

Fig. 6. DiGraph representation of human genome annotations dataset using dictionary.

This above graph also represents the nodes and edges in an understandable format. All the sequence types are surrounded with sequences associated with them. One cluster depicts sequence ids connecting scaffolds and biological region. Cluster of chromosomes is also connected with all the sequence ids which contain part of chromosomes inside them.

Multipartite Graph: A multipartite graph is a graph whose vertices are or can be divided into n different subsets of independent sets. Implementation of this algorithm on dataset, several subsets can be identified. These are sequence types as subset origin and all the sequence ids are connected with these. Sequence ids are shared by all these subsets (Fig. 7).

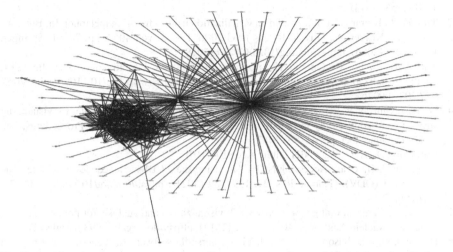

Fig. 7. Multipartite Graph representation of human genome annotations dataset using dictionary.

Here in representation, the above graphs conclude that how the type of elements inside genome are distributed across sequences and their connections with each other. Almost all the sequences starting with K are containing scaffolds. A cluster of these can be seen just like a flower in the graph image. These also share some sequences with biological_region which also shows a cluster of sequences. Next come Exons. These are also connected with K series sequence names sharing connections with biological region sequences. Also these share connections with Y chromosome and MT chromosome. All other chromosomes are highlighted in centre of the graph which contain dense connections with almost all the elements of genome.

All the results can be found at github repo: https://github.com/aarunbhardwaj/human-genome-graph-representation.

5 Conclusion

Using above code, generated graphs shows some clusters of genome elements and sequence types. DiGraph plots all the sequence types surrounded with sequences associated with them. Multipartite graph represents subsets like scaffolds at center, biological_region, chromosomes and other sequence types of human genome. This community detection makes clear understanding of distribution of genome sequences over different genome element types. Also one can understand how the elements of human genome are connected with each other. This relationship can further help in exploring the complex structure of human genome and life. In future, hierarchy of genome elements can get further deep. This can get really high on data size and computation resources.

References

1. Biesecker, L.: Hypothesis-generating research and predictive medicine. Genome Res. **23**(7), 1051–1053 (2013)
2. Therón, R.: Hierarchical-temporal data visualization using a tree-ring metaphor. In: Butz, A., Fisher, B., Krüger, A., Olivier, P. (eds.) SG 2006. LNCS, vol. 4073, pp. 70–81. Springer, Heidelberg (2006). https://doi.org/10.1007/11795018_7
3. Zheng, B., Sadlo, F.: On the visualization of hierarchical multivariate data. In: IEEE Pacific Visualization Symposium, pp. 136–145 (2021). https://doi.org/10.1109/PacificVis52 677.2021.00026
4. Dang, T., Murray, P., Etemadpour, R., Forbes, A.G.: A user study of techniques for visualizing structure and connectivity in hierarchical datasets. In: CEUR Workshop Proceedings, vol. 1947, no. September, pp. 45–59 (2017)
5. Karolchik, D., Kent, W.J.: NIH Public Access (2010)
6. Rangwala, S.H., et al.: Accessing NCBI data using the NCBI sequence viewer and genome data viewer (GDV). Genome Res. **31**, 159–169 (2021). https://doi.org/10.1101/gr.266932. 120.This
7. Fiume, M., et al.: Savant genome browser 2: visualization and analysis for population-scale genomics. Nucleic Acids Res. **40**, 615–621 (2012). https://doi.org/10.1093/nar/gks427
8. Homann, O.R., Johnson, A.D.: MochiView : versatile software for genome browsing and DNA motif analysis Software (2010)
9. Cancer, T., Atlas, G., Commons, G.D.: Visualizing and interpreting cancer genomics data via the Xena platform. Nat. Biotechnol. **38**(6), 675–678 (2020). https://doi.org/10.1038/s41587-020-0546-8
10. Connors, J., et al.: Circos: an information aesthetic for comparative genomics. Genome Res. **19**(604), 1639–1645 (2009). https://doi.org/10.1101/gr.092759.109.19
11. An, J., Lai, J., Sajjanhar, A., Batra, J., Wang, C., Nelson, C.C.: J-Circos: an interactive Circos plotter. Bioinformatics **31**, 1463–1465 (2015). https://doi.org/10.1093/bioinformatics/btu842
12. Tanyalcin, I., Al Assaf, C., Gheldof, A., Stouffs, K., Lissens, W., Jansen, A.C.: I-PV: a CIRCOS module for interactive protein sequence visualization. Bioinformatics **32**, 447–449 (2016). https://doi.org/10.1093/bioinformatics/btv579
13. Drori, E., Levy, D., Rahimi, O.: Genome analysis CircosVCF: circos visualization of whole-genome sequence variations stored in VCF files. Bioinformatics **33**, 1392–1393 (2017). https://doi.org/10.1093/bioinformatics/btw834
14. Cui, Y., et al.: BioCircos. js: an interactive Circos Javascript library for biological data visualization on web applications. Bioinformatics **32**, 1740–1742 (2016)
15. Carvalho, L.M.: BioNetComp : a Python package for biological network development and comparison (2021)
16. Que, X., Checconi, F., Gunnels, J.A.: Scalable community detection with the Louvain algorithm (2015). https://doi.org/10.1109/IPDPS.2015.59
17. Traag, V.A., Waltman, L., Van Eck, N.J.: From Louvain to Leiden : guaranteeing well-connected communities. Sci. Rep. **9**(2), 1–12 (2019). https://doi.org/10.1038/s41598-019-41695-z

18. Ozaki, N., Tezuka, H., Inaba, M.: A simple acceleration method for the Louvain Algorithm. Int. J. Comput. Electr. Eng. **8**(3), 207–218 (2016). https://doi.org/10.17706/ijcee.2016.8.3. 207-218

19. Zhang, Z., Pu, P., Han, D., Tang, M.: Self-adaptive Louvain algorithm: fast and stable community detection algorithm based on the principle of small probability event. Physica A **506**, 975–986 (2018). https://doi.org/10.1016/j.physa.2018.04.036

20. Sattar, N.S., Arifuzzaman, S.: Parallelizing Louvain algorithm : distributed memory challenges. In: 2018 IEEE 16th International Conference on Dependable, Autonomic and Secure Computing, 16th International Conference on Pervasive Intelligence and Computing, 4th International Conference on Big Data Intelligence and Computing and Cyber Science and Technology Congress, pp. 695–701 (2018). https://doi.org/10.1109/DASC/PiCom/DataCom/ CyberSciTec.2018.00122

21. Jia, X.I., Song, Q.I.: LinkLPA: a link-based label propagation algorithm for overlapping community detection in networks. Comput. Intell. **33**, 308–331 (2016)

22. Coscia, M., Pedreschi, D.: DEMON: a local-first discovery method for overlapping communities, pp. 615–623 (2012)

23. Choumane, A., Awada, A., Harkous, A.: Core expansion: a new community detection algorithm based on neighborhood overlap. Soc. Netw. Anal. Min. **10**(1), 1–11 (2020). https://doi. org/10.1007/s13278-020-00647-6

Transfer Learning Architecture Approach for Smart Transportation System

Sujatha Krishnamoorthy[✉]

Assistant Professor School of Science and Technology, Wenzhou Kean University, Zhejiang, China
sujatha@wku.edu.cn

Abstract. An intelligent and smart transportation system aims at effective transportation and mobility usage in smart cities. In recent years, modern transportation networks have undergone a rapid transformation. This has resulted in a variety of automotive technology advances, including connected vehicles, hybrid vehicles, Hyperloop, self-driving cars and even flying cars, as well as major improvements in global transportation networks. Because of the open existence of smart transportation system as a wireless networking technology, it poses a number of security and privacy challenges. Information and communication technology has long aided transportation productivity and safety in advanced economies. These implementations, on the other hand, have tended to be high-cost, customized infrastructure systems. To address these challenges, a novel machine learning method developed for a transportation system is reused for making it more generic and smart for intelligent carriage. This type of transfer learning enables rapid progress on the task with enhanced results. In this work, together with domain adaptation, a novel weighted average approach is used to build models related to the smart transportation system. A smart system comprising of interconnected sensors along with the gateway devices can lead the way to a more efficient, viable and robust city centers. Finally, in this paper also provides a view of current research in smart transportation system along with future directions.

Keywords: Smart transportation · Transfer learning · Spatial and temporal characteristics · Connected world · Machine learning models · Homogeneous and heterogeneous transfer learning

1 Introduction

An intelligent transportation system refers to advanced application that helps to provide novel services related to various modes of transport along with traffic management, allowing consumers to be better educated and making the use of transport networks safer, more coordinated and smarter. In the recent years, many deep learning models are developed and have become an integral part of realizing the intelligent transportation [1]. This includes transportation traffic, the complex interactions and environmental elements and so on as shown in Fig. 1 below. Transfer learning helps in this smart transportation system through model features that are learned in diverse tasks by making them general:

© Springer Nature Switzerland AG 2022
A. K. Luhach et al. (Eds.): ICAICR 2021, CCIS 1575, pp. 162–181, 2022.
https://doi.org/10.1007/978-3-031-09469-9_15

Intelligent transportation system (ITS) includes a variety of services like traveller information systems, road traffic management, public transit system management and autonomous vehicles [2].

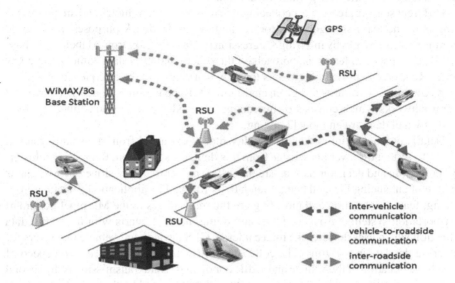

Fig. 1. A typical intelligent transportation system scenario

While smart transportation applications have been empowered by unprecedented progresses in computing, sensing and wireless technology, they will also have a wide variety of problems due to their scalability and varied quality-of-service requirements, as well as the enormous volumes of data they will generate. During the recent times, Machine Learning (ML) methods have gained significant attention in this field enabled by different technologies, including cloud- and edge computing [16]. ML has been used by a varied applications set, similar to ITS services, having a wide range of requirements.

In specific, ML models such as reinforcement and deep learning have been beneficial tools to explore underlying structures and configurations in big datasets for forecast and precise decision-making [3]. The different benefits of smart transportation system and ML approach to it are detailed below.

A. Communication

Intelligent transportation system helps create interconnected transport systems with the help of open communication that happens between different devices and vehicles.

B. Vehicle management

Managing traffic systems that in turn helps to keep the public transportation on time without any delay.

C. Real time information

Citizens have access to different real time information about the vehicular movement, traffic and other public transportation conditions.

Different sensors are used for collecting the data from the vehicles and are processed using machine learning algorithms for prediction and feedback purposes. Supervised learning methods works by inferring a regression or classification from a labeled database [4, 17]. Unsupervised learning approach on the other hand infer data without using any labels. Reinforcement Learning works towards learning to make a sequence of actions for maximizing the rewards in a given environment. Deep learning models uses artificial neural networks which consists of interconnected nodes offering non- linearity, high flexibility and data-driven model building.

Data is one of the important commodity that is extracted from the smart systems. ML try to further discover knowledge from this data. Classification, Regression, clustering, prediction and decision-making are the different features provisioned by ML that is capable of enhancing ITS and being foundations for the ITS application's. Data preprocessing, feature extraction and modeling are the main stages in the ML pipeline. Smart transportation system consists of four main components. It starts with the traffic data collection which uses devices like road cameras, GPS devices and vehicle identifiers for gathering the data in real time. The collected information provides details on speed of the vehicle, location of the vehicle and traffic conditions. Data transmission is the second stage in the pipeline which helps to transmit the data collected by the sensors to the network or the processing center where it is further treated and forwarded to applications. Data is further analyzed and the feedback is provided for the end users.

The different internet of things use cases related to this work include connected cards, vehicle tracking system, public transport management and traffic management. All of them involves usage of machine learning algorithms either at the source place where the data is collected or in the cloud. Since each use case involves multiple modules and most of them can be shared across applications with minor changes, hence use a new transfer learning approach for smart transportation system is proposed.

Transfer Learning (TL) is an artificial intelligence approach to the problem of learning where a prototype is reclaimed as the initial point for the new task that is already created [5, 18]. Developing a prototypical approach and a pre-trained model are the two common methods used for TL. In first approach need of selecting the source task is important to develop the source model, reuse the model and tune it as per the application. In the latter approach, select the source model and reuse the model and tune the model. This is very commonly used in the deep learning field.

The rest of the paper is organized as follows: Sect. 2 discusses the methods relevant to this work in the literature, Sect. 3 describes the data-based modelling of the intelligent transportation system, Sect. 4 deals with proposed transfer learning architecture, Sect. 5 shows the experimental outcomes and as a final point Sect. 6 concludes the work with further scope of study related to this topic.

2   Related Work

Emerging technology and the processing of big data have enabled the collection, analysis, storage and processing of multi-source data by systems. Cars, pedestrians, and even utilities will collect and exchange information in this area using a peer-to-peer procedure or a telecommunication network. Vehicle-to-vehicle (V2V), vehicle-to-infrastructure (V2I), pedestrian-to-infrastructure (P2I) or vehicle-to-pedestrian (V2P) interactions or knowledge transfer are all possible in this model. The authors [6] have reviewed the present trends in smart transportation applications along with insights in to connected vehicle environment for these systems.

When using the double loop detectors now used in traffic control centers, traffic practitioners prefer to calculate the time mean value rather than the space mean speed. The authors [7] feel that the relationship between the two speeds is important in smart transportation systems and hence have developed a probabilistic technique for appraising the space mean value from the time mean speed. They have also experimented the idea near Barcelona in real time and able to prove that the methodology can estimate with comparative fault as low as 0.5% through the proposed model.

With deep neural networks, TL begins with the process of preparing the base system on a given data set and then moving the structures to a target data set on the second network. The generalization capabilities of the deep neural network get improved with this approach. They are also useful in the time series classification problems. The researchers [8] investigated on how to handover the deep neural networks for the time series task. UCR archive that is publicly available and containing 85 datasets is used as the TSC benchmark for evaluating the potential of the transfer learning in this work. They have pre-trained a model for every dataset that is present in the archive, which is later fine-tuned on other datasets to construct different deep neural networks. At the end of the experimentation, the authors could prove that the TL can improve the predictions of the prototype depending on the transfer dataset used.

In various real-world applications, data mining along with machine learning techniques are used. Most approaches to machine learning demand that data from training and testing come from the same domain, which makes the space of the input function and the characteristics of the distribution of data the same. This assumption does not hold well when the training data is expensive to collect or unavailable. Hence high performance learners that can get trained with the data collected from different domains is needed. The authors [9] have surveyed different transfer learning process available in the literature along with their applications. The survey is made independent of the size of the data and can be useful for big data processing.

The majority of previous heterogeneous models of TL methods investigate a cross-domain feature plotting based on a small cross-domain instance-correspondence between different feature spaces, with these instances assumed to be characteristic in the source and target domains. The bias issues in this approach makes the assumptions to not hold good. As a result, the researchers [10] developed a new transfer learning method called Hybrid Heterogeneous Transfer Learning (HHTL), which allows for bias in either the source or target field in the resultant events across domains. The relationship between the source and the target has a significant impact on the effectiveness of transfer learning. The source side brute force leveraging will decrease the performance of the classifier. The authors [11] have hence devised an approach that makes use of extending the boosting framework for knowledge transfer from different sources rather than just one. Task-TrAdaBoost and MultiSource-TrAdaBoost are the two different algorithms discussed in this work which on experimentation proved that the performance is greatly improved by reducing the negative transfer. This is a fast algorithm enabling rapid retraining over new targets.

Utpal Paul et al. have conducted a measurement analysis with the help of large-scale data set that is collected through 3G cellular data network [22]. Individual subscriber behaviour is analysed and a significant variation in network is studied by the authors. The different implications with respect to protocol design, pricing parameters, resource and spectrum management are described in detail in this work. Different mobile networking networks have been developed in recent times in such a way that they have highly complex infrastructure and advanced range of related devices along with resources, as well as more diverse network formations, due to the firm development of current industries focused on mobile and Internet technology. As a result, Xiaofei Wang and others have discussed artificial intelligence-based methods for developing heterogeneous networks [23], as well as the current state of the art, prospects, and challenges.

The wireless communication techniques advancements along with mobile cloud computing, intelligent terminal technology and automotive domains are driving the evolution of automobile networks into the Internet of Vehicles paradigm. The vehicle routing problem hence gets changed based on the static data that is towards the real time traffic prediction. In this research, the authors Jiafu Wan et al. first address the classification of cloud-assisted IoV from the perspective of the service association between IoV and cloud computing [24]. After that, they assess traditional traffic prediction, which is used in both V2V and V2I communications.

The numerous traffic-related accidents that occur on expressways in a developed world are calculated to be closely related to previous traffic conditions, which are actually time-varying. To predict the likelihood of crashes, volume, speed, and occupancy-related parameters are used. These parameters are invalid for roads where traffic conditions are estimated using speed data. A dynamic Bayesian network model is designed by Jie Sun and others which models the time sequence traffic data and they have also investigated the relationship between dynamic speed condition data and the crash occurrence itself [25]. The authors have collected and used 551 different crashes data along with their corresponding speed related information from the expressways present in Shanghai, China. They developed the DBN models using time series speed condition data as well as different state combinations. The experimentation results from the authors show that the proposed DBN model offers a prediction exactness of 76.4% with a failure rate of 23.7% with only speed condition related data along with the nine traffic state blends. The results of the transferability verification show that the DBN models discussed are suitable for other related expressways, with a crash prediction accuracy of 67.0%.

With the ever-increasing global number of road traffic accidents, street traffic safety has become a serious issue for smart transportation systems. The identification of high-probability locations where major traffic incidents occur, so that precautions can be implemented efficiently, is a crucial step toward improving road traffic safety. The major limitations in this solutioning includes location accuracy and data availability.

To address these issues, researchers Lanyu Shang, Yang Zhang, Daniel Zhang, Yi-wen Lu and Dong Wang created RiskSens, a multi-view learning method that uses social data and remote sensing data to identify dangerous traffic locations [26]. This is shown in Fig. 2 above. The authors' experimentation findings show that the RiskSens approach proposed in this paper significantly outperforms other state-of-the-art baselines for identifying different risky traffic locations in a region.

In developing countries, a lack of reliable data is a significant impediment to sustainable growth, disaster relief, and food security. Poverty data, for example, is typically scarce, labor-intensive to obtain, and has limited scope. Remote sensing data is becoming gradually available and low-priced as well. However, such data is highly unstructured, and there are currently no tools for extracting valuable insights to inform policy decisions and guide charitable efforts. A TL method [27] has been discussed by Marshall Burke, Neal Jean, David Lobell, Michael Xie and Stefano Ermon, where night-time light power is used as a data-rich substitute. The authors trained a completely convolutional neural network (CNN) model to predict night time lights using daytime imagery while studying characteristics that can be used to predict poverty. The researchers show that these learned features are extremely useful for poverty plotting, even precluding the prognostic presentation of field-collected survey data.

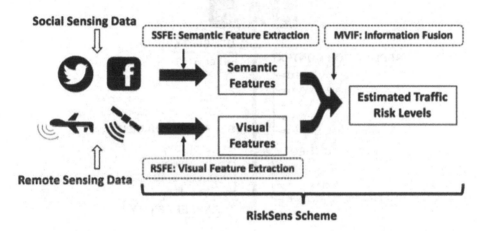

Fig. 2. RiskSens scheme

3   Data Based Modeling for Smart Transportation System

For implementing an intelligent transportation application, five different data processing stages have to be considered. Figure 3 below shows the different functional requirements for a smart transportation system. It is a list of possibilities that can help to make a model actionable and it includes usability, self-sustainability, application context, traffic theory and transferability.

1) Data collection through devices and sensors

Together with state-of-the-art and sophisticated microchip, RFID (Radio Frequency Identification) and low-cost smart beacon sensing technologies [12, 19], technical advances in information technology and telecommunications have strengthened procedural capabilities that will simplify motor safety assistance for smart transportation systems worldwide. Such sensing systems for smart transportation include infrastructure and vehicle based networked systems. These infrastructure sensors are long-lasting instruments that are fixed or installed in the driving road or surrounding path as required. They can be manually distributed by sensor injection machinery for fast positioning or by preventive road erection maintenance. Vehicle-sensing strategies include the placement of electronic communications beacons for vehicle-to-infrastructure and infrastructure-to-vehicle and can also deploy video-based automatic number plate segmentation or vehicle magnetic signature recognition technologies at preferred intervals to improve continuous monitoring of vehicles operating in sensitive world zones. The data collected through such sensing systems needs to be pre-processed and stored before further analysis.

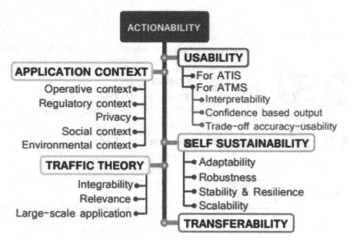

Fig. 3. Functional requirements for a smart transportation system

2) Data Pre-processing

The data comes from the sensors and devices in different forms and formats which needs pre-processing before modelling [13, 20]. Also, the corrupted instances present in the captured data can distort the databased model outputs and hence an actionable data pre-processing must emphasis not only on refining the captured data quality in terms of regularity and completeness, but also on giving valuable insights about the essential phenomena yielding corrupted, missing and/or outlying data, along with their effects on modelling. The study of possible pre-processing stages of data using experiential knowledge of domain features can be used as a method to increase the performance of the target learner, in addition to resolving inconsistencies in the domain varying step for dissemination. The heuristic knowledge will be characterized by a set of complex rules or connections that traditional transfer learning methods cannot explain. In certain instances, this heuristic knowledge will be exhaustive for each domain, resulting in no standard solution. If such a pre-processing phase, however, may lead to better target learner performance, then the effort is probably worth it.

3) Modelling

Modelling phase works towards extracting knowledge from the pre-processed data by constructing a model [14] that characterizes the distribution of the data. If this modelling can be generalized through transfer learning, then it can be used across domain rather than limiting to a particular domain. Machine Learning algorithms are hence put in to use in this stage which allow for modelling automation for instance, to understand patterns relating to the input data to a set of supervised outputs directing to automatically label unseen new data, to forecast future values based on the previous inputs, or to examine the output formed by a model when processing the data that is provided as input. In our use case, where the goal is to model data communications within complex systems such as transportation grids, the modelling choice routes to groups of diverse learner types.

A key feature of this modelling is the generalization of the established model to new unforeseen data. So the design goal would be to find the trade-off between the generalization and the model performance. For smart transportation, the accuracy in prediction can be improved by analysing different models and picking the right architecture or by combining different models for the new system. Optimization needs to be taken care when different models are combined together thereby increasing the system computational complexity.

4) Adaptation

A real time ITS environment is provided for the trained model to see how it adapts and behaves. Actions taken from the outcome result of a data-based model can aid for tactical, strategical or in operational decision making [15]. The output of the prior data-based modelling stage can be used to quantitatively evaluate the fitness or quality of the system. Finally, the suggested actionable data handling workflow contemplates model adaptation as a new processing level that can be applied over various modelling stages in the pipeline. Adaptations can be observed from two standpoints: automatic versions that the system is prepared to do when some circumstances happen, or the adaptations that are derived due to user changes.

Different models for following the vehicle patterns in the same lane can be studies through Gazis-Herman-Rothery (GHR) model. In this model, a vehicle fast-tracks in reaction to the velocity and front vehicle distance. The GHR model in its most general form is represented as:

$$a_n(t+T) = \alpha \frac{v_n^m(t)}{(X_{n-1}(t) - X_n(t))^l} (V_{n-1}(t) - V_n(t)) + K_i a_{n-1}(t) + K_2 a_n(t) \qquad (1)$$

where $a_n(t + T)$ refers to the speeding up of next car at any given time denoted by $t + T$,
   T = Actual Time
   V_n = Following car velocity
   V_{n-1} = Leading car velocity
   X_n = Follower car longitudinal position
   X_{n-1} = Leading car longitudinal position
   A = Acceleration at any given time t for both cars
   Alpha, m, l, k1 and k2 are the other related parameters.

This model provides a general stimulus response and it is observed that the follower's acceleration is relational to the comparative speed between the trailing vehicle and the leading vehicle, whereas the actual data analysis is again inversely proportional. This model is derived from different basic prototypes such as G-H-P model, C-H-M system and basic GHR model.

The purpose of the calibration technique is to reduce the discrepancies between the driving behaviour simulated and the driving behaviour measured. This measured difference is referred to as the relative error, which is defined in Eq. 1 below, with variable 'a' designated as the error dimension.

When comparing the calibrated variables, it is important to evaluate the compassion of various constraints of the objective function, which is how much the value of the objective deviates when adding a slight adjustment to the original parameter. Data-driven modelling along with simulation technique is a noteworthy research focus. Compared to traditional knowledge-based modelling and mechanism modelling approaches, it demonstrates numerous advantages in operability and accuracy. Nevertheless, when implementing such modelling methods in practice, it is still doubtful since data-driven display is occasionally bad in description and data noises can also cause additional errors during modelling.

4   Proposed Transfer Learning Architecture

The case of smart transport domain usage that is considered defined by the letter 'D' and has two parts: a function vector space denoted by X and a marginal distribution of probability of the same by P (X). Here X = {x1,...,xn} X. If the machine learning algorithm can classify defects and each software metric in the algorithm is considered a function, then xi is the i-th feature instance conforming to the i-th module in the software, n is the total number of feature vectors present in X, Y is the space of all likely feature vectors, and X is a particular learning sample in this environment.

Once the source area is trained for a certain application, now that can extend the same for a different transportation related application through transfer learning instead of training it from scratch. This new transport domain is represented by DS with the resulting source task TS, along with the target area DT with the analogous TT task. TL refers to the procedure of refining the target projecting function fT() with the help of related information from TS and DS, where TS = TT or DS = DT. This symmetric transformation mapping is represented in Fig. 4 below.

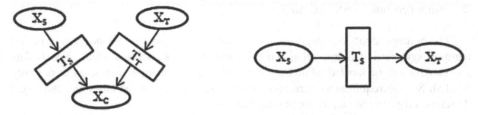

Fig. 4. Symmetric transformation mapping between source and target domains

If the distributions of the transport area are not found to be identical, then additional steps for domain revision are required. The type of data transfer is another essential feature of this transfer learning technique. This include four categories namely transfer learning through instances, learning through features, learning through shared parameters and finally transfer information created on some distinct association among the basis and target areas. This is presented in Fig. 5 below:

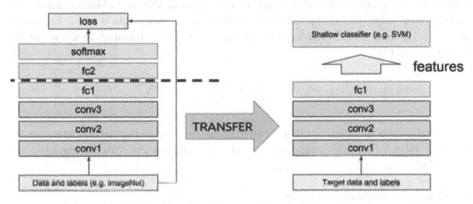

Fig. 5. System architecture for transfer learning

The proposed architecture of transfer learning addresses the following: What kind of data should be transferred between tasks, when to transfer this data and how to transfer it effectively without increasing the complexity of the system. The proposed algorithm takes advantage of the source domain's inductive biases to improve the target task effectively. Depending on the application, the learning could either be self-teaching or multitasking. It is suggested the use of four different forms of transfer, including the transfer of instances, the transfer of feature representations, the transfer of parameters and the transfer of relational information. The algorithm infers a mapping from the trained examples set. The inductive bias or conventions can be classified based on a variety of variables, including the hypothesis space within which it confines the method and the search procedure within that space. Hypothesis biases have an effect on how the algorithm has learned from the model on a particular mission.

D. Homogeneous transfer learning

The homogeneous TL categories can be built on parameters, instances, asymmetric features, symmetric features, relational or hybrid (both instance and feature based). The source data will be labeled while the target data can be labeled, unlabeled or partially labeled. So, the requirement here is to bridge the gap among the basis and the target domains. Proposed Strategies for this problem is

(a) Correct the marginal distribution differences in such a way that (P (Xt) = P (Xs)).
(b) Correct the conditional distribution differences in such a way that (P (Yt|Xt) = P (Ys|Xs)).
(c) A hybrid method of correcting both the above mentioned distribution differences.

In this method, reweight the samples collected in the source domain that helps to precise the marginal distribution changes. It uses these reweighted occurrences for training in the target domain. The conditional distribution should remain same in both the domains for better performance. The weights are adjusted based on the statistical values such as the mean and variance of the data that is under test. Maximum Mean Discrepancy is a distance metric that is applied on the probability measures space which has found different applications in nonparametric testing and machine learning, as shown in the following Eq. (2).

$$Disat(P(x_s), P(X_T)) = \left| \frac{1}{n_s} \sum_{i=1}^{n_s} \varphi(xs_i) - \frac{1}{n_T} \sum_{j=1}^{n_r} \phi(xT_i) \right|_H \tag{2}$$

Based on the statistics and their contributions to the classification accuracy in the target domain, part of the source domain labeled data can therefore be reused in the target domain as well after re-weighting.

E. Heterogeneous transfer learning

Different feature spaces are used to describe the basis and target areas in the case of heterogeneous transfer learning. The characteristics are used for learning by reducing the difference in the latent space between the various distributions. Data label obtainability is one of the functions of the primary application. Heterogeneous transfer learning solutions aims towards bridging the gap between the different feature spaces and change the problem to a homogeneous transfer learning one where additional distribution that could be either conditional or marginal differences will need to be modified. Machine learning algorithms have already shown promising results in the transportation industry, where it has demonstrated better performance compared to the traditional solutions. Nevertheless, the transportation issues are still rich in relating and leveraging machine learning techniques and need more attention. The fundamental goals for these models are to decrease congestion, increase safety and reduce human errors, optimize energy performance, lessen unfavorable environmental influences, and progress the productivity along with surface transportation efficiency. The machine learning pipeline and the interaction between ITS and ML is shown in Fig. 6:

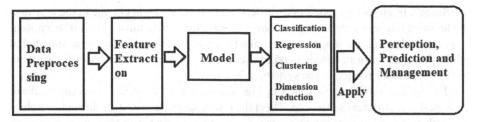

Fig. 6. ML pipeline and interaction with ITS system

The raw data could also be obtained, apart from the sensors, by triangulation process, vehicle re-identification, GPS-based methods and rich monitoring based on smartphones. Mobile operators across the world are also are becoming an important player in these value chains as they provide dedicated apps which can be used for making mobile payments, provide insights in to data and navigation tools, offer discounts and incentives to the end customer, and act as a digital e-commerce medium as well.

The proposed system has two models namely the convolutional base and the classifier. The convolutional base consists of a pooling stack and convolution layers. Development of image features is the main objective of this convolution base. Typically, the classifier used in this method is generated by completely linked layers. Using the detected features and classifying the image is the main objective of the classifier. A completely related layer is a layer whose neurons have a total effect on all previous activation of the layer. Once the system is trained with the model, it can re purpose a pre-trained model by removing the actual classifier and then introduce the new classifier that fits the ITS purpose and fine tune it through one of the following strategies:

(a) Train the full model: the pre-trained model's design is used and trained as per the ITS dataset in this case. The model is learned from scratch and thus needs a considerable amount of dataset.

(b) Train some layers while leaving the rest frozen: The general features are referred in the lower layers which are problem independent and the higher layers refer to precise features which are problem dependent. The weight of the network is adjusted and the frozen layer present in the model does not change during the training stage. If there are large number of parameters and the dataset is small, then there will be more frozen layers to avoid the problem of overfitting. On the other hand, if the dataset is huge with lowered parameters, then by training more layers to the new task, that can increase the model output as the issue of overfitting is not a problem.

(c) Freeze the complete convolutional base. This situation relates to the serious state of the freeze and train trade-off. In this method, the key concept is to maintain the convolutionary base as such and then re-use only the output as input for the classifier. Feature extraction happens through the pre-trained model and it is useful when the computational power is low, the provided dataset is small, or when the pre-trained model can solve multiple problems.

Since it is a hyper-parameter that is dependent on the weight change in the network, the learning rate associated with the convolutional component must be carefully chosen. In general, the high learning rate can make the system to lose the previous knowledge while the small learning rate is good to use. This will also make sure that the weights are not adjusted too often in the system.

The system model is presented in Fig. 7 where a set of vehicles on the road are equipped with different sensors to collect the raw data and transmitted through a mobile network to the edge computing device. Data accumulation provides the strength for analyses to capture some data insights that would not be conceivable from single sensors. The sensed data is transmitted frequently and the vehicles interacts with the gateway devices on every transmission. Based on the intended service, the gateway device will collect and handle the data accordingly. Transportation efficiency, vehicle security, travel safety, environment monitoring, are just few samples of types of services that can be offered. Before the feedback is provided to the vehicles or the end users, the machine learning algorithms can be run either on the edge computing system or on the cloud. The concept of transfer learning is also realized on the gateway device or on the cloud depending upon the application.

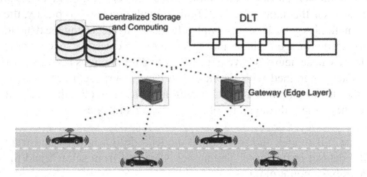

Fig. 7. System model for smart transportation system

For the purpose of smart transportation system, select the pre-trained model of convolutional neural network (CNN) which has a 4-layer architecture and then deep-belief network (DBN) model was employed to distinguish between the various associated activities. The dataset used for experimentation in this system is divided into three diverse groups such as speed limit overrun, immediate line overrun and yellow-line driving. This method can be used for different category features for different kinds of vehicles without training them independently.

Size similarity matrix is one which control the different choices in the system. Based on the size of the dataset, this matrix helps to classify the computer vision problem. This matrix is also useful for fine-tuning the model and repurposing the previously trained method. We have also performed weight transfusion based experiments, in which only a pre-trained weights subset of the system is transferred, with the remainder of them being just initialized randomly. While comparing the convergence speeds of these weight transfused models with full transfer learning, it is observed that the reuse of the extracted features are happening only at the lowest layers of the system.

The transfer learning scenario can be considered as a set of segments of the road "n" that are built with speed sensors. Each of the sensors "i" can provide the traffic speed at any given point of time "t" and is represented as vi[t]. Transfer learning is applied to this use case in order to predict the future speed of traffic at a given time. Historical data can be generally used for future value prediction but when such values are not available, then the concept of transfer learning helps.

The model proposed in this work will exploit this dataset for some source areas and then will build a prediction model for target location where there is only little or no available data. The data format consists of the road network represented through links and nodes. Each node in the network characterizes the latitude and longitude properties. Every link in the network will help to connect nodes and most streets consists of multiple links. The average traffic speed is given by the row values of a particular link at any given point of time. Different spatial and temporal features are extracted from the given data which will act as the essential constituents of the proposed approach. Once the features are extracted, different machine learning methods such as support vector machines, linear regression, convolutional neural networks etc. are used for training the system followed by testing on a new dataset not related to the training as such.

For smart transportation networks, various types of wireless communications technologies have been proposed. Radio mobile communication on VHF and UHF frequencies are extensively used for long and short range communication within ITS. This proposed intelligent transportation system based on transfer learning can be applied for various use cases, including Controlling traffic flow (traffic lights, measuring traffic flow, analysing traffic flow, and controlling guidance equipment), and managing public transportation (highway and tunnels, parking lots, expressway, railway and subway, bus, taxi and truck), Publication of Traffic Data (LED plate release information, SMS, radio station and television, terminal and website for public inquiry), Control of Traffic Offenses (over speed, red light running, wrong direction, occupied lane), Management of the Vehicle and Driver (vehicle information, driver information, driving route tracing, violation record and penalty), Statisticians and research (record demand, log, user management and simulation), daily tasks and emergency management (command centre, resource dispatch, pre-plan and daily task management) as well as real-time traffic status monitoring (accident, traffic jam and abnormal status).

5   Experimentation and Results Discussion

The availability of models developed for the source task and also tested is one of the significant criteria for the successful use of transfer learning. There are several advanced deep learning frameworks for TL and research purposes available across domains. Different pre-trained prototypes are typically shared in the parameters/weights form which is attained while being qualified to a stable state. For smart transportation system, the popular computer vision models include VGG-19, VGG-16, XCeption, Inception V3 and ResNet-50. One of the such model for training and testing is used in this method.

The identified Dataset is first divided into two categories — namely the training set and the testing set. Three different scenarios namely the no transfer task, cross transfer task and the local transfer task are considered for testing. The first one will predict the future speed based on the history of the data, second one will build a model first and then test on another target region that is not completely related while the last one will also have model training with the exception being testing from the same set.

Freight management, arterial and freeway management, transit management systems, regional multi modal and traveller information systems, incident and emergency management systems, and information management systems are all major areas of intelligent transportation systems in metropolitan deployments. Its applications are not limited to highway traffic alone, with electronic toll collection, highway data collection, traffic management systems, vehicle data collection, and transit signal priority being among them.

Open source library for machine learning purposes which includes grid based search tests and helps us to find the best performing model along with the appropriate hyper parameters. Our system has: 6 Hidden layers, 6 Neurons per layer, learning rate is 0.01 and minimum error is 0.01.

Wireless communications, inductive loop detection, sensing technologies, bluetooth detection, computing technologies and video vehicle detection are some of the enabling technologies used in this research. During the initial stages, the larger networks needs more number of epochs to fit the data. Conversely after some number of epochs, it exceeds the smaller ones and achieves the best score.

When it comes to transfer learning, the proposed network is first pre-trained using simulation and then applied on the real data. When compared to the control network, these approaches work well. The convergence time is also much faster with this proposed approach. Some iterations are required for the random initialization network in order to fit the new weights in it. The complexity of the neural network, the predictive capabilities and the size of the gap between the simulation and real data will decide on the success of the different approaches discussed. An empirical study was conducted in South Indian districts, using three types of traffic datasets: floating cars, annual average daily traffic and public transportation routes.

Table 1. Comparison of transfer performance

Location	RMSE	MAE
Bellary	10.63	7.62
Parbhara	5.74	4.33
Hampi	4.91	3.04
Guntur	8.11	5.65
Jaina	11.32	8.92

There are two metrics used in this work to calculate the precision of continuous variables, namely the mean absolute error and the root-mean-square error. The first one deals with the error average magnitude in the prediction set without direction consideration.

$$MAE = \frac{1}{n} \sum_{j=1}^{n} \left| y_j - \widehat{y}_j \right| \quad (3)$$

The latter one called as the Root Mean Square Error is a quadratic scoring rule. It also helps to measure the average magnitude of the error. This is calculated as the square root of the average of prediction and actual values squared differences.

$$RSME = \frac{1}{n} \sum_{j=1}^{n} \left| \left(y_j - \widehat{y}_j \right)^2 \right| \quad (4)$$

The average model prediction error is expressed through these two metrics MAE and the RMSE. They can range between 0 to infinity. They are both indifferent to the error direction. The lower the value, the better the output, and so on, as both scores are negative. RMSE will give more importance to large errors due to squaring of errors when compared to MAE. Table 1 gives the transfer performance across different locations in Karnataka, India in terms of MAE and RMSE. From this table, we observed that larger regions that has different kinds of links gave us better performance when compared to the other locations nearby. This is also represented through a graph in Fig. 8 below.

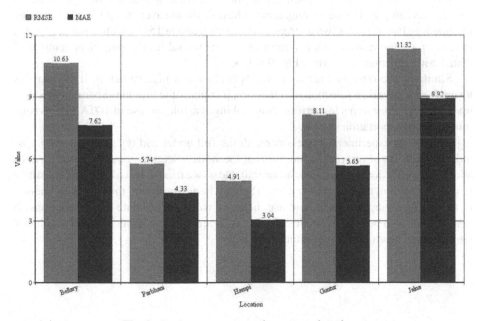

Fig. 8. Performance comparison across locations

Below shows the results and summarized statistics along with the error rates for the proposed method vs. other architecture for ITS in the literature that resorts to DLT features. The proposed transfer learning based smart transportation system outperforms in terms of performance when compared to simple pre-train CNN system that uses PCA in the same selected dataset (Table 2).

Table 2. Results for 60, 120 and 240 vehicles based on latency and error rates

Vehicles	Method	Average latency	Error rate
65	Fixed Random	72.68 s	14.36 %
	Dynamic Random	57.1 s	18.26%
	Proposed Method	20.40 s	0.70%
120	Fixed Random	86.85 s	24.48%
	Dynamic Random	67.5 s	18.99%
	Proposed Method	24.90 s	1.0%
240	Fixed Random	187.62 s	42.80%
	Dynamic Random	128.19 s	44.85%
	Proposed Method	71.37 s	6.45%

It is clear from the above table that both the error ate as well as the average latency is very less as compared to the existing approaches. While the average rate for the proposed method is ~ 1%, the other two approaches have well above 15% which is not acceptable in case of a smart transportation system and hence unusable. The empirical cumulative distribution function is shown in Fig. 9 below.

Similarly, the error rate across methods is shown in Fig. 10 below. It is clear that through an appropriate selection of full nodes, it is plausible to achieve consistent ledger updates or in other terms low errors, thus making feasible the use of IOTA to provision intelligent transportation system.

During our experimental assessment, all the full nodes had typically a low computational load. However, results indorse that the node selection is quite relevant. As an additional validation of this claim, in our initial tests we tried to feat a heuristic, substitute to those offered in the previous section. The idea here was to find the best N full nodes, in terms of existing resources, and use them to provide or validate the transactions. A gateway can also be used to employ an edge computing model as an alternative solution which would be an interesting future work.

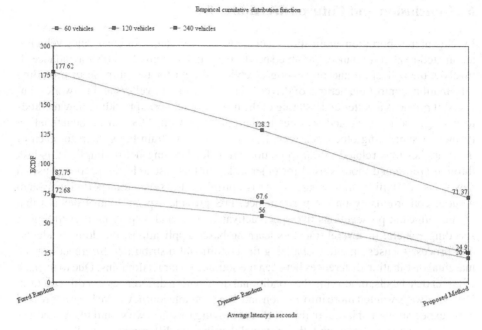

Fig. 9. Empirical cumulative distribution function

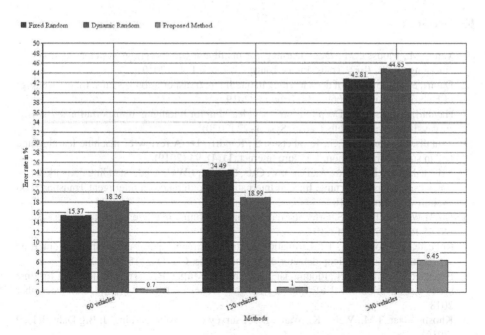

Fig. 10. Error rate analysis across methods

6   Conclusion and Future Directions

Intelligent transportation applications include warning systems for emergency vehicles, automated road compliance, variable speed limits and systems for crash avoidance. It involves the collection and processing of collected data for the purpose of providing information, control the actions of drivers, fleet operators, travellers and network managers. It provides a better understating of the transport network, providing new methods to manage the network and services to the public as well. ITS can be beneficial on its own or supporting other measures. It is not so easy to train the system for each of these applications related to transportation. Transfer learning helps simplify this task through pre-trained models used for other tasks. In this research, the proposed uses a new transfer learning architecture which is optimized for smart transportation system without compromising on the performance. ITS provides speed control devices that are not aimed at prosecutions like speed activated signs and displaying registration of speeding vehicle. In several transfers learning-based applications, the domain adaptation process focuses on either changing the conditional distribution differences or the marginal distribution differences between the source and target domains. Due to the lack of target data labels, modifying the conditional distribution differences is a difficult task. Drivers always wanted more information and more reliable journeys. We have addressed these expectations and issues in this work and moving forward, we would like to address the other issues associated with the marginal distribution differences as well.

References

1. Veres, M., Moussa, M.: Deep learning for intelligent transportation systems: a survey of emerging trends. IEEE Trans. Intell. Transp. Syst. **21**, 1–17 (2019)
2. Dabiri, S.: Application of deep learning in intelligent transportation systems. In: proceedings of Dabiri, Corpus ID: 86693644, February 2019
3. Haydari, A., Yasin, Y.: Deep reinforcement learning for intelligent transportation systems: a survey. IEEE Trans. Intell. Transp. Syst. 1–22 (2020)
4. Zantalis, F., Koulouras, G., Karabetsos, S., Kandris, D.: A review of machine learning and IoT in smart transportation. J. Future Internet, **11**(4), 94 (2019)
5. Krishnakumari, P., Perotti, A., Pinto, V., Cats, O., Lint, J.W.C.: Understanding network traffic states using transfer learning. In: 21st International Conference on Intelligent Transportation Systems, December 2018
6. Ho, H.W., Agachai, S.: Smarter and more connected: future intelligent transportation system. IATSS Res. **42**(2), 67-71 (2018)
7. Robuste, F., Soriguera, F.: Estimation of traffic stream space mean speed from time aggregations of double loop detector data. Transp. Res. C **19**(1), 115–129 (2011)
8. Forestier, G., Fawaz, H.I., Idoumghar, L., Weber, J., Muller, P.A.: Transfer learning for time series classification. In: IEEE International Conference on Big Data (Big Data), December 2018
9. Khoshgoftaar, T.M., Weiss, K., Wang, D.: A survey of transfer learning. J. Big Data, **3**(1), 9 (2016)
10. Tsang, I.W., Zhou, J.T., Yan, Y., Pan, S.: Hybrid heterogeneous transfer learning through deep learning. In: Proceedings of the National Conference on Artificial Intelligence, vol. 3, pp. 2213–20 (2014)

11. Doretto, G., Yao, Y.: Boosting for transfer learning with multiple sources. In: Proceedings of the IEEE Computer Society Conference on Computer Vision and Pattern Recognition, pp. 1855–62 (2010)
12. Fong, S.L., Bakar, A.A.A.B.A., Ahmed, F.Y., Jamal, A.: Smart transportation system using RFID. In: 8th International Conference on Software and Computer Applications (2019)
13. Zelaya, C.V.G.: Towards explaining the effects of data preprocessing on machine learning. In: 35th International Conference on Data Engineering (ICDE), April 2019
14. Islam, M.S., Okita, T., Inoue, S.: Evaluation of transfer learning for human activity recognition among different datasets. In: IEEE Intl Conf on Dependable, Autonomic and Secure Computing, August 2019
15. Yu, C., Wang, J., Chen, Y., Huang, M.: Transfer learning with dynamic adversarial adaptation network. In: IEEE International Conference on Data Mining (ICDM), November 2019
16. Pan, S.J., Yang, Q.: A survey on transfer learning. IEEE Trans. Knowl. Data Eng. **22**, 1345–59 (2009)
17. Lai, T.M., Bui, T., Lipka, N., Li, S.: Supervised transfer learning for product information question answering. In: IEEE International Conference on Machine Learning and Applications (ICMLA), December 2018
18. Zhang, Y., Hongxiao, W., Daniel, Z., Dong, W.: DeepRisk: a deep transfer learning approach to migratable traffic risk estimation in intelligent transportation using social sensing. In: International Conference on Distributed Computing in Sensor Systems (DCOSS), May 2019
19. Shah Singh, M., Pondenkandath, V., Zhou, B., Lukowicz, P., Liwicki, M.: Transforming sensor data to the image domain for deep learning -an application to footstep detection. arXiv Computer Vision and Pattern Recognition, July 2017
20. Jelena, F., Maksims, F., Jörg, M.: Big data processing and mining for next generation intelligent transportation systems. Jurnal Teknologi **63**(3), 21–38 (2013)
21. Walker, S.J.: Big data: a revolution that will transform how we live work and think. In Int. J. Advertising **33**(1), 181–183 (2014)
22. Subramanian, A.P., Das, S.R., Paul, U., Buddhikot, M.M.: Understanding traffic dynamics in cellular data networks. In: Proceeding of IEEE INFOCOM, pp. 882–890, April 2011
23. Leung, V.C.M., Li, X., Wang, X.: Artificial intelligence-based techniques for emerging heterogeneous network: state of the arts opportunities and challenges. IEEE Access, **3**, 1379–1391 (2015)
24. Liu, J., Wan, J., Shao, Z., Imran, M., Zhou, K., Vasilakos, A.V.: Mobile crowd sensing for traffic prediction in internet of vehicles. Sensors **16**(1), 88 (2016)
25. Sun and Sun: A dynamic Bayesian network model for real-time crash prediction using traffic speed conditions data. Transp. Res. Part C: Emerg. Technol. **54**, 176–186 (2015)
26. Wang, D., Zhang, Y., Shang, L., Lu, Y., Zhang, D.: Risksens: a multiview learning approach to identifying risky traffic locations in intelligent transportation systems using social and remote sensing. In: IEEE International Conference on Big Data (Big Data), pp. 1544–1553 (2018)
27. Lobell, D., Xie, M., Burke, M., Ermon, S., Jean, S.: Transfer learning from deep features for remote sensing and poverty mapping. In: Thirtieth AAAI Conference on Artificial Intelligence (2016)
28. Bellone, M., Caltagirone, L., Wahde, M., Svensson, L.: Lidar-based driving path generation using fully convolutional neural networks. In: IEEE International Conference on Intelligent Transportation Systems (ITSC) (2017)
29. Liu, J., et al.: Resume Parsing based on Multi-label Classification using Neural Network model. In: 2021 6th International Conference on Big Data and Computing (2021)
30. Wang, X., Wang, L., Zhang, Y., Wang, J.: 3D-lidar based branch estimation and intersection location for autonomous vehicles. In: IEEE Intelligent Vehicles Symposium (IV), pp. 1440–1445, June 2017

Machine Learning Approach
for Detection of Cardiology Diseases

Gunupudi Rajesh Kumar(✉) , Nimmala Mangathayaru , Aditya Kolli,
Avinash Komatineni, Srihitha Reddy, and Shivani Reddy

Department of Information Technology, VNR Vignana Jyothi Institute
of Engineering and Technology, Hyderabad, India
gunupudirajesh@gmail.com
http://vnrvjiet.ac.in/itfaculty.php

Abstract. Heart plays essential part in living creatures. Heart disease
is one of the most major causes of death in the world today. Prediction of
this cardiac disease is most difficult part in the field of medical data analysis. Diagnosis and forecast of heart linked disorders need greater accuracy, perfection and correctness since a small error may create tiredness
issue or death of the person, there are countless death cases connected
to heart and their counting is rising geometrically day by day. As the
outside world is developing a lot but why have not the software that
many people have developed are not showing good performance, then
with a lot of research we have found that machine learning is the correct
way which serves our purpose. Machine learning has been demonstrated
to be successful in aiding in generating judgments and predictions from
the huge amount of data generated by the healthcare business. Various
research provide merely a peep towards forecasting heart disease using
ML approaches. Here, we construct a model that aims at detecting key
characteristics by using machine learning methods resulting in enhancing the accuracy in the prediction of heart disease. There are various
methods to perform this job effectively, but how effective are they? Our
major target is to provide an increased performance level with the excellent accuracy level via the prediction model for heart disease using the
SVM, Naive Bayes, Extreme learning machine, logistic regression and
Random Forest techniques.

Keywords: Accuracy · ML models · Heart disease · Prediction · Web
application · Graph

1 Introduction

Heart Disease is extensively known all over the world and it is a series of disorders
that arise when heart and blood arteries aren't performing the way they should.
It is estimated that on an average over 17 million people die of cardiovascular
illnesses each year, which is nearly one third of overall fatalities throughout
the world. In our day-to-day life we say many people who are suffering from

A. K. Luhach et al. (Eds.): ICAICR 2021, CCIS 1575, pp. 182–191, 2022.
https://doi.org/10.1007/978-3-031-09469-9_16

this heart disease. Doctors can treat these kind of disease after they were being encountered. But so many scholars around the world are developing various software for early detection of these kind of diseases. Before developing a software with different models we have seen so many models for our idea of understanding about how the diagnosis process is being done and what all the methods are being used by the people around different parts of world. In the present methods, early diagnosis of probable cardiac illnesses is not more feasible and effective use of different obtained data is time intensive and the projections are frequently erroneous. We strive to anticipate any possible cardiovascular hazards ahead and thereby averting dangerous scenarios. We also assess several ML models and their performances in fulfilling the objective. The main objective of the project is to implement a methodology in which we use different algorithms to predict the heart disease. The results that are obtained include accuracy, precision of that particular model used. Also we showcase the accuracy graphs where we can find out the difference in between the models used.

1.1   Literature Survey

[1] Introduces a new data mining model with the help of random forest classifier, also here the authors were successful in predicting the risk factors related to the heart disease [2]. Here in this study, the authors have decided in producing the best rules in the view of diagnosis of heart disease. The authors have used "Particle Swarm Optimization algorithm" whereas the random rules are being generated at the starting and then they are being optimized. Later on the achieved results are being compared with "C4.5 algorithm" [3]. Mainly in this study, the authors have compared various models as they have implemented "HRFLM model" which means it is a combination of both the linear method and random forest classifier. They achieved good accuracy with that algorithm while compared to other models. Also they have used the "Cleveland dataset" and they have plotted the graphs of the models that they have worked with [4]. Artificial Neural Network named "ANN" was introduced for this diagnosis of heart related disease whereas with the help of this ANN, authors were able to produce the best results and overall this model have delivered a great performance [5]. In this study, the new tool named "TPOT" was being introduced where this was an "automated tool of machine learning". Automatically picking of the suitable algorithm is the specialty of this tool and then it fits that algorithm to the data. Also they have confirmed that, the algorithm is still in the phase of development but it gives good accuracy which solely depends upon problem statement. Here also the authors have compared various models including this new tool that they have introduced [6]. Mainly as per the study, a novel approach based on back propagation Network of MLP has been used. Here also the same Cleveland dataset has been used which consists of 13 attributes for predicting the disease [7]. Here in this paper, the authors gives us a brief that there are very less methods in finding the connections and all these kind of several patterns in the data. So, the introduction of some data mining methods are being introduced in here. In machine learning the volume of the dataset plays

very important role. Various data preprocessing and dimensionality reduction the approaches discussed in [8–27] exhibits promising results.

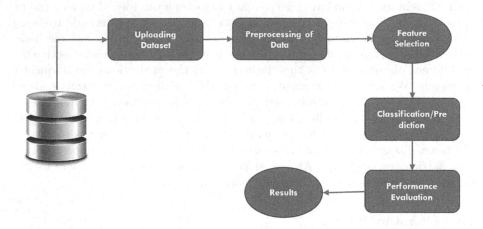

Fig. 1. System architecture of our software.

2   System Architecture

Generally there are so many prediction methods for various diseases in the field of this health-care. As we are daily seeing or hearing that most of the people around us are suffering from this heart disease, but there are doctors on field for this diagnosis and treatment of the disease. But examining the dataset and predicting the heart disease is difficult for the doctors to perform. So as more number of researchers contribute their work towards in this field, we also have decided to develop a web application in which we have used several models to predict the disease and also to find the model's accuracy for that particular dataset. Here we have developed a web application using flask framework and in that our software consists of nine modules in which at uploading of the dataset, then that particular dataset consists of raw data, whereas we use data preprocessing techniques to preprocess that raw data i.e. the data which does not contain numerical values are being discarded. Then after the clean dataset is being achieved after all this, then the main task of training and testing the model will take place where in that we train eighty percent of data from the cleaned dataset, the other twenty percent of the dataset is used for testing the model. So, we train the test different supervised learning models which are "SVM, Naïve Bayes, Logistic regression, ANN, Hybrid model of the combination of random forest and linear method, Extreme learning machine model". Figure 1 presents teh system architecture. Whereas Fig. 2 presents the flow diagram. All the accuracy that is being generated by the model is plotted with the help of accuracy graphs where we can directly examine which model is performing well.

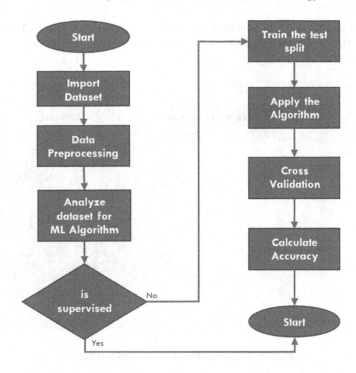

Fig. 2. Flowchart regarding the flow of our web application.

3   Implementation and Results

The implementation of our system is explained clearly here. Here, mainly the dataset we used for this purpose was "Cleveland heart disease". The dataset contains so many records which are non-numerical, so our primary goal is to discard all these records and only retain the numerical values. To discard the values, we use data preprocessing techniques where we remove the values that are non-numerical. Then, we move the entire dataset which we got finally into another file and then use that dataset in the new file for all the prediction and all. At first after data preprocessing we have to split the dataset into two halves, where we use majority of the data for training purpose where the minority of the data is used for testing purpose like 80% for training purpose and 20% of the data for testing. After this, we have to build the model and then train the model with our dataset which we have split. Then we can test the model and then we also generate the accuracy graphs, classification reports and all. As we have developed the web application using flask framework, we can easily generate the graphs. Also while comparing all the models that are being developed "hybrid model which was a combination of linear method and random forest" has given good accuracy which is consistent. Also extreme learning machine shown good accuracy when compared with the other models. Finally after this completion of the work we can come to a conclusion that both the "extreme learning machine method" and the "hybrid method" has given us good accuracy. Also we have generated the accuracy graphs by which we can analyze the model.

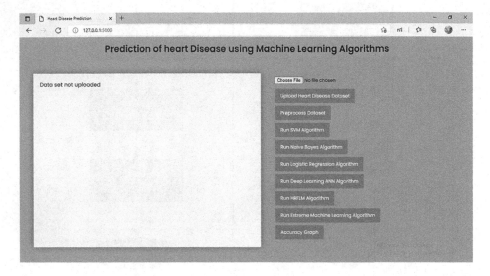

Fig. 3. User interface of our application.

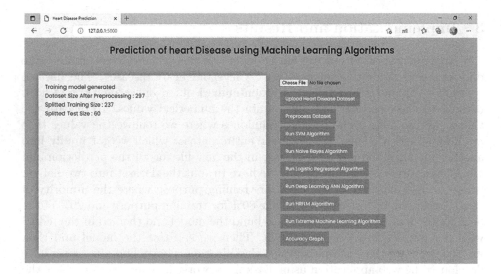

Fig. 4. Data prepossessing.

The steps involved are as followed:

Step 1: Dataset Collection.

Step 2: Performing Data preprocessing on the dataset as it consists of non-numerical values.

Step 3: Train and test split of the dataset.

Step 4: Training the model.

Step 5: Evaluating the model with the help of the test split dataset.

Step 6: Predicting the heart disease as it shows predicted value if disease is positive (1) or it shows (0).

Step 7: Generating the classification report.

Step 8: Finding the accuracy of the model.

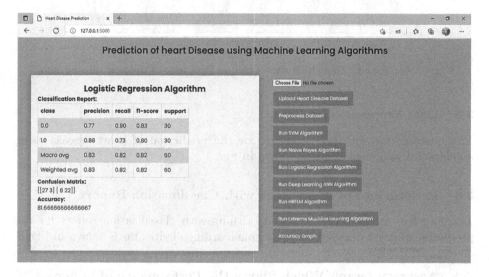

Fig. 5. Performance of algorithms with classification report.

All the above steps that are being followed in our project for predicting the disease and finding accuracy of the models can be better explained using the following screenshots of our product.

3.1 User Interface of Our Application

The user interface for the prediction of heart disease using machine learning algorithms is shown in Fig. 3.

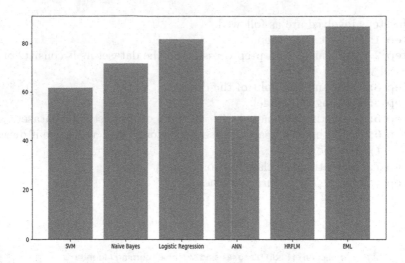

Fig. 6. Accuracy Graph which shows the performance of different algorithms.

3.2 Data Prepossessing

The interface for data prepossessing for the prediction of heart disease using machine learning algorithms is shown in Fig. 4.

3.3 Performance of Algorithms with Classification Report

The interface for Performance of algorithms with classification report for the prediction of heart disease using machine learning algorithms is shown in Fig. 5.

3.4 Accuracy Graph Which Shows the Performance of Different Algorithms

The Accuracy Graph which shows the performance of different algorithms for algorithms used in the prediction of heart disease using machine learning algorithms is shown in Fig. 6.

4 Conclusions

By identifying the entire process that the raw data related to this heart disease is going through, this particular approach will help in saving lives and also detection of these heart diseases are done somewhat early. Mainly with the help of these particular machine learning techniques that are being used in our project, these help to process the raw data and then provide a good approach in prediction of the disease. As we know that prediction of heart disease is more important and also with the early prediction of heart disease death rate can be slightly controlled because measures that are used for prevention can be employed in the next step. Also more and more variety of algorithms should be equipped as we have used several algorithms to compare and find out which one is more accurate. While building such predictive models, it's necessary to ensure the data we feed our models is of very good quality because it is essential to train the models to perfection and we need to ensure we leave no stone unturned since we're expected to deal with a 100% accuracy and nothing less.

References

1. Abdullah, A.S., Rajalaxmi, R.R.: A data mining model for predicting the coronary heart disease using random forest classifier. In: Proceedings of the International Conference in Recent Trends in Computational Methods, Communication and Controls, April 2012, pp. 22–25 (2012)
2. Alkeshuosh, A.H., Moghadam, M.Z., Al Mansoori, I., Abdar, M.: Using PSO algorithm for producing best rules in diagnosis of heart disease. In: Proceedings of the International Conference on Computer and Applications (ICCA), September 2017, pp. 306–311 (2017)
3. Mohan, S., Thirumalai, C., Srivastava, G.: Effective heart disease prediction using hybrid machine learning techniques. IEEE Access **7**, 81542–81554 (2019). https://doi.org/10.1109/ACCESS.2019.2923707
4. Cheng, C.-A., Chiu, H.-W.: An artificial neural network model for the evaluation of carotid artery stenting prognosis using a national-widedatabase. In: Proceedings of the 39th Annual International Conference of the IEEE Engineering in Medicine and Biology Society (EMBC), July 2017, pp. 2566–2569 (2017)
5. Sowjanya, K., Krishna Mohan, G.: Predicting heart disease using machine learning classification algorithms and along with TPOT (AUTOML). Int. J. Sci. Technol. Res. **9**(4), 3202–3210 (2020)
6. Durairaj, M., Revathi, V.: Prediction of heart disease using back propagation MLP algorithm. Int. J. Sci. Technol. Res. **4**(8), 235–239 (2015)
7. Gandhi, M., Singh, S.N.: Predictions in heart disease using techniques of data mining. In: International Conference on Futuristic Trends on Computational Analysis and Knowledge Management (ABLAZE) 2015, pp. 520–525 (2015). https://doi.org/10.1109/ABLAZE.2015.7154917
8. Kumar, G.R., Mangathayaru, N., Narsimha, G.: An approach for intrusion detection using novel gaussian based kernel function. J. Univ. Comput. Sci. **22**(4), 589–604 (2016). ISSN: 0948–6968
9. Narsimha, G., Kumar, G.R., Mangathayaru, N.: Intrusion detection - a text mining based approach. Int. J. Comput. Sci. Inf. Secur. (IJCSIS) **14**, 76–88 (2016). Special issue on "Computing Application"
10. Kumar, G.R., Nimmala, M., Narsimha, G.: A novel similarity measure for intrusion detection using Gaussian function. Tech. J. Faculty Eng. TJFE **39**(2), 173–183 (2016)
11. Gunupudi, R.K., Nimmala, M., Gugulothu, N., Gali, S.R.: CLAPP: a self constructing feature clustering approach for anomaly detection. Future Gener. Comput. Syst. **74**, 417–429 (2017)
12. Kumar, G.R., Mangathayaru, N., Narsimha, G.: A feature clustering based dimensionality reduction for intrusion detection (FCBDR). IADIS Int. J. Comput. Sci. Inf. Syst. **12**(1), 26–44 (2017)

13. Radhakrishna, V., Kumar, G.R., Aljawarneh, S.: Optimising business intelligence results through strategic application of software process model. Int. J. Intell. Enterp. **4**(1/2), 128–142 (2017)
14. Kumar, G.R., Mangathayaru, N., Narasimha, G.: An approach for intrusion detection using text mining techniques. In: Proceedings of the The International Conference on Engineering & MIS 2015 (ICEMIS 2015). ACM, New York (2015). https://doi.org/10.1145/2832987.2833076. Article no. 63, 6 pages
15. Radhakrishna, V., Kumar, G.R., Aljawarneh, S.: Strategic application of software process model to optimize business intelligence results. In: Proceedings of the the International Conference on Engineering & MIS 2015 (ICEMIS 2015). ACM, New York (2015). https://doi.org/10.1145/2832987.2833053. Article no. 44, 6 pages
16. Kumar, G.R., Mangathayaru, N., Narasimha, G.: Intrusion detection using text processing techniques: a recent survey. In: Proceedings of the the International Conference on Engineering & MIS 2015 (ICEMIS 2015). ACM, New York (2015). https://doi.org/10.1145/2832987.2833067. Article no. 55, 6 pages
17. Kumar, G.R., Mangathayaru, N., Narasimha, G.: An improved k-means clustering algorithm for intrusion detection using Gaussian function. In: Proceedings of the the International Conference on Engineering & MIS 2015 (ICEMIS 2015). ACM, New York (2015). https://doi.org/10.1145/2832987.2833082. Article no. 69, 7 pages
18. Kumar, G.R., Mangathayaru, N., Narsimha, G.: An approach for intrusion detection using fuzzy feature clustering. In: 2016 International Conference on Engineering & MIS (ICEMIS), Agadir, pp. 1–8 (2016). https://doi.org/10.1109/ICEMIS.2016.7745345
19. Mangathayaru, N., Kumar, G.R., Narsimha, G.: Text mining based approach for intrusion detection. In: International Conference on Engineering & MIS (ICEMIS) 2016, Agadir, Morocco. Publisher IEEE (2016). https://doi.org/10.1109/ICEMIS.2016.7745351
20. Kumar, G.R., Mangathayaru, N., Narsimha, G.: Design of novel fuzzy distribution function for dimensionality reduction and intrusion detection. In: 2016 International Conference on Engineering & MIS (ICEMIS), Agadir, pp. 1–6 (2016)
21. Nagaraja, A., Gunupudi, R.K., Saravana Kumar, R., Mangathayaru, N.: Optimization of access points in wireless sensor network: an approach towards security. Intell. Syst. Cybern. Autom. Theory **348**, 299–306 (2015)
22. Kumar, G.R., Mangathayaru, N., Narsimha, G., Reddy, G.S.: Evolutionary approach for intrusion detection. In: 2017 International Conference on Engineering & MIS (ICEMIS), Monastir, pp. 1–6 (2017). https://doi.org/10.1109/ICEMIS.2017.8273116
23. Aljawarneh, S.A., RadhaKrishna, V., Kumar, G.R.: A fuzzy measure for intrusion and anomaly detection. In: 2017 International Conference on Engineering & MIS (ICEMIS), Monastir, pp. 1–6 (2017). https://doi.org/10.1109/ICEMIS.2017.8273113
24. Kumar, G.R., Mangathayaru, N., Narsimha, G., Cheruvu, A.: Feature clustering for anomaly detection using improved fuzzy membership function. In: Proceedings of the Fourth International Conference on Engineering & MIS 2018 (ICEMIS 2018). ACM, New York (2018). https://doi.org/10.1145/3234698.3234733. Article no. 35, 9 pages
25. Vangipuram, R., Gunupudi, R.K., Puligadda, V.K., Vinjamuri, J.: A machine learning approach for imputation and anomaly detection in IoT environment. Expert Syst. **37**(5) (2020). https://doi.org/10.1111/exsy.12556

26. Nagaraja, A., Uma, B., Gunupudi, R.: UTTAMA: an intrusion detection system based on feature clustering and feature transformation. Found. Sci. **25**(4), 1049–1075 (2019). https://doi.org/10.1007/s10699-019-09589-5
27. Rajesh Kumar, G., Mangathayaru, N., Narasimha, G.: Similarity function for intrusion detection. In: ICEMIS 2019: Proceedings of the 5th International Conference on Engineering and MIS, June 2019, pp. 1–4 (2019). https://doi.org/10.1145/3330431.3330460. Article no. 28

Efficient Entity Resolution
for Bibliographic Data Using MapReduce

Dolly Mittal[1]([✉]), Anjana Sangwan[2], and Veena Yadav[3]

[1] Department of IT, SKIT, Jaipur, India
dolly.mittal@skit.ac.in
[2] Department of CSE, SKIT, Jaipur, India
anjana@skit.ac.in
[3] Department of CSE, PCE, Jaipur, India
veena.yadav@poornima.org

Abstract. Entity resolution is a process to identify all objects/entities referring to the same real-world object. The standard process to extract matches is to compare every entity with all the available entities using some similarity computation technique. It results into inefficient quadratic time complexity for huge datasets. To reduce the number of comparisons for entity pairs, blocking techniques thus become necessary. The objective of this research is to provide an approach for entity resolution to overcome the challenges like scalability of big data, reduce the time for matching process and making it cost effective. An efficient implementation for entity resolution can be achieved by combining the use of blocking and distributed computing framework for massive datasets. The proposed hybrid blocking approach uses the MapReduce model because of it's particular partitioning technique along with the solution to the data skew problem associated with traditional blocking approach.

Keywords: Entity resolution · Blocking · MapReduce · Partitioning

1 Introduction

Entity Resolution is a complex problem and has a great impact on data quality and data integration. The entity resolution process identifies matches and merges records that correspond to the same entities from several data sources. The entities in this process can be humans, such as students, customers, authors, or travelers, along with this various consumer products, research publications and citations can also be used as entities. In entity matching process, we generally match combination of all possible record pairs with the help of various similarity measures, e.g., Hamming distance, N-gram, Edit distance, Jaccard Comparison and judge whether there is any similarity among entities [1].

Entity resolution can also be defined as entity matching, duplicate identification de-duplication, or record linkage. Generally, structured or tabular data is processed by entity resolution and it compares that structured data (either entity or database record) with existing entities present in the knowledge base.

A. K. Luhach et al. (Eds.): ICAICR 2021, CCIS 1575, pp. 192–200, 2022.
https://doi.org/10.1007/978-3-031-09469-9_17

Entity resolution is considered as a significant challenge in various data analysis technique like information retrieval, database management, natural language processing, machine learning and statistics. Entity resolution is a problem of cleaning, extracting, matching entities stored in structured and unstructured data. Various domains are highly affected by accuracy and speed of entity resolution process like security, commercial and scientific domain. In this era of big data, the requirement for high-quality and highly efficient entity resolution is emerging to clean, integrate and match a large amount of data. In many cases, ER is performed in a static mode or in batch processing form where all matching operations are performed at once. ER can also be carried out in real-time, where a query is given to the task to find the most similar record(s).

The most significant use case of entity resolution is the quality maintenance of bibliographic databases. To create and maintain bibliographic databases lot of efforts are required and have to deal with several challenges. Ever increasing the size of these databases is one major problem, as some of the larger publications databases containing well above 25 million publications. The biggest problem is that it is a very common situation that a database can have several researchers and scholars with the same surname and the same initials, or some even working in the same research domain. Even after providing full given names, it is still not easy to identify if two research publications were authored by the same person or not. Also, sometimes conference and journal names are written in short-form and they do not adhere to a standardized format. Hence, it is possible to find many variations of the reference of same research publication in a database.

The standard technique to find duplicates in n input records is to compare each record with all other records. However, it produces intolerable execution times for large datasets with the quadratic complexity of $O(n^2)$. Thus to decrease the number of entity/record comparisons with ensuring match quality, blocking techniques have become necessary. Despite the use of blocking, it is observed that ER is a costly process with high execution time. Due to the data skew blocks, it may take many hours or days to end up processing. Load imbalance is a major issue engaged with entity matching because of skewed data blocks. The matching process performs for all the entities inside the block and skewed blocks will take more execution time to finish. Therefore a better solution for an efficient entity resolution with load balancing and reduced running time is required.

ER is a computationally expensive process that can take large amount of time, which can be either in hours or sometimes in days for matching large datasets in Big Data applications. With the growing size of modern databases, it becomes necessary to increase the computation power and storage resources for deduplicating or matching. Here, the modern parallel and distributed computing environments come into the picture. The employment of parallel programming environments is capable of reducing the time needed to perform large-scale data matching.

MapReduce(MR) model is one among many parallel programming models which is part of Hadoop- a distributed processing paradigm. MapReduce is a best suitable framework for the parallel execution of complex task like entity resolution. MapReduce model is a programming paradigm based on python and java presented by Google in 2004 [2]. MapReduce provides a platform for parallel & distributed data-intensive processing in cluster environments having several nodes. The MapReduce framework makes use of the concept of split and redistribution of data [3]. Entities are defined in the form of (key, value) pair. Computations in MapReduce paradigm are performed with the help of two function which can be defined as [4]:

The standard entity resolution workflow can be easily implemented with MapReduce framework. In the MapReduce based ER, map function is used to implement blocking phase reduce function is used for similarity computation phase. Blocking key is generated by map function for every input entity. Map function produces output in the form of a (blocking_key, entity) pair. These blocking keys are given as input to the partitioning function that distributes key-value pairs to various reducing tasks. Same reducer task is assigned to all entity pair with the same blocking key. Lastly, for every reducer task, similarities for every entity pair within that reduce block are computed . The effective load balancing between the all available nodes is a major factor to get the higher performance and productivity of MapReduce implementation. The biggest challenge here to prevent from data skew, because it may lead to memory bottlenecks and it may result in more computation complexity by the node under execution.

This rest of the paper is organized as follows: Work already done in the field of MapReduce and entity resolution is discussed in Sect. 2. Proposed approach of entity resolution using the concept of hybrid blocking key is described in Sect. 3, followed by Implementation Results and finally the last section concludes the paper with some future aspects to our work.

2   Related Work

Various researchers have studied the Blocking techniques for entity resolution. Newcombe et al. [5] proposed the idea of blocking key. It divides the full Cartesian product of record comparisons into mutually exclusive blocks. The target of their approach is to minimize the number of comparisons in similarity computation step, without missing any possible similar entity pair. These blocking aims cause a trade-off and make blocking phase a difficult task.

Elmagarmid et al. [6] described a "naive" approach for detecting similar records in a database. In this approach they computed hash value for every record in the database using a hash. Authors have given an alternative wherein the algorithm for duplicate detection is executed multiple times and they used a different blocking key for each iteration. This approach reduces the false positivity rate at the cost of slight increment in the execution time.

Hernandez et al. [7] described the popular sorted neighborhood approach. This approach has three major steps: create key, sort key and merge. A blocking key for each record/entity in the input list is generated by retrieving the relevant attributes or parts of attributes. Using this blocking key the entities in the entire dataset is then sorted. Sorting of records is based on a key that is defined as a segment of some attributes or a series of substrings from the available attributes. Further, a window of fixed size is slid on the sequential list of records. This process reduces the comparisons as each record is compared only with records present in that window.

Monge et al. [8] tried to improve the quadratic time complexity based on an assumption that duplicate detection is transitive. They described the problem of matching records in a database under the assumption of transitivity. According to them the duplicates can be described as connected components in an undirected graph. This approach can decreased the total number of record matching, if an entity p is not identical to an entity q present in the same block, then entity p will be dissimilar to all the entities in that block.

Aizawa et al. [9] presented a technique for blocking for huge scale record deduplication. This method is known as suffix array blocking. This is an efficient and less time consuming blocking method for huge amount of data. Suffix Array blocking follows a procedure to insert values of blocking key and associated variable length suffixes into an inverted index structure based on suffix array. Vries et al. [10] presented an improved version of the Suffix Array blocking technique. The authors performed a deep analysis, effectiveness of their method is proved for both natural and processed data.

Baxter et al. [11] presented a comparison of new blocking techniques with the existing method on the basis of accuracy and execution time. They used Standard Blocking as existing blocking technique, the Bigram Indexing, Sorted Neighborhood and Canopy Clustering as new blocking methods. These blocking techniques are compared with TF-IDF. Many blocking techniques are evaluated and compared by Christen et al. [12]. They proposed modifications in two of them. When the same data set is used for testing of different blocking methods, the experimental results showed that different techniques generate a different number of truly matched candidate record pairs. It was also determined that most of these methods showed unstable behavior with the selected parameter values. It had resulted that n-gram based indexing could achieve better-blocking quality results than both Sorted Neighborhood and standard blocking approach.

Kolb et al. [13, 14] presented a Hadoop MapReduce based easy to use tool for parallel entity resolution with many functionalities, blocking methods and similarity computation strategies. Dedoop provides support for several high level load balancing techniques to handle the data skew issues and assures an improved performance. They presented analysis for 20 ER strategies. The result shows the effectiveness of Dedoop to solve challenging match tasks. Kolb et al. [15] investigated the parallel execution of Sorted Neighbourhood blocking and entity resolution using MapReduce Paradigm. The presented approach required particular partitioning criteria of the MapReduce paradigm and implemented a accurate sliding window assessment of entities. The authors described how the MapReduce framework can be used for the implementation of workflow of standard entity resolution, wherein blocking and similarity computation phase are executed in parallel.

Kolb et al. [16] proposed two load balancing methods, BlockSplit and Pair-Range. These methods are compatible with the widely available MapReduce framework and provide parallel blocking-based entity resolution. Kolb et al. [17] have shown the effective parallelization of single and multi-pass Sorted Neighborhood blocking. The authors presented 2 single pass Sorted Neighborhood implementation on the basis of MapReduce paradigm and a demonstration of their scalability and efficiency in evaluating the real datasets was given.

A load balancing approach named BlockSlicer is presented by Mestre and Pires [18]. This method showed compatibility with distributed computing environment e.g. well-known MapReduce framework and provided parallel entity matching. The proposed method is to provide efficient load balancing method to an entity resolution process for large datasets.

Hsueh et al. [19] proposed an algorithm to provide a solution for the entity resolution process incorporating the concept of big data analytics, using the Hadoop MapReduce model. The usage of multiple blocking keys by different attributes of entities is presented and utilized them for effective key based blocking. Their approach has the issue of comparing an entity pair multiple times, also enumeration of every probable combination of title words increases the space and time requirement of the algorithm.

3   Proposed Work

The main objective of this work is to provide load balancing and thus, decrease the memory bottleneck problem. The impact of the key based skew can be reduced and balanced partitions can be generated by selecting an efficient partitioning function that is capable of assigning a different number of keys to the individual reduce tasks. Hadoop has functionalities like InputSampler and TotalOrderPartitioner that allow sampling the output of a MapReduce job. By estimating a suitable partitioning function p, it can avoid diversity in the size of map output partitions and ensures totally sorted keys.

The presented approach consider particular partitioning requirements of the MapReduce paradigm and some internal optimization to find similar entities on the bases of distance based learning. The implementation of partitioning method with TotalOrderPartitioner was done and found that generated partitions were balanced and not vulnerable to data skew problem. To reduce the number of candidate records matching some optimization thresholds were applied while calculating distance between different attributes of various records. In this work a combination of workflow of standard entity resolution, consisting a blocking and similarity computation phase, with a distributed computing framework for the parallel execution on large bibliographic data is demonstrated.

Key Points of this work are:

– A modified traditional blocking technique by applying TotalOrderedPartitioner to assign multiple keys to the individual reduce tasks to overcome the key skew problem was presented.

- A combination of traditional blocking with sliding window in mapreduce framework was given. The obtained results shows that the execution time taken by this combination is less than the traditional blocking.
- To avert irrelevant computations an internal optimization is performed by avoiding the execution of the rest of the matchers, if the similarity value computed by the execution of the first matcher was very less (i.e. $\theta \leq 0.5$) in order to reach out the combined similarity threshold.

In this paper the issue of entity resolution (de-duplication) for one source is considered. The input dataset $E = \{e_i\}$ consist set of entities e_i, which are finite. The objective is to detect all entity pair $P = \{(e_i, e_k)|e_i, e_k \in E\}$ which are considered as similar pair. Figure 1 depicts a proposed entity resolution workflow. This consists of a blocking and a similarity computation phase. Blocking semantically divides a data source E into disjoint balanced partitions (blocks) B_i, with $E = \cup B_i$. In the Fig. 1 for example a data source S has 15 records to be checked whether they are duplicate or not. Initially given input will split into 3 parts and each will assign to individual map tasks. Mapper's output will be a blocking key for each individual entity with a value as entire record or entity. Mapper's output will assign to totalorderpartitioner function,which will generate equally distributed balanced blocks sorted across all partitions. Here, 2 partitions are generated and assigned to 2 reduce tasks for parallel matching. In the reduce phase for example if records with the same key are equal to or more than 4 then a sliding window of size 3 will apply for matching, otherwise each record will match with each record as in traditional blocking.

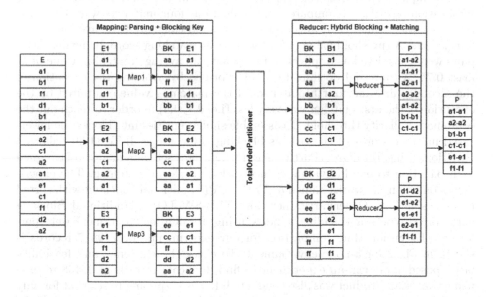

Fig. 1. Entity resolution workflow

In the Fig. 1 all the entities with the same blocking key for example "aa" will compare with each other in sliding window manner to find matches. All the other entities with same blocking key e.g. "bb", "cc", "dd", "ee", "ff", will match each other without sliding window.

In this work a publications dataset consists of Title, Year, Venue and Authors have been used. So four matchers are applied on individual attribute value for entities pairs and average of all matchers have been calculated to get similarity value. The match decision will be taken on the basic of computed similarity value.

In mapper function for proposed approach the concatenation on first two words of Title is used to generate blocking key. In reducer function the first threshold is used to decide blocking technique. In this work $\theta_1 = 5000$ is taken, if there are more than 5000 records with same key in a partition then blocking with window size 100 will apply otherwise traditional blocking will apply. Here, another threshold is used, in which if an average similarity score for entity pair is at least $\theta_2 = 0.75$ then it will be regarded as match.

4   Implementation Result

Our experiments are conducted in a cluster of three nodes. Each node run Ubantu-14.04LTS (64 bit), 7 openjdk-amd64 and Hadoop 2.7.1. Each node is equipped with an Intel Core i5(3.20 GHz), 3.7 GB RAM. The DFS block size is set to 128 MB.

The input DBLP data-set [20] for the experiments contains about 749817 publication records. To compare two publications four matchers were (edit distance on title, venue, year, authors) executed and calculated the average of the four results. A threshold value of 0.75 was set as matching score. It means entity pairs were considered as duplicates if they have an average matching value of at least 0.75. An internal optimization is performed by avoiding the execution of the second, third and fourth matchers, if the matching value computed by the execution of the first matcher was very less (i.e. $\theta \leq 0.5$) in order to reach out the combined similarity threshold. To assemble similar entities into blocks the lower-cased first two words of the title as blocking key were used. Total 30 balanced partitions using TotalOrderPartitioner of whole data-set were made and assigned each partition to one individual reduce task to perform matching. The experiments on two frameworks named as TSB-TOP(Traditional Blocking with sorted blocks using TotalOrderPartitioner) and TSB-SW-TOP (Traditional Blocking with sorted blocks and sliding window using TotalOrderPartitioner) were performed. Execution time comparison for our experiments for 749817 records is shown in Fig. 2 for 3-node environment. To check the efficiency and feasibility of proposed approach, an experiment to find duplicate records in 27438 records using Cartesian Product was also conducted. It was surprising to see that for only 27438 records Cartesian Product (sequentially) computation took 17628.785 s which was much higher than MapReduce based computation.

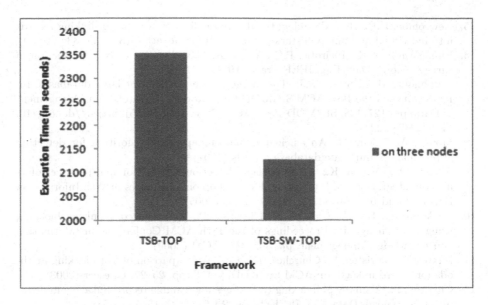

Fig. 2. Execution time comparison for TSB-TOP & TSB-SW-TOP

5   Conclusion and Future Work

The problem with standard blocking method is that, blocking keys generated using the erroneous records might place records into the wrong block. In this work blocking key was chosen very carefully to overcome the above mentioned situation. Another issue with traditional blocking technique was data skew, to reduce the impact of data skew we applied a partitioner which generate almost equal sized partitions and thus less vulnerable to memory bottleneck. In future this work can be extended to build a custom partitioning function similar to TotalOrderPartitioner and prepare an efficient evaluation environment using machine learning algorithms.

References

1. Christen, P.: Data Matching: Concepts and Techniques for Record Linkage, Entity Resolution, and Duplicate Detection. Springer Science & Business Media, Berlin (2012)
2. Ghemawat, S., Gobioff, H., Leung, S.T.: The google file system. In: Proceedings of the Nineteenth ACM Symposium on Operating Systems Principles, pp. 29–43. SOSP 2003, ACM, New York (2003)
3. Shvachko, K., Kuang, H., Radia, S., Chansler, R.: The hadoop distributed file system. In: Proceedings of the 2010 IEEE 26th Symposium on Mass Storage Systems and Technologies (MSST), pp. 1–10. MSST 2010, IEEE Computer Society, Washington, DC, USA (2010). https://doi.org/10.1109/MSST.2010.5496972
4. Dean, J., Ghemawat, S.: Mapreduce: simplified data processing on large clusters. Commun. ACM **51**(1), 107–113 (2008)

5. Newcombe, H.B.: Record linking: the design of efficient systems for linking records into individual and family histories. Am. J. Hum. Genet. **19**(3 Pt 1), 335 (1967)
6. Elmagarmid, A.K., Ipeirotis, P.G., Verykios, V.S.: Duplicate record detection: a survey. Knowl. Data Eng. IEEE Trans. **19**(1), 1–16 (2007)
7. Hernández, M.A., Stolfo, S.J.: The merge/purge problem for large databases. In: Proceedings of the 1995 ACM SIGMOD International Conference on Management of Data, pp. 127–138. SIGMOD 1995, ACM, New York (1995). https://doi.org/10.1145/223784.223807
8. Monge, A., Elkan, C.: An efficient domain-independent algorithm for detecting approximately duplicate database records (1997)
9. Aizawa, A., Oyama, K.: A fast linkage detection scheme for multi-source information integration. In: International Workshop on Challenges in Web Information Retrieval and Integration, pp. 30–39. IEEE (2005)
10. De Vries, T., Ke, H., Chawla, S., Christen, P.: Robust record linkage blocking using suffix arrays. In: Proceedings of the 18th ACM Conference on Information and Knowledge Management, pp. 305–314. ACM (2009)
11. Baxter, R., Christen, P., Churches, T., et al.: A comparison of fast blocking methods for record linkage. In: ACM SIGKDD, vol. 3, pp. 25–27. Citeseer (2003)
12. Christen, P.: A survey of indexing techniques for scalable record linkage and deduplication. Knowl. Data Eng. IEEE Trans. **24**(9), 1537–1555 (2012)
13. Kolb, L., Thor, A., Rahm, E.: Dedoop: efficient deduplication with hadoop. Proc. VLDB Endowment **5**(12), 1878–1881 (2012)
14. Kolb, L., Rahm, E.: Parallel entity resolution with dedoop. Datenbank-Spektrum **13**(1), 23–32 (2013)
15. Kolb, L., Thor, A., Rahm, E.: Parallel sorted neighborhood blocking with mapreduce. arXiv preprint arXiv:1010.3053 (2010)
16. Kolb, L., Thor, A., Rahm, E.: Load balancing for mapreduce-based entity resolution. In: Data Engineering (ICDE), 2012 IEEE 28th International Conference on, pp. 618–629. IEEE (2012)
17. Kolb, L., Thor, A., Rahm, E.: Multi-pass sorted neighborhood blocking with mapreduce. Comput. Sci. Res. Dev. **27**(1), 45–63 (2012)
18. Mestre, D.G., Pires, C.E.S.: Improving load balancing for mapreduce-based entity matching. In: 2013 IEEE Symposium on Computers and Communications (ISCC), pp. 000618–000624. IEEE (2013)
19. Hsueh, S.C., Lin, M.Y., Chiu, Y.C.: A load-balanced mapreduce algorithm for blocking-based entity-resolution with multiple keys. In: Proceedings of the Twelfth Australasian Symposium on Parallel and Distributed Computing, vol. 152, pp. 3–9. Australian Computer Society, Inc. (2014)
20. Dataset. https://aminer.org/citation, (Online)

Networks

Securing of Identification System Data Transmission Using Deep Autoencoders and Data Hiding

Drishti Agarwal[1], Anand Nayyar[2]([✉]), and Preeti Nagrath[1]

[1] BharatiVidyapeeth's College of Engineering, New Delhi, India
preeti.nagrath@bharatividyapeeth.edu
[2] Duy Tan University, Da Nang, Vietnam
anandnayyar@duytan.edu.vn

Abstract. The reliability of any identification systems depends on the level of security provided to the storage of sensitive data. These identification systems provide information about people working in any organization which is intended to help the organization keep track and monitor their activity. Databases of such systems need to be fast, reliable and highly secured. Apart from providing authorization layer to the databases the data itself can be encoded and stored in a simple as well as easy form such that the data itself is secure and does not go through lossy transformation. In this paper, the data is encoded with the help of DAE (Deep Autoencoder) models and these encoded data are then merged with the images of respective people using RDH (Reversible Data Hiding) which is then stored as a simple image data. The data is then retrieved when required and decoded using the same autoencoder mode and checked for loss in the data. This helps us to easily store and send the data as a simple image and improves the security of the system. The models perform good on all datasets with simple autoencoders gives the best result with a loss of only 1.5% loss in data as compared to 3% and 7% by deep autoencoder and convolutional autoencoder respectively Keywords: Identification system, authorization, security, Deep Autoencoder, Reversible Data hiding, storage, transformation.

Keywords: Autoencoders · Convolution Neural Networks · Data hiding · Text vectorization

1 Introduction

National Common Identification Cards are used to tie all sensitive and personal information about a person, their fingerprints and other biometric data together which increases its vulnerability to security attacks. From using IC chips in plastic cards to using encrypted digital certificates [3], considerable work has been put into it over the years to make identification systems more secure [8]. But these methods were still prone to security attacks ranging from physical attacks to attacks that exploit weakness of the card's software or hardware [13]. Usual goal of these attacks was to expose the private

A. K. Luhach et al. (Eds.): ICAICR 2021, CCIS 1575, pp. 203–220, 2022.
https://doi.org/10.1007/978-3-031-09469-9_18

encryption key and then read/manipulate the user's data. Securing such databases is an increasing concern proven by the evident rise in the count of reports of loss of valuable data or unauthorized access to vulnerable information. As the volume and sensitivity of important data collected, stored and shared via channels expands, the requirement to upgrade their security expands [21].

At its base, database security is responsible to ensure that no unauthenticated users perform any unauthorized activities at unauthorized times. It counts the systems, group of processes, and sets of protocols that safeguard a database from any form of suspicious activity. The Defense Information Systems Agency (DISA) of the US Department of Defense (DoD), guides the database Security, has clearly stated that database security system should be able to provide "Restricted and protected access to the information of your database while, preserving the integrity, consistency, and overall quality of your data" [21]. While understanding that database security involves a wide range of security and control topics, notwithstanding, physical and network security, encryption as well as authentication, our work aims at improving the encryption process by including deep learning methods and data hiding techniques simultaneously, this gives more control to the end parties over their data, hence increasing the security [22]. This paper puts one step forward in this domain with the help of data hiding and encoding using deep learning algorithms and techniques, thus creating a highly advanced and secured system for identification [28]. All relevant data of an individual can be kept secure in an encrypted form and can only be accessible by authorized personnel and its data should be retrieved and stored in a safe way using data hiding techniques which are discussed in this paper, Dataset which we used for our research is an amalgamation of two separate open-source datasets from Kaggle ("LFW-People Face Recognition" and "People Wikipedia Data"). The former dataset consists of several images of various personalities labelled with their names [35], while the latter dataset contains URIs, names of people and text from their Wikipedia [34] pages. The two datasets are employed to serve the following objectives:

- Using deep learning-based Convolutional Neural Network approach for improving data hiding and data security.
- Designing an AI-based Deep Autoencoder for encryption as well as decryption of vulnerable images.
- Implementation of Reversible data hiding contains two steps, encoding the images and de-coding the merged image.

The research paper is organized into multiple sections, starting with Sect. 1, the introduction. Section 2, related works summarize the previous research methodologies and solutions provided in data security, followed by Sect. 3, materials and methods that give a brief idea about models used in this research. Section 4 explains the proposed methodology that presents the workflow of the research, model architecture and development. Further, Sect. 5 presents the results and discussions of the proposed method, with a significant comparison between the different models developed. Finally, Sect. 6 concludes the purpose and the results of the research work discussing the scope for future advancements.

2   Related Works

Several Research works and studies have been put forth on encoding the data to secure them in a better and efficient way. These findings are discussed in this section of our study of securing identification databases. [5] and [6] discussed and approached image encryption and decryption models originated from improved logistic chaotic map and phase-truncated short-time fractional Fourier transform and hyper- chaotic system to suppress interference. Algorithm possessed infinite key space, plus the key sensitivity is high, which results in the resistance to the attack through the exhaustion method analysis. The STFrFT (short-time fractional Fourier Transform) with relatively higher concentration and in absence of cross terms could provide concrete support for the signals while eliminating any interference. The feedback system in the diffusion operation enabled the encryption algorithm to suppress interference. Meriwani [9] proposed a deep autoencoder based deep neural network enhancing model on small datasets since neural networks start to have issues like noise and overfitting. Overfitting is resolved and the accuracy increases with a deep autoencoder. Accuracy for the model that used encoded input was higher for heart attack and Autism Diagnosis while it was -4. Malekzadeh [10] proposed a replacement autoencoder model which is a privacy algorithm on sensory data analysis on time-series data in order to provide utility while protecting user's privacy. Since Replacement Auto-Encoder (RAE) was trained to transform blacklisted sections into same-size sections that were very similar to gray-listed activities, therefore only non-sensitive gray-listed activities can be inferred. Number of false positives was near zero which increased QoS. RAE can automatically transform features corresponding to black-listed data while retaining the features corresponding to white activities unchanged. Kaur [13] and Juneja [14] discussed steganography for linking data into images to form a stego image so as to develop efficient and accurate steganography algorithms either by combining the existing techniques or by developing new techniques and detecting suspicious activity over the web. In this, basically Video steganography techniques were discussed. All the techniques discussed by them are able to secure the hidden data. Some algorithms, on the contrary, have a very high time complexity and very less amount of data stored in the images. The researchers in [17, 18] and [16] proposed a reversible data hiding algorithm to retrieve the original image from the stego/marked image without loss of data after the data has been extracted. Reversible Data Hiding in these cases achieved higher embedding capacity and better image quality on retrieval. The proposed scheme can hide the secret data in layers that improved the hiding capacity. The proposed method can achieve a hiding capacity of more than 4 bpp with a PSNR value greater than 51 dB for all cover images. After the secret data has been extracted, original image can be recovered without any distortion from the stego image. The above-mentioned research works were a breakthrough in the field of data encryption. Thus, the paper presents an improved method for implementing data hiding for embedding secret message bits in the least significant byte of non-adjacent and random pixel locations. The model developed in this research is derived from previous works done in this field. Also, the paper presents a meticulous comparison between the three models developed over the dataset.

3   Materials and Methods

3.1   Autoencoders

Autoencoders are mainly used as an algorithm for dimensionality reduction (or compression) with some of the important properties:

1. Data-specific: Autoencoders efficiently compress data using unique training techniques than the standard zipping algorithm of data compression. These encoders are trained on the selected features, filtered out from the training dataset.
2. Lossy Algorithm: Another property of autoencoders is Lossy compression. Here, the input data or information gets reduced due to the preprocessing of encoders, the output is not the same as the input.
3. Unsupervised: Autoencoders follow an unsupervised learning technique. These encoders learn and compress information only when raw input data is provided to them. Another way to look at these encoders is that they follow a self-supervised learning technique where they develop their labels from the training data (Fig. 1).

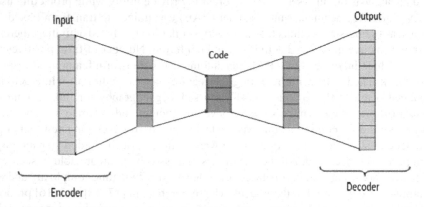

Fig. 1. A simplistic representation of autoencoder

The first step is feeding the input to the encoder, which is a fully connected ANN (Artificial Neural Network), to produce the code. The decoder, which has similar ANN architecture, decodes the output by using the code. This process aims at retrieving the output similar to the input. The only requirement is that the dimensions of our inputs and received outputs need to be equal. The rest of the parts of the model in the middle can be modified according to need. There are four hyperparameters to fine-tune before training an autoencoder:

1. Code size: It is the count of nodes in the middle layer. The smaller size of the nodes results in more compression.
2. The number of layers: layers to the autoencoder can be laid according to our requirements. In Fig. 1, we have two layers in encoder and decoder.

3. The number of nodes per layer: This value decreases with every layer of the encoder, whereas it increases in the decoder. Also, the layer structure of the decoder is symmetric to that of the encoder.
4. Loss Function: This depends on the input value, as if it is in the range of [0,1], then we apply cross-entropy and, for the others, mean squared error.

3.2 Simple Autoencoder

The autoencoder is the three layers network, which is a neural network with only one hidden layer, which is the simplest conceivable autoencoder. The input and output are identical; hence the model must be learned to reconstruct the input using the Adam optimizer and the mean squared error loss function. Because the hidden layer dimension (1024) is smaller than the input, autoencoder is used (99974). Our neural network is forced to learn a compressed representation of data as a result of this limitation. In the model we separate the encoder model as well as the decoder model in Deep fully-connected autoencoder (Fig. 2).

Latent Representation

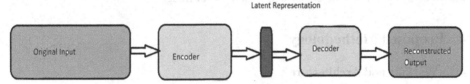

Fig. 2. Architecture of a simple autoencoder

3.3 Convolutional Autoencoder

Convolutional Autoencoder is an Autoencoder variant of Convolutional Neural Nets that are utilized as tools for unsupervised learning in case of convolution filters. They generally are utilized in the task of image reconstruction in order to minimize the errors by learning from the optimal filters. Once they are trained for this particular task, they can be applied on any input data in order to extract and select features. Convolutional Autoencoders are designed as a general-purpose feature extractor and vary from general autoencoders which completely ignore the fact about 2D image structure. To implement a deep convolutional autoencoder, our encoder will be composed of stacks of both Conv2D and MaxPooling2D layers. The decoder will have the stacks of Conv2D and UpSampling2D layers. To train our model, we had to use the dataset with shape (shape = (22, 106, 1)), and we had to normalize pixel values between 0 and 1.

3.4 Reversible Data Hiding

Reversible data hiding contains two major steps, encoding the images and decoding the merged image. Encoder: The channels of each pixel that is red, green and blue in an image is represented by an 8-bit value. To make our secret image discrete, we hide it in a cover image. We substitute the n least significant bits of the cover image pixel value with the same amount of most significant bits from the secret image pixel value. Example, using 3 hidden bits:

- Cover pixel: (167, 93, 27) = = (10100111, 01011101, 00011011).
- Secret pixel: (67, 200, 105) = = (01000011, 11001000, 01101001).
- Output pixel: (162, 94, 27) = = (10100010, 01011110, 00011011).

The pixel of the output is almost unidentical and different from the cover pixel, but holds extra information to extract of the value of hidden pixel, which is then padded with 0 bits to cover for the absent bits, so comes out to (64, 192, 96) == (01000000, 11000000, 01100000). Using a larger number of hidden bits not only to produces a higher-quality concealed image, but it also makes it much easier to detect the hidden image.

Decoder: The decoding part in data hiding is fairly simple but not obvious when first encountering an image. To gather the two original images, we again go through the three RGB channels and retrieve the n lest significant images. This data is then again divided in two arrays giving us the cover images and secret image.

4 Proposed Methodology

4.1 Working and Architecture

In this section, the research work is explained in detail. Initially, the personal details that are the name, mobile number, address, email etc. of a total 4000 people dataset is an input to the model. After the analysis of data, the data gets Text vectorization and Transformation for the three different autoencoders: simple autoencoder, deep fully-connected au- to encoder and deep convolutional autoencoder. After that, pass through their respective encryption function to encode the data and save the encrypted data separately. After the encryption, we change the data to a suitable QR code for easy image on image reversible data hiding algorithm and use data hiding techniques. After hiding the encryption, we created a smart card. This card had a photo and barcode where our data was hidden. After that we scan the photo or barcode to extract the hidden data. After extraction we decrypt the data for the respective autoencoder. After decryption we compare with our original dataset and create a data loss table and compare the result (Fig. 3).

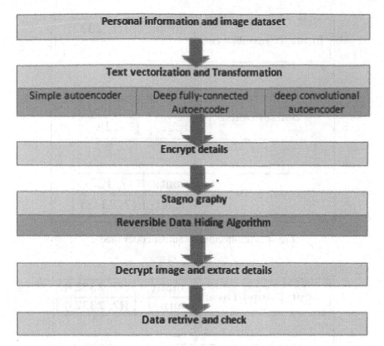

Fig. 3. Flow of the research

4.2 Model Architecture

This is the simplest implementation of the model in which two dense layers are inserted. According to the shape of the vector obtained after the vectorization step, an input layer of compatible shape is defined using the keras library, and then two more dense layers are added to the mode to adjust the weight and biases assigned to the parameters of the input vector. These two dense layers act as the encoder layer of the autoencoder model. The figures given below give the summary of all the layers in the models i.e. the simple autoencoder, fully connected autoencoder, and convolutional autoencoder (Fig. 4, 5 and 6).

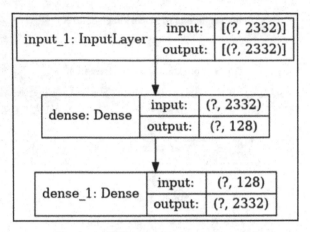

Fig. 4. Architecture of autoencoder model

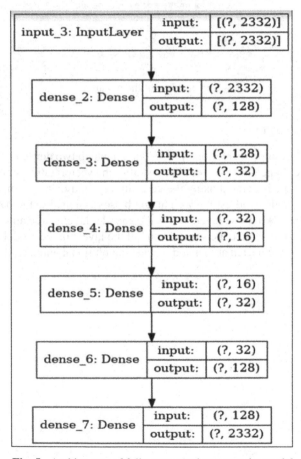

Fig. 5. Architecture of fully connected autoencoder model

```
Model: "functional_38"
```

Layer (type)	Output Shape	Param #
input_18 (InputLayer)	[(None, 22, 106, 1)]	0
conv2d_43 (Conv2D)	(None, 22, 106, 16)	160
max_pooling2d_18 (MaxPooling	(None, 22, 106, 16)	0
conv2d_44 (Conv2D)	(None, 22, 106, 8)	1160
max_pooling2d_19 (MaxPooling	(None, 22, 106, 8)	0
conv2d_45 (Conv2D)	(None, 22, 106, 8)	584
max_pooling2d_20 (MaxPooling	(None, 22, 106, 8)	0
conv2d_46 (Conv2D)	(None, 22, 106, 8)	584
up_sampling2d_18 (UpSampling	(None, 22, 106, 8)	0
conv2d_47 (Conv2D)	(None, 22, 106, 8)	584
up_sampling2d_19 (UpSampling	(None, 22, 106, 8)	0
conv2d_48 (Conv2D)	(None, 22, 106, 16)	144
up_sampling2d_20 (UpSampling	(None, 22, 106, 16)	0
conv2d_49 (Conv2D)	(None, 22, 106, 1)	145

```
Total params: 3,361
Trainable params: 3,361
Non-trainable params: 0
```

Fig. 6. Architecture of convolutional autoencoder model

4.3 Dataset Description

The two datasets that are taken in this study are LFW-people (Face recognition) dataset and people Wikipedia data dataset freely available on Kaggle repository. LFW dataset contains labelled images of various individuals which in our case will be considered as ID images of people. The people Wikipedia dataset in our case is considered as the data of the people and its 'Text' field is assumed as the sensitive data to be encoded and later merged with the image. The people Wikipedia dataset is utilized in training the autoencoder models and the encoder model is applied on the text field which is then merged with lfw image by using the reversible data hiding algorithm.

4.4 Text Vectorization and Transformation

Machine learning tools and approaches operate on numeric features, which are input as a 2D array with rows representing instances and columns representing extracted features in this phase. To run algorithms, we must first convert our text data to a vector format. This is referred to as vectorization. There are text files for the dataset's name, address, and email address, among several other items. From a sequence of words to a set of points in a high-dimensional semantic space. Points in this area can be packed tightly or uniformly distributed, and they can be near together or far apart. As a result, semantic space is mapped in such a way that documents with similar interpretations are kept closer together and those with different interpretations are kept farther apart. The bag-of-words model is the simplest way to encode a semantic space, with the main concept being that meaning and similarity are both encoded in the vocabulary. We use three different types of autoencoders in this paper, with deep-convolutional being the most complex and basic autoencoder being the simplest. A data compression algorithm in which the encoding and decoding functions are data-specific, follow a lossy algorithm, and are learned automatically is known as an auto encoder. The vectorization function is applied to the dataset's text field, which converts it to vector format. A feature array of the vector function is also retrieved in order to later transform the vector form back into text form in order to test the model's efficiency.

4.5 Model Optimization and Metrics

After the data preparation the data is reshaped and divided into test and training dataset. The training data set is used to train our subsequent models that are simple autoencoder, fully connected deep autoencoder and convolutional autoencoder, the hyperparameters of these models are fine-tuned to get the best results and a best suitable optimizer is selected to get better learning curve. Adam optimizer is used and the loss function used is binary cross entropy. The metrics used in the same compile function are accuracy, precision, recall and mean squared error. These metrics can be used later to discuss the performance of the models on the data and monitor any case of underfitting or overfitting.

4.6 Data Hiding and Retrieval

The encoded Data is converted to a QR code to that the proposed image on image data hiding can be done. Image from dataset of pictures is taken and is treated as the cover image whereas the QR code is taken as the secret image and hidden using the cover image's least significant bit in each pixel. The merged image can be sent across the channel which when received can be decoded and split into the QR code and the cover image by the authorized user at the receiving end.

5 Results and Discussion

After training the three models their subsequent accuracies, mean square errors and precision as well as recall were recorded for each epoch in the following table. The epochs were increased until a stagnation in the improvement of the model was observed. The above table tells us some important information about the models. The simple model although didn't perform well in initial cycles but its performance saw a continuous improvement even up to higher number of cycles. Other models could only manage to given number epochs before reaching stag- nation in improvement. In all these models simple autoencoder perform the best (Table 1).

Lets further have a look at the different values of metrics for each model graph ically (Fig. 7, 8, 9 and 10).

The graph clearly shows that even though the simple autoencoder has lower learning rate. Its performance improved after multiple cycles and ends up performing better than other two models. Now we move to the more important part, encoding the data using

Table 1. Training of autoencoder models

Model	No of epochs	Accuracy (%)	Mean square error	Precision	Recall
Simple autoencoder	5	60.17	0.11	0.12	0.06
	15	70.22	0.08	0.31	0.38
	25	90.25	0.09	0.28	0.39
	50	94.5	0.08	0.45	0.56
	100	97.2	0.03	0.60	0.63
Fully-connected autoencoder	5	91.23	0.17	0.12	0.14
	15	92.01	0.13	0.11	0.17
	25	92.03	0.14	0.12	0.18
Convolutional autoencoder	5	89.23	0.41	0.32	0.21
	15	95.44	0.28	0.31	0.24
	25	95.55	0.21	0.35	0.26

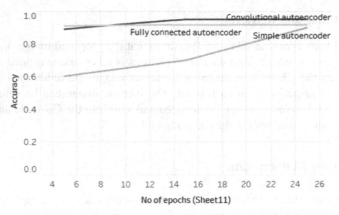

Fig. 7. Accuracy vs no. of epochs

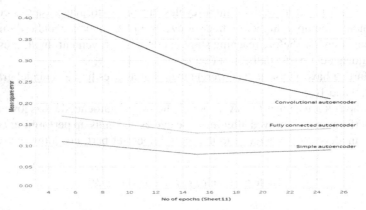

Fig. 8. Mean squared error vs no of epochs

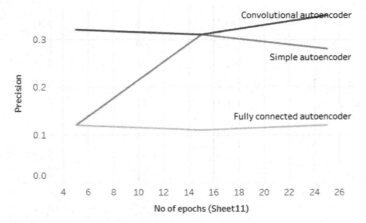

Fig. 9. Precision vs No. of epochs

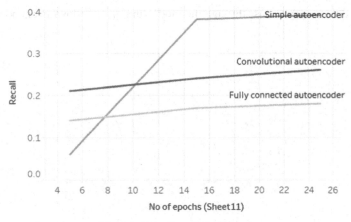

Fig. 10. Recall vs No. of epochs

both autoencoder and data hiding algorithm. The original data looks something like this (Fig. 11, 12, 13, 14 and 15):

```
In [7]: text=df1['text'][0]
        text

Out[7]: 'digby morrell born 10 october 1979 is a former australian rules footballer who played with the kangaroos and carlton in the au
        stralian football league aflfrom western australia morrell played his early senior football for west perth his 44game senior ca
        reer for the falcons spanned 19982000 and he was the clubs leading goalkicker in 2000 at the age of 21 morrell was recruited to
        the australian football league by the kangaroos football club with its third round selection in the 2001 afl rookie draft as a
        forward he twice kicked five goals during his time with the kangaroos the first was in a losing cause against sydney in 2002 an
        d the other the following season in a drawn game against brisbaneafter the 2003 season morrell was traded along with david teag
        ue to the carlton football club in exchange for corey mckernan he played 32 games for the blues before being delisted at the en
        d of 2005 he continued to play victorian football league vfl football with the northern bullants carltons vflaffiliate in 2006
        and acted as playing assistant coach in 2007 in 2008 he shifted to the box hill hawks before retiring from playing at the end o
        f the season from 2009 until 2013 morrell was the senior coach of the strathmore football club in the essendon district footbal
        l league leading the club to the 2011 premier division premiership since 2014 he has coached the west cohurg football club also
        in the edflhe currently teaches physical education at parade college in melbourne'
```

Fig. 11. Secret data to encode

After preprocessing and data preparation the above data looks like this.

```
0, 0, 0, 0, 0, 0, 0, 0, 0, 1, 0, 0, 0, 0, 0, 0, 0, 0, 0, 0, 0, 0, 0, 0, 0, 0, 0, 0, 0, 0, 0,
0, 0, 0, 0, 0, 0, 0, 0, 0, 0, 0, 0, 0, 0, 0, 0, 0, 0, 0, 0, 0, 0, 0, 0, 0, 0, 0, 0, 0, 0, 0,
0, 0, 0, 0, 0, 0, 0, 0, 0, 0, 0, 0, 0, 0, 0, 0, 0, 0, 0, 0, 0, 0, 0, 0, 0, 0, 0, 0, 0, 0, 0,
0, 0, 0, 0, 0, 0, 0, 0, 0, 0, 0, 0, 0, 0, 0, 0, 0, 0, 0, 0, 0, 0, 0, 0, 1, 0, 0, 0, 0, 0, 0,
0, 0, 0, 0, 0, 0, 0, 0, 1, 0, 0, 0, 0, 0, 0, 0, 0, 0, 1, 0, 0, 0, 0, 0, 0, 0, 0, 0, 0, 0, 0,
0, 0, 0, 0, 0, 0, 0, 0, 0, 0, 0, 0, 0, 0, 0, 0, 0, 0, 0, 0, 0, 0, 0, 0, 0, 0, 0, 0, 0, 0, 0,
0, 0, 0, 0, 0, 0, 0, 0, 0, 0, 0, 0, 0, 0, 0, 0, 0, 0, 0, 0, 0, 0, 0, 0, 1, 0, 0, 0, 0, 0, 0,
0, 0, 0, 0, 0, 0, 0, 0, 0, 0, 0, 0, 0, 0, 0, 0, 0, 0, 0, 0, 0, 0, 0, 0, 0, 0, 0, 0, 0, 0, 0,
0, 0, 0, 0, 0, 0, 0, 0, 0, 0, 0, 0, 0, 0, 0, 0, 0, 0, 0, 0, 0, 0, 0, 0, 0, 0, 0, 0, 0, 0, 5,
0, 0, 0, 0, 0, 0, 0, 0, 0, 0, 0, 0, 0, 0, 0, 0, 0, 0, 0, 0, 0, 0, 0, 0, 0, 0, 0, 3, 1, 0, 0,
0, 0, 0, 0, 0, 0, 0, 0, 0, 0, 0, 0, 0, 0, 0, 0, 0, 0, 0, 0, 0, 0, 0, 0, 0, 0, 0, 0, 0, 0, 0,
0, 0, 0, 0, 0, 0, 0, 0, 0, 0, 0, 0, 0, 0, 0, 0, 0, 0, 0, 0, 0, 0, 0, 0, 0, 0, 0, 0, 0, 1, 0,
0, 0, 0, 0, 0, 0, 0, 0, 0, 0, 0, 0, 0, 0, 0, 0, 0, 0, 0, 0, 0, 0, 0, 0, 0, 0, 0, 0, 0, 0, 0,
0, 0, 0, 0, 0, 0, 0, 0, 0, 0, 0, 0, 0, 0, 0, 0, 0, 0, 0, 0, 0, 0, 0, 0, 0, 0, 0, 1, 0, 0, 0,
0, 0, 0, 0, 0, 0, 0, 0, 0, 0, 0, 0, 0, 0, 0, 0, 0, 0, 0, 0, 0, 0, 0, 0, 0, 0, 0, 0, 0, 0, 0,
0, 0, 0, 0, 0, 0, 0, 0, 0, 0, 0, 0, 0, 0, 0, 0, 0, 0, 0, 0, 0, 0, 0, 0, 0, 0, 0, 0, 0, 0, 0,
0, 0, 0, 0, 0, 0, 0, 0, 0, 0, 0, 0, 0, 0, 0, 0, 0, 0, 0, 0, 0, 0, 0, 0, 0, 0, 0, 0, 0, 0, 0,
```

Fig. 12. Data after going through data preprocessing

Above data is easy to pass through the model and gives following encoded data.

```
k=[0.00000000e+00, 1.42113052e+02, 1.94057884e+01, 1.35818157e+01,
    8.74176025e-02, 1.80673096e+02, 1.40716324e+02, 1.52196808e+02,
    1.76931931e+02, 1.30182449e+02, 0.00000000e+00, 8.73346567e-01,
    3.86145439e+01, 1.91695038e+02, 1.10020966e+02, 8.31712532e+00,
    1.57618246e+01, 4.62567635e+01, 4.81921291e+00, 4.15383911e+00,
    1.03339205e+01, 5.54965515e+01, 0.00000000e+00, 0.00000000e+00,
    1.70156174e+02, 8.71312408e+01, 1.10403748e+01, 6.02194595e+01,
    1.59961639e+02, 1.52389404e+02, 1.41960327e+02, 7.16746712e+00,
    3.61093445e+01, 1.54326767e+02, 1.10056465e+02, 3.04767742e+01,
    0.00000000e+00, 0.00000000e+00, 3.62478523e+01, 1.11617088e+02,
    3.60928011e+00, 0.00000000e+00, 1.95583286e+01, 1.68275177e+02,
    1.59350342e+02, 4.05859604e+01, 1.40938705e+02, 3.94215703e+00,
    1.51008110e+01, 3.78948669e+01, 1.68527328e+02, 1.26059860e+02,
    1.64440506e+02, 9.36533570e-01, 5.21194496e+01, 0.00000000e+00,
    1.44179504e+02, 1.33173431e+02, 5.29334927e+00, 3.01522293e+01,
    2.84747429e+01, 1.64814499e+02, 1.32726868e+02, 0.00000000e+00,
    3.27787247e+01, 1.62380203e+02, 9.61818924e+01, 2.53202171e+01,
    1.66909103e+02, 5.09925041e+01, 1.30079365e+01, 0.00000000e+00,
    1.84943657e+01, 2.09781957e+00, 1.66825455e+02, 2.49533176e+01,
    5.32720337e+01, 1.87635689e+01, 1.76427841e+02, 5.75390701e+01,
    8.37914467e+00, 1.60068207e+01, 1.45669785e+02, 1.34400757e+02,
    1.72473801e+02, 1.75031876e+02, 1.51205597e+02, 5.44540215e+01,
    1.56159912e+02, 1.59006863e+01, 2.10125999e+01, 1.62554993e+02,
    1.18387384e+01, 3.91569214e+01, 0.00000000e+00, 2.88872185e+01,
    1.45413010e+02, 1.40952072e+02, 2.09340172e+01, 1.52817566e+02,
    1.66047607e+02, 1.91121857e+02, 1.46614243e+02, 0.00000000e+00,
    1.59544220e+02, 1.70226624e+02, 1.48927231e+02, 0.00000000e+00,
    1.04536293e+02, 0.00000000e+00, 8.01468849e-01, 0.00000000e+00,
    1.93724594e+02, 1.46865891e+02, 9.31743698e+01, 2.19491792e+00,
    1.26472244e+02, 5.94546890e+00, 1.22238792e+02, 9.17005310e+01,
    1.68702526e+01, 1.07886002e+02, 1.63386139e+02, 2.00170563e+02,
    1.30108353e+02, 1.51900192e+02, 3.41581612e+01, 5.43721352e+01]
```

Fig. 13. Encoded data

The given encoded data is still unable to be used as an image because of its numerical array form. Conversion to QR code is a great solution to implement an image-on-image data hiding algorithm.

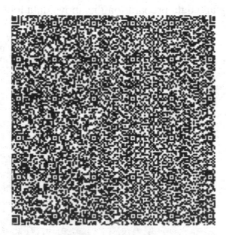

Fig. 14. QR code of encoded data to be used as secret image

After this a cover image is taken and then these two images are merged using the reversible data hiding technique. Giving the following merged image will be sent on the channel to the authorized end user.

Fig. 15. Merged image after data hiding

After the decoding of above image, the QR code is obtained again and is used to get the encoded data which is then passed through the autoencoder's decoder to get the original data. This data is then compared with the original data to check for loss in the encryption and is recorded in the following table (Table 2):

Table 2. Loss of information in each autoencoder model

Model	Similarity Percentage (%)	Loss of information (%)
Simple Autoencoder	98.5	1.5
Fully connected Autoencoder	97	3
Convolutional Autoencoder	93	7

Above table gives the good idea about how good the encoder and decoder part of the simple autoencoder to minimize the loss of data as compared to the other two models. Clearly simple autoencoder serves as the best model along with data hiding algorithm to send encrypted data across any channel without any intrusion.

6 Conclusion

The field of data security requires innovations to improve the secure data transfer of sensitive information across any network. Countless cryptographic algorithms are in the making to encode data in a unique and secure form to avoid any unauthorized access. Our research work aimed at contributing towards this field by employing deep learning in data hiding techniques. The model worked over a combined dataset containing an image of an individual along with the identification data. For secure transmission, the data was turned into a single merged file for transmission to an authorized end-user. This data can be safely decoded back to its original form. The autoencoder models employed for reducing the dimensions of the datasets and intrusion detection in a system performed appreciably. Simple Autoencoder performed better than deep and convolutional autoencoder in terms of performance metrics. The simple autoencoder with reversible data hiding algorithms suffered the lowest loss value with only 1.5% whereas, the other two models had a loss value of 3% and 7%. Hence the best combination that implemented two-level encoding on our dataset was simple autoencoder and RDH algorithm. Although this study performed exceedingly well on a given dataset, the loss for such vulnerable and valuable data is significantly high, which can be highly disadvantageous for organizations associated with it. This research has an opportunity for advancement in future, as specific designing of data can be performed to train the model well, and parameters of models can be modified to suffer minimum or no loss at all, thus, improving the accuracy and precision. Also, the combination of other data hiding techniques can be employed where the difference between the dimension of the cover image doesn't need to be larger than the dimension of the secret encoded image without going any loss of data while decoding the encoded data from the merged image.

References

1. Al-qershi, O.M., Ee, K.B.: An overview of reversible data hiding schemes based on difference expansion technique (2009)
2. Nasser, Y., Hassouni, M.E., Brahim, A., Toumi, H., Lespessailles, E., Jennane, R.: Diagnosis of osteoporosis disease from bone X-ray images with stacked sparse autoencoder and SVM classifier. In: 2017 International Conference on Advanced Technologies for Signal and Image Processing (ATSIP), pp. 1–5 (2017). https://doi.org/10.1109/ATSIP.2017.8075537
3. Jayesh, S.: Comparative Analysis of LSTM Sequence-Sequence and Auto Encoder for real-time anomaly detection using system call sequences. Int. J. Innov. Res. Comput. Commun. Eng. (2019)
4. Zavrak, S., I˙skefiyeli, M.: Anomaly-based intrusion detection from network flow features using variational autoencoder. IEEE Access, **8**, 108346- 108358 (2020). https://doi.org/10.1109/ACCESS.2020.3001350
5. Chunyan, H.: An image encryption algorithm based on modified logistic chaotic map. Optik, **181**, 779–785 (2019), ISSN 0030–4026
6. Yu, S.S., Zhou, N.R., Gong, L.H., Nie, Z.: Optical image encryption algorithm based on phase-truncated short-time fractional Fourier transform and hyper- chaotic system. Optics Lasers Eng. **124**, 105816 (2020), ISSN 0143–8166
7. Chen, G., Wang, C., Chen, H.: A novel color image encryption algorithm based on hyper-chaotic system and permutation-diffusion architecture. Int. J. Bifurcation Chaos, **29**, 09 (2019)
8. Liang, Y.H., Haoran, F., Li.: An asymmetric and optimized encryption method to protect the confidentiality of 3D mesh models. Adv. Eng. Inform. **42**, 100963 (2019). https://doi.org/10.1016/j.aei.2019.100963
9. Meriwani, O.: Enhancing Deep Neural Network Performance on Small Datasets by using Deep Autoencoder. An Assignment in Data Science CSEE University of Essex (2019)

10. Malekzadeh, M., Clegg, R.G., Haddadi, H.: Replacement autoencoder: a privacy-preserving algorithm for sensory data analysis. In: 2018 IEEE/ACM Third International Conference on Internet-of-Things Design and Implementation (IoTDI) (2018)
11. Principi, E., Rossetti, D., Squartini, S., Piazza, F.: Unsupervised electric motor fault detection by using deep autoencoders. IEEE/CAA J. Automatica Sinica **6**(2), 441–451 (2019). https://doi.org/10.1109/JAS.2019.1911393
12. Muhammad, K., Ahmad, J., Farman, H., Jan, Z., Sajjad, M., Baik, S.W.: A secure method for color image steganography using gray-level modification and multi-level encryption. KSII Trans. Internet Inf. Syst. **9**(5), 1938–1962 (2015). https://doi.org/10.3837/tiis.2015.05.022
13. Kaur, H.R., Jyoti.: A survey on different techniques of steganography. MATEC Web of Conferences. **57**, 02003 (2016). https://doi.org/10.1051/matecconf/20165702003
14. Juneja, M.S., Parvinder.: An improved LSB based steganography technique for RGB color images. Int. J. Comput. Commun. Eng. **2**, 513–517 (2013). https://doi.org/10.7763/IJCCE.2013.V2.238
15. Alqadi, J., Khisat, Z., Yousif, M.E.: Message Segmentation and Image Blocking to Secure Data Steganography. 75–82 (2020)
16. Malik, A., Singh, S., Kumar, R.: Recovery based high capacity reversible data hiding scheme using even-odd embedding. Multimedia Tools Appl. **77**(12), 15803–15827 (2017). https://doi.org/10.1007/s11042-017-5156-1
17. Sahu, A.K., Swain, G.: Dual Stegoimaging based reversible data hiding using improved LSB matching. Int. J. Intell. Eng. Syst. **12**, 63–74 (2019). https://doi.org/10.22266/ijies2019.1031.07
18. Aziz, F., Ahmad, T., Malik, A.H., Uddin, M.I., Ahmad, S., Sharaf, M.: Reversible data hiding techniques with high message embedding capacity in images. PLoS ONE **15**(5), e0231602 (2020)
19. Zeng, N.Z., Song, H., Liu, B., Li, W., Abdullah, Y., Dobaie.: Facial expression recognition via learning deep sparse autoencoders. Neurocomputing (2017). https://doi.org/10.1016/j.neucom.2017.08.043
20. Alanazi, N., Alanizy, A., Baghoza, N., Al Ghamdi, M., Gutub, A.: 3-layer PC text security via combining compression, AES cryp tography 2LSB image steganography. J. Res. Eng. Appl. Sci. **03**, 118–124 (2018). https://doi.org/10.46565/jreas.2018.v03i04.001
21. Murray, M.C.: Database security: what students need to know. J. Inf. Technol. Educ. **9** (2010)
22. Abadi, M., Budiu, M., Erlingsson, U., Ligatti, J.: Control-flow integrity principles, implementations, and applications. ACM Trans. Inf. Syst. Secur. (2009)
23. Bao, T., Burket, J., Woo, M., Turner, R., Brumley, D.: BYTEWEIGHT: learning to recognize functions in binary code. In: 23rd USENIX Security Symposium (2014)
24. Bekrar, S., Bekrar, C., Groz, R., Mounier, L.: A taint based approach for smart fuzzing. In: 2012 IEEE Fifth International Conference on Software Testing, Verification and Validation. IEEE (2012)
25. Dahl, G.E., Stokes, J.W., Deng, L., Yu, D.: Large-scale malware classification using random projections and neural networks. In: IEEE International Conference on Acoustics, Speech and Signal Processing (ICASSP). IEEE (2013)
26. Dai, Y., Li, H., Qian, Y., Lu, X.: A malware classification method based on memory dump grayscale image. Digit. Investig. (2018)
27. David, O.E., Netanyahu, N.S.: DeepSign: deep learning for automatic malware signature generation and classification. In: 2015 International Joint Conference on Neural Networks (IJCNN). IEEE (2015)
28. Godefroid, P., Peleg, H., Singh, R.: LearnFuzz: machine learning for input fuzzing. In: 2017 32nd IEEE/ACM International Conference on Automated Soft- ware Engineering (ASE). IEEE (2017)

29. Phan, A.V., Nguyen, M.L., Bui, L.T.: Convolutional neural networks over control flow graphs for software defect prediction. In: 2017 IEEE 29th International Conference on Tools with Artificial Intelligence (ICTAI). IEEE (2017)

30. Zhang, S., et al.: Syslog processing for switch failure diagnosis and prediction in datacenter networks. In: 2017 IEEE/ACM 25th International Symposium on Quality of Service (IWQoS). IEEE (2017)

31. Yun, I., Lee, S., Xu, M., Jang, Y., Kim, T.: QSYM: a practical concolic execution engine tailored for hybrid fuzzing. In: 27th USENIX Security Symposium (2018)

32. Yuan, X., Li, C., Li, X.: DeepDefense: identifying DDoS attack via deep learning. In: 2017 IEEE International Conference on Smart Computing (SMARTCOMP). IEEE (2017)

33. Rosenberg, I., Shabtai, A., Rokach, L., Elovici, Y.: generic black-box end-to-end attack against state-of-the-art api call based malware classifiers. In: Research in Attacks, Intrusions, and Defenses. Springer (2018)

34. Guo, W., Mu, D., Xu, J., Su, P., Wang, G., Xing, X.: Lemna: explaining deep learning based security applications. In: Proceedings of the 2018 ACM SIGSAC Conference on Computer and Communications Security (2018)

35. Sameer, M.: People Wikipedia Data, Version 1, November 2017, https://www.kaggle.com/sameersmahajan/people-wikipedia-data

36. Atul, A.J.: lfw-People (Face recognition), Version 3, March 2018, https://www.kaggle.com/atulanandjha/lfwpeople

37. Wang, Y., Wu, Z., Wei, Q., Wang, Q.: NeuFuzz: efficient fuzzing with deep neural network. IEEE Access 7 (2019)

Review on IoT Based Real-Time Healthcare Monitoring System

Amit, Chander Kant, and Suresh Kumar[✉]

University Institute of Engineering and Technology, MD University, Rohtak, Haryana, India
amit.deswal141197@gmail.com,
sureshvashist.uiet.ece@mdurohtak.ac.in

Abstract. In today's modern medical fields, the emerging trends are wearable's, which are connected to IoT (Internet of things) & thus helps in the process of patients monitoring. The main advantages of wearable devices are continuous tracking of the health status of the patients wearing them. Thereby, ultimately it results in better treatment by having an insight for the doctors about health status of the patient. Also there in the real time approach results in lower cost of operation & increased chances of improvement in patient's health. With the advancement in the field of Cloud, AI (Artificial Intelligence) & IoT, it is now possible to track the health parameters of the patients by the doctors. This has resulted in proactive and timely alerts available to remotely located person by measuring their live record being fed to the cloud server via internet. After systematic analysis of this data with medical history & finding the best possible treatment can be administered using various Machine Learning (ML) techniques. Critical situation can be avoided as forecasted in the beginning is possible. It assists the health workers & family members to monitor & controls the health criterion of patients in an efficient way. This review paper, focused on analysis of IoT based wearable devices used for continuous health monitoring, benefits, challenges, future scope, & applications.

Keywords: Health monitoring · IoT · Wearable devices · ML · Cloud

1 Introduction

In good old times, the sole method to diagnose sickness was through a physical examination of the figure in an exceedingly hospital. This forced the patients to remain physically in hospital for treatment, increasing care and prices. Also the diagnosis of human body can only be possible through physical examination by the doctor. Health care costs increased many folds because the exhaustion of health facilities in rural & remote areas. The technological advances achieved over the years made it attainable to diagnose various diseases & monitor health with miniaturized devices like good watches. The technological progress achieved over these years now permits the identification of varied diseases & health management with miniaturized devices such as smart watches. Various clinical tests (O2 level, blood pressure, glucose level etc.) are allotted and monitored without the assistance of a medical professional. In addition, advanced telecommunication services will facilitate delivery of clinical knowledge and care facilities in remote

© Springer Nature Switzerland AG 2022
A. K. Luhach et al. (Eds.): ICAICR 2021, CCIS 1575, pp. 221–231, 2022.
https://doi.org/10.1007/978-3-031-09469-9_19

areas too. These communication services along with advanced technologies such as ML, data analytic, cloud computing, IoT & wireless sensing has improved the accessibility of medical facilities.

IoT advancements over the past few decades have made healthcare systems accessible even in remote areas and improved the overall health of the individuals. IoT based technology is advancing rapidly in healthcare system. Because the health sector expands, it expects to have direct identification that permits simple observation & management of the knowledge. The futuristic goal is to integrate IoT with emergency services, residential areas & hospitals [1]. With the assistance of artistic movement algorithms & protocols, the IoT has become a crucial contributor to world communication because it connects various wireless sensors, household appliances & electrical devices to the network [2]. The applications of IoT can also be observed in the field of agriculture, automotive, household & healthcare. The growing quality of the IoT is because of its capability of displaying more accurate, lower cost, & AI based data analytics. In addition, better data of package & applications, the advancement of mobile & computing technologies, the easy accessibility of wireless technology & the rise of the digital economy have all contributed to the speedy revolution of the IoT [3]. IoT devices like sensors & actuators are integrated with physical devices to observe & share data through numerous communication protocols like Bluetooth & Wi-Fi etc. Especially in healthcare applications, sensors are mostly employed to collect physiological information such as temperature, heart rate, and pulse rate from the user's body [4]. In addition, outside information such as temperature, humidity is also recorded. This knowledge facilitates to draw meaning & precise conclusions regarding the patient's state of health. The stored data in the IoT system from various sources such as sensors, applications & mobile phone plays crucial role. The information from the detection device is created accessible to doctors, nurses & approved parties. Knowledge with care suppliers via cloud or server permits speedy identification of patients &, if necessary, medical intervention. Continues transmission between the user and medical employees is assisted. However, the most concern in developing an IoT system is embracing the confidentiality of data exchange, security, cost, responsibility & availability. This paper covers IoT-based health systems & provides a scientific summary of the basic technologies, services & applications.

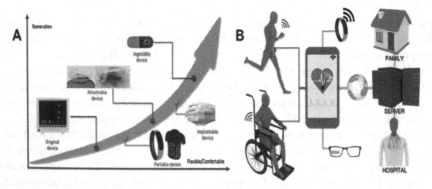

Fig. 1. (A) Wearable gadgets (B) IoT based wearable gadgets used in health monitoring

2 System Analysis

There are various components for the system architecture such as input, information processing, ML, decision making, & output. By using this type of portable system & sensor, healthcare surveillance of a patient living in a remote area can be performed as it would have been not easy for the patients to visit health cares or have regular check-ups. This system will minimize risk of life & improve a person's health. Various types of motion sensors are used for sending the information, which will measure body temperature, blood sugar, pressure & pulse [5].

Wearable technologies such as the wireless Body Area Network (BAN) have been used in health-related research. Real-time condition monitoring by handheld gadgets operate the classification approach for series of time analysis. Previously, Zigbee was used for communication between mobile systems & physiological gadgets. Recent research studies in this area shows that a far-flung of IoT-facilitated gadgets, wearable bracelet sensors, watches & fabric are operated. Many of the research reports achieved using various techniques for routing such as Bluetooth, Wi-Fi, ZigBee, RFID for real/actual-time healthcare surveillance in wearable gadgets. Generally this kind of research uses fitness trackers, smart jacket, shoes & gloves, etc.

2.1 Methodology

Step1: Collection of information & preparation of information
This will include the gathering of measured physiological wave using portable gadgets with motion sensors.

Step2: To Develop a ML Algorithm for healthcare surveillance
A ML algorithm is developed using automatic Artificial Neural Networks (ANN) to calculate judgment with reference to the patient's health status. The ANN is chosen as it has ability to create a vigrious classifier, as the information to be created is in the form of series of time & also has great notion effects that allow it to continuously classify original information.

Step3: Training & Experimenting with information sets
Healthcare surveillance model, which is a ML algorithm, is trained on information set to accurately perform health surveillance & then inform the patient.

Step4: Implementation & analysis in real/actual life scenario

3 Devices

With the onset of 21st century, wearable devices such as wrist mounted devise, head mounted, body cloths & body sensory control devices have made health services personalized. With the development of microelectronics and communication technology the wearable devices are miniaturized and made portable. These portable wearable devices are deeply embedded in our day to day life as shown in Fig. 2 below.

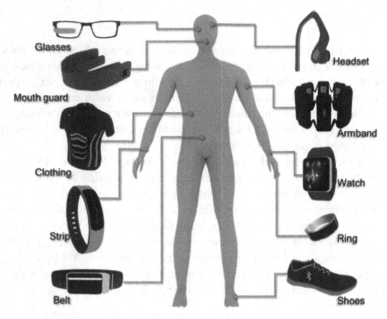

Fig. 2. Wearable healthcare devices

3.1 Portable Gadgets

Wrist-mount gadgets for physiological observation are developed commercially. This helped improvement in battery life and miniaturization and are able to convert signals from human body to real-time communication data. Physiological indicators like BP, heart rate are most important indicators of an individual's health status. Conventional sensors are bulky and ergonomic. With the advancement in technology, devices that can be worn on the wrist have been developed. New age fitness bands & smart watches come loaded with tiny sensors to check pulse rate, blood pressure & various other physiological indicators. With the technological advancement sensors are miniaturised, increasing their scope of usage.

Head-mounted devices such as accelerometers, gyroscopes, altimeters & GPS can be placed in nose pads of a smart glass. Smart goggles are equipped with computer and sensors to continuously monitor & display users health status during activities likes running or riding.

Smart fabrics are being developed which are capable of monitoring human physiological signals, biomechanics & physical activities. This smart fabric generally consists of a conductive devices & clothing materials. An example to smart fabrics are smart clothing, head gear & shoe being developed for defence forces to monitor soldiers physiological traits & biomechanics in real time.

3.2 Attachable Devices

These are considered as next generation portable personal healthcare devices with skin like adaptability features & flexibility thereby offers accurate sensing even without hindering natural movement & comfort. **Wearable Patches** with sweat, cardiovascular & temperature sensors are gaining popularity as ideal wearable's due to their accuracy in sensing data and ease of wearing. Latest advances in sensors technology, microelectronics & data analysis are enabling manufacturing of cost effective advanced & real time data capturing devices. These smart devices are important components in health monitoring systems. These devices use wide range of sensors such as piezoelectric, resistive & capacitive sensors to gather physiological to BP, heart rate & body temperatures. **Smart contact lenses** enable physiological monitoring of the eyes, non-invasively. These smart contact lenses uses optical an electrical inputs to monitor the eyes. These sensors analyses the chemical nature of tear fluid and reflectivity of primary diffraction light.

3.3 Implantable and Ingestible Devices

MEMS technology fusion with biology and chemistry has made wireless medical measurement possible. These devices are used in diagnosing and treatment of diseases by detecting the possible changes observed in body.

An **implantable electronic device includes** pacemakers, ICDs & deep brain simulators. These devices are made of batteries for power and biocompatible materials embedded as pre-programmable circuitry.

The **ingestible pill contains** sensors that are capable of passing the lumen of digestive track & reach organs around the abdomen. These sensors can monitor enzymes, hormones, electrolytes, microbes and metabolites and delivers biometric information. Figure 3 depicts the application of smart pill and patches.

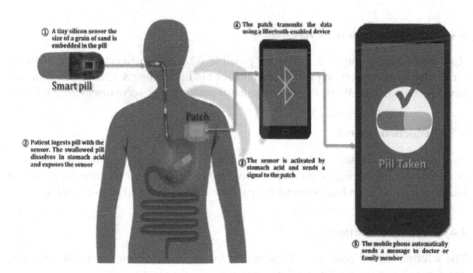

Fig. 3. Ingestible pill system (smart pill & Patch)

4   Benefits of IoT in Healthcare

4.1   Monitoring and Reporting

Connected devices make it simple to draw the attention of professionals to watch patient's heath, conjointly period observance can be rescued the lives during healthcare emergency. Appreciate polygenic disorder attack, heart failure, asthma attack, & so forth by means that of an intelligent healthcare device are connected to apps. Assembling healthcare data & alternative necessary medicative data isn't a challenge if connected properly. IoT devices gather & transmit medicative data such as BP, element & level of glucose, weight & ECG. The info gathered by the devices is stored within the cloud & may be accessed by a certified Individual who can also be doctor, company of insurance, health care company, or outside consultant, no matter location, time, or device used.

4.2   Assortment of Data and Its Analysis

Without application of cloud, it is not possible to deposit massive amounts of knowledge gathered from smartphone devices & health care apps. In addition, it's quite rugged for healthcare employees to gather information from numerous gadgets & sources. In such type of situation, the IoT gadgets will gather, report & data analyzation in actual time [6].

4.3   Tracking and Alerts

The circumstances which are life threatening, timely warnings become very important. For addressing such kind of state, healthcare IoT gadgets & apps can collect critical information & broadcast it to experts & medical staff for monitoring in real or actual time, the critical conditions of the patient regardless of place & time.

4.4   Far-Flung Healthcare Assistance

Reaching a doctor remote is almost not possible for lonely patients in an exceedingly medical emergency, however with the appliance of IoT in tending & alternative connected devices, it's possible. Workers also can monitor patients to observe diseases on the way.

4.5   Reduction in Cost

By exploitation IoT-facilitated gadgets, clinicians will keep an eye on the patients in real or actual time. Therefore, method of period of time observation in numerous locations can facilitate patients scale back supernumerary doctor visits, hospital stays & readmissions.

4.6   Enhanced Treatment

The information collected by IoT gadgets helps doctors & clinicians build informed, proof-based choices & offers total transparency.

4.7 Speedy Diagnosis of Disease

Due to continues patients watching & time period information tracking, doctors will diagnose sickness in the beginning or maybe before disease really evolves supported symptoms.

4.8 Reduction in Error

The information generated by connected gadgets facilitates to form correct & effective selections & conjointly guarantee sleek operation with fewer errors, rejections & costs.

5 Applications

Medical services /concepts are employed to create various IoT based health system. With the advancement of IoT technology, microelectronic & communications, economical and user friendly implantable, ingestible, and wearable sensors and devices have emerged. These systems can be used to gather data, diagnose and track patient's heath. It can also send out alarms in case of any medical emergency. This part will look at some of the most recent commercially available gadgets.

5.1 Monitoring of ECG

Heart muscles atria and ventricles functions in rhythms which are represented on electrocardiogram (ECG). The observed electrical activity, which takes place because to basic heart muscles rhythm will depicts cardiac abnormalities. The IoT technology aids in early detection of cardiac anomalies. The IoT based ECG analysis consists of wircless data acquisition module with a receiving processor. This detects cardiac anomalies in real time. A low-power & portable ECG monitoring system built into fabric has been proposed in [7]. It contains a biopotential chip to gather ECG data & transmit to end users. In [8] the author have attempted to solve the power consumption problem through compression detection [9] using a cloud & mobile application. It is designed to provide real-time monitoring of patients.

5.2 Monitoring the Glucose Level

Diabetes is one among the foremost common human diseases in which blood sugar levels in the body remain high for a long time. Generally there are, three types of diabetes are found (i) type I diabetes, (ii) type 2 diabetes, & (iii) gestational diabetes. These are identified by three tests (i) the random plasma glucose test (ii) the fasting plasma glucose test, & (iii) the oral glucose tolerance test. The IoT technologies uses several handheld blood glucose meters that are non-invasive, comfortable, convenient, & safe instead of widely used diagnostic method i.e., finger prick followed by measuring the blood sugar level. A non-invasive IoT-based glucometer to monitor blood sugar levels in real time was proposed. Here, wearable sensors & healthcare providers are wirelessly connected. In another study the IoT architecture for measuring glucose levels in human body uses optical sensors [10].

5.3 Monitoring of Temperature

Human body maintains a particular temperature. A slight change of body temperature could be considered signal for some diseases hence temperature is one of the most important indicator of human body health. Tracking changes in temperature over time helps clinicians draw conclusions about the patient's health. The traditional method of temperature measurement is to use a thermometer. Comfortability & high risk of infection are always a problem with this method. IoT-based technologies have suggested several solutions to this problem. In [11] an infrared sensor based 3D-printed wearable device is proposed to measure the core temperature of human body. The integrated device can be influenced by environmental factors & other physical activities. In [12] another study used portable & lightweight sensors to measure infant body temperature in real time. You can also warn parents if the temperature rises above a critical level.

5.4 Monitoring of BP

Measuring blood pressure (BP) is one of the mandatory diagnostic procedures. The integration of IoT & sensors has changed the way the BP was monitored previously. In [13], a portable cuff-less device has been proposed that can evaluate systolic as well as diastolic pressure. The data can be saved and retained in the cloud. Also, ECG & PPG is used for the measurement of BP. In [14] microcontroller module is used to calculate BP and cloud storage is used to record the data.

5.5 O_2 Level Monitoring

Saturation of Blood oxygen is considered as an important parameter for health analysis. Previously Pulse oximetry test is used to measure blood oxygen saturation. A non-invasive tissue oximeter resulting from the mixing from IoT based technology has been proposed to measure blood oxygen saturation alongwith pulse rate. The recorded data can be transmitted to medical authorities. In [15] another study patient can be warned regarding their oxygen saturation level by an alarm system. In [16] an inexpensive remote monitoring system for patients with low power consumption has been suggested.

6 Challenges

6.1 Data Privacy and Security

As the IoT gadgets & smartphone apps will gather & send information in real/actual time, there is a risk of privacy of data & protection being compromised. In healthcare, the majority of IoT gadgets lack standards & data protocols. The data is vulnerable to theft, cybercrime & fraud, putting doctors' & patients' personal health information at danger [17].

6.2 Devices and Protocols

Various gadgets surely act as barrier in the deployment of IoT in the healthcare arena. This is because of the absence of standards & networking communication protocols. As a result, regardless of whether gadgets are connected, there will always be a discrepancy in communication protocol, which complicates & inhibits the entire process.

6.3 Data Overload and Accuracy

Data aggregation becomes complicated due to the many standards & protocols. It is challenging for doctors to make timely quality decisions due to massive volume of information acquired by smartphone apps & IoT-facilitated gadgets.

6.4 Price

In many ways, IoT is ahead of the other economical packages, but it is still not as economical for the average person as it is for large healthcare organizations.

6.5 Connectivity

IoT gadgets rely on & run on the internet, a lack of Wi-Fi access in the locations where IoT is desired the most will cause the concept of IoT devices to fail. It is still feasible for hospitals to go without internet access, but there is no guarantee for patients.

6.6 Availability

IoT devices are supposed to work round the clock. It sets the responsibility of healthcare institutions to provide maintenance round-the-clock & if they don't, it will be impossible to receive accurate information from patients on time.

7 Future Scopes

7.1 Home Healing

With the advancement of technology & the development of IoT health monitoring systems, healing at home has become a viable option. Patients do not need to be beneath the hospital's roof because of the collaboration of real/actual time monitoring & numerous specific modules. As a result, the technology has a bright future ahead of it, giving independent & monitoring health by gadgets while minimizing stress of having to see experts & other healthcare professionals.

7.2 Remote Health Monitoring

IoT enables continues monitoring, recording & tracking the changes in various health parameters of remotely located patients. It enhances the access of patient's health data to medical authorities to prevent any emergencies and readmissions. This monitoring minimizes the routine checkup and hospital stays. The accuracy and reliability of the data provides better precision in treatment. The IoT technology comprising of various sensors installed in the house or on the patients collects real time health parameters sending alarms in event of any crisis.

7.3 Taking Medicines at the Appropriate Time

How many times have you forgotten to acquire your medications when they were due? If you answered "many times," you are correct. IoT surveillance gadgets that will maintain track of patient's recommended drug habit has solved this problem. The technology has been shown to be most effective for patients with Alzheimer's or dementia disease. For example, Med Signals' IoT operated solution. A novel solution using a pill cases that lights up when it's time for the patient to take their medicine.

8 Conclusion

In this paper, the role of real time health monitoring wearable devices in medical field & their technological up gradation are studied. The emphasis is on IoT involved in these different medical devices used for sensing & sending patient health conditions to any location connected via server. Overall timely & continuous tracking by medical experts results in lesser fatal cases & better health conditions with overall reduced maintenance health cost. It results in an increase of medical services accessibilities. This paper gives a look on all the advancement going on IoT based medical technologies up to date. Also the concept of HIoT & its various perspectives are also included with their involvements in various applications.

References

1. Rashmi, I., Sahana, M., Sangeetha, R., Shruthi, K.: IOT based patient health monitoring system to remote doctors using embedded technology. Int. J. Eng. Res. Technol. https://www.academia.edu/download/64225849/iot-based-patient-health-monitoring-system-IJERTCONV8IS13058.pdf. Accessed 14 Nov 2021
2. Khan, M., Han, K., Karthik, S.: Designing smart control systems based on Internet of Things and big data analytics. Wireless Pers. Commun. **99**(4), 1683–1697 (2018). https://doi.org/10.1007/s11277-018-5336-y
3. Jagadeeswari, V., Subramaniyaswamy, V., Logesh, R., Vijayakumar, V.: A study on medical Internet of Things and big data in personalized healthcare system. Health Inf. Sci. Syst. **6**(1), 1–20 (2018). https://doi.org/10.1007/s13755-018-0049-x
4. Peng, H., Tian, Y., Kurths, J., Li, L., Yang, Y.: Secure & energy-efficient data transmission system based on chaotic compressive sensing in body-to-body networks. IEEE Trans. Biomed. Circ. Syst. **11**(3), 558–573 (2017). https://ieeexplore.ieee.org/abstract/document/7921444. Accessed 14 Nov 2021
5. Real-Time Health Monitoring Using Wearable Devices Problem Statement. https://play.google.com/store/apps/details?id=org.imperial.activemilespro. Accessed 14 Nov 2021
6. What is the Future Scope of IoT in Healthcare? - Appventurez. https://www.appventurez.com/blog/iot-healthcare-future-scope. Accessed 14 Nov 2021
7. Wu, T., Redouté, J., Yuce, M.: A wearable, low-power, real-time ECG monitor for smart t-shirt & IoT healthcare applications, Springer (2019). https://doi.org/10.1007/978-3-030-02819-0_13.pdf. Accessed 14 Nov 2021
8. Amira, A., Djelouat, H., Bensaali, F., Kotronis, C., Politi, E.: Real-time ECG monitoring using compressive sensing on a heterogeneous multicore edge-device (2019). https://dora.dmu.ac.uk/h&le/2086/18499. Accessed 14 Nov 2021

9. Al-Kababji, A., et al.: IoT-based fall & ECG monitoring system: wireless communication system based firebase realtime database (2019). https://ieeexplore.ieee.org/abstract/document/9060353. Accessed 14 Nov 2021

10. Sunny, S., Kumar, S.S.: Optical based non invasive glucometer with IoT (2021). https://ieeexplore.ieee.org/abstract/document/8379597. Accessed 14 Nov 2021

11. Ota, H., et al.: 3D printed 'earable' smart devices for real-time detection of core body temperature. ACS Sens. **2**(7), 990–997 (2017). https://doi.org/10.1021/ACSSENSORS.7B00247

12. Zakaria, N.A., Binti, N., Saleh, M., Azhar, M., Razak, A.: IoT (Internet of Things) based infant body temperature monitoring, ieeexplore.ieee.org (2018). https://doi.org/10.1109/ICBAPS.2018.8527408

13. Xin, Q., Wu, J.: A novel wearable device for continuous, non-invasion blood pressure measurement. Comput. Biol. Chem. **69**, 134–137 (2017). https://www.sciencedirect.com/science/article/pii/S1476927117302803. Accessed 14 Nov 2021

14. Dinh, A., Luu, L., Cao, T.: Blood pressure measurement using finger ECG & photoplethysmogram for IoT. IFMBE Proc. **63**, 83–89 (2018). https://doi.org/10.1007/978-981-10-4361-1_14

15. Agustine, L., Muljono, I., Angka, P.R., Gunadhi, A., Lestariningsih, D., Weliamto, W.A.: Heart rate monitoring device for arrhythmia using pulse oximeter sensor based on & roid, https://ieeexplore.ieee.org/abstract/document/8711120. Accessed 14 Nov 2021

16. Larson, E.C., Goel, M., Boriello, G., Heltshe, S., Rosenfeld, M., Patel, S.N.: SpiroSmart: using a microphone to measure lung function on a mobile phone (2012). https://dl.acm.org/doi/abs/10.1145/2370216.2370261. Accessed 14 Nov 2021

17. Elansary, I., Darwish, A., Hassanien, A.E.: The future scope of internet of things for monitoring and prediction of COVID-19 patients. In: Hassanien, A.E., Darwish, A. (eds.) Digital Transformation and Emerging Technologies for Fighting COVID-19 Pandemic: Innovative Approaches. SSDC, vol. 322, pp. 235–247. Springer, Cham (2021). https://doi.org/10.1007/978-3-030-63307-3_15

A Blockchain-Based Solution for Electronic Medical Records System in Healthcare

Shubham Sharma$^{(\boxtimes)}$, Sakshi Kaushal, Shubham Gupta, and Harish Kumar

Department of Computer Science and Engineering, University Institute of Engineering and Technology, Panjab University, Chandigarh 160014, India
shubhamsharma0040@gmail.com

Abstract. Healthcare has come out as an emerging field for technologies like IoTs, cloud computing, big data, etc. lately. However, keeping the healthcare records secure and private is still a big issue. Due to this, its widespread adoption is something that might take a few more years. For past few years, blockchain technology has shown its capability to be a preferred technology to provide better security and privacy. Recent breakthroughs in various technologies have improved medical transactions, health insurance claims, and secure records keeping, with the help of its decentralized and distributed nature. In this paper, several algorithms and methods are proposed to improve limitations in the current healthcare system using blockchain technology. It further proposes architecture and tools to measure the performance of the system. Finally, the results and future directions for the research in the healthcare domain are discussed.

Keywords: Blockchain · Electronic Medical Records · Healthcare · Ethereum · Binance Smart Chain · IPFS

1 Introduction

For past few years, the evolution of technologies like the Internet of Things (IoT), etc. has created a smart ecosystem where various entities interconnect to facilitate capturing, storing, sharing, and communicating the information. Technologies like Bluetooth, wi-fi, RFID, etc. have been a major catalyst in the transformation and improvements of traditional systems into smart systems [1–4]. With this advancement, all the major sectors like education, agriculture, transportation, etc. are shifting from transitional approaches to smart systems [5, 6]. Similarly, the healthcare industry is also developing into a Smart Healthcare System (SHS) where all the participants are interconnected to achieve holistic and ubiquitous healthcare facilities. This transformation has led to expansion in investments and awareness leading to becoming increasingly competent at enabling faster identification, handling large chunks of data, determining illness at a faster pace, with suggestions and treatment comparisons [7].

© Springer Nature Switzerland AG 2022
A. K. Luhach et al. (Eds.): ICAICR 2021, CCIS 1575, pp. 232–243, 2022.
https://doi.org/10.1007/978-3-031-09469-9_20

The Healthcare industry has come a long way over the years and has seen some major technological changes from Healthcare 1.0 to the current Healthcare 4.0 [8]. Started in the 1970s the Healthcare industry has gone from using paper-based records to blockchain-enabled Electronic Medical Records (EMRs). The Fig. 1 shows the features of all 4 versions of the industry. The current era aims at enhancing virtualization and enabling personalized healthcare in real-time by building blockchains with a focus on convergence.

Healthcare data contains the private data of its patients, so it is obvious that it needs a high level of privacy and security. This requires a formation of standards and a trust among healthcare providers with the creation of agreed policies. Various security standards like Health Insurance Portability and Accountability Act (HIPAA), Digital Information Security in Healthcare Act (DISHA), and Control Objectives for Information and Related Technologies (COBIT) have been introduced to tackle this issue [8]. Healthcare security is of utmost importance to protect patient's private data. Access control management of the information, modification and removal of the previously stored data, and safety from unauthorized users, etc. are included in this [9]. With the increase in healthcare databases, the need for security mechanisms to safeguard the data has also been increased a lot.

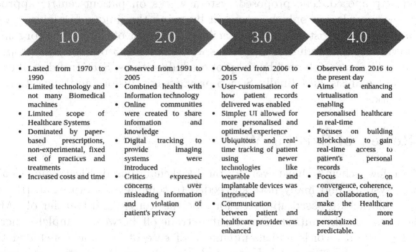

Fig. 1. Versions of healthcare industry

1.1 Blockchain Technology

In recent years, due to the increase in popularity of cryptocurrencies like Bitcoin [10] and Ethereum [11], research related to blockchain or the distributed ledger technology has gained worldwide popularity. Blockchain can be defined as a decentralized, distributed, and immutable ledger technology that provides data transparency and simultaneously, user privacy, removing middleman and not requiring a central dependency for checking transactions [12–14]. The concept of blockchain is based on the peer-to-peer system where the blocks (data) are connected to each other using chains (cryptographic techniques). There is an absence of central authority and the transactions or the immutable ledger is open to everyone connected to the network. All the valuable and invaluable information can be stored in the form of blocks where each block will have its own unique hash. These hashes are created on the basis of stored data inside them, therefore tampering is not possible since, with a change in data, the hash will also be changed [7].

1.2   Blockchain in Healthcare

The Healthcare sector, with this rapidly increasing data, is struggling with challenges like access to data, security, and access of the data outside the healthcare facility [8]. Blockchain can be one technology that can help in improving the verification and integrity of the data. Its decentalization, distributed, and immutable features can help healthcare industry transform.

The main contributions of this research are described as follows. Firstly, using distributed ledger technology, a Binance blockchain-based system to store EMRs in an immutable ledger form to provide better security, privacy, and decentralization is proposed. The proposed system works on patient-centric approach where the records can only be accessed by using the unique IDs given to the patients and at a registered medical facilities. The rest of the paper is organized as follows: Sect. 2 examines the previous works. Section 3 presents the proposed system architecture, followed by the proposed algorithms. Section 4 describes the results and analysis, and, finally, Sect. 5 provides conclusions and suggestions for future work.

2   Review of Existing Work

Quite a few schemes have worked on blockchain-based Electronic Medical Records systems and many have succeeded to some level. Vora et al. [15] presented a blockchain-based approach for efficient storage and transfer of EMRs. In their results, the authors found out a trade-off between complete encryption of patient's records and maintenance of ease of use and concluded that both cannot go hand-in-hand. Kaur et al. [16] proposed a solution and gave a future direction to store heterogeneous medical data in cloud environments on a blockchain-based system. The cloud environment is incorporated to mitigate the scalability issues which come with storing the data on the blockchain itself. Chen et al. [9] proposed a blockchain-based novel system for medical information sharing with a complete business process. In the proposed system, the information systems were combined with blockchain technology in which authorized users could jointly maintain the information in the network using a consensus mechanism. Li et al. [17] presented a novel data preservation system (DPS) that provides a reliable storage solution to ensure the stored data's primitiveness and verifiability while also users' privacy preservation. The proposed system could deal with situations of data loss and tampering.

Tripathi et al. [7] proposed a Secure and Smart Healthcare System (SSHS) framework, based on blockchain, to provide a healthcare system which is secure and private. The authors took the various IoT devices into consideration and proposed a framework to constantly monitor the patient's health and store the data in the blockchain.

Sun et al. [18] proposed a blockchain-based EMR system that enables doctors to add and encrypt patients' data with access policies and then upload the encrypted data to IPFS. For searching particular encrypted data records, keyword index searching is also employed. Tanwar et al. [8] proposed a distributed ledger system architecture and algorithms for a patient-centric approach to provide an access control policy to different healthcare providers. The authors were successful in eliminating the centralized authority and a single-point of failure in the system. Usman and Qamar [19] presented an EMR preservation system based on blockchain, providing efficient, reliable, and secure storage, to better the availability and accessibility of medical records. In the proposed system, patients can actively manage their records and control access to their data. Huang et al. [20] presented a blockchain-based scheme for privacy preservation. The scheme employs the secure sharing of healthcare or medical data between entities like patients, doctors, research institutions, and semi-trusted cloud servers. The main contribution to the research is the employment of Zero-Knowledge proof which helps in verification of whether the patient's medical records meets the requirements proposed by research institutions without revealing the patient's data or records to achieve data availability and consistency among both parties. Shamshad et al. [21] presented a novel blockchain-based protocol managing the privacy and security of patient's health records for improved diagnosis and efficient treatments in Telecare Medicine Information System (TMIS). Pandey and Litoriya [22] presented challenges faced during the implementation of healthcare services on a large scale (specifically India) and proposed AarogyaChain, based on blockchain technology. The authors employed Hyperledger fabric to form a model to store patient's EMRs and tested the throughput of the system analyzing the scalability of the system.

After extensive research, it was found out that blockchain is indeed a rising technology that can help in improving the healthcare sector to a significant level. Table 1 shows the comparison of the proposed model with existing models based on similar principle.

3 Proposed Methodology

In this section, a blockchain-based approach for EMR sharing is introduced. Consequently, the blockchain-based system architecture for EMR sharing is also proposed.

Table 1. Comparison of the proposed system with similar models

S. No.	Paper	Patient centric	Access control	IPFS used	Performance evaluation	Blockchain used
1	Sun et al. [18]	✗	✗	✓	✓	Ethereum
2	Vora et al. [15]	✓	✓	✗	✗	Ethereum
3	Tanwar et al. [8]	✓	✓	✗	✓	Hyperledger fabric, Composer
4	Tripathi et al. [7]	✓	✓	✗	✗	Public and private blockchain
5	Usman et al. [19]	✓	✓	✓	✗	Hyper ledger Fabric, Composer
6	Omar et al. [23]	✓	✗	✗	✗	Not specified
7	Proposed system	✓	✓	✓	✓	Binance Smart Chain

3.1 System Architecture

In the proposed system, there are 3 main entities: (1) The deployer, (2) the doctor, and (3) the patient. Unlike the traditional system, where all the rights of adding, updating, and deleting the records were with the administrator of the system, here, the patient is the sole owner of his/her records. Whereas the deployer is responsible for deploying the smart contracts on the blockchain network, the doctors is responsible for adding new patients and records to the system. In the proposed system, underlying blockchain technology enables the EMR to be distributed with other entities. In the proposed system, various smart contracts are defined, which are: HospitalContract, and PatientContract.

The system workflow is easy to use and access. Doctors are registered in the network by the deployer using a password and the public address of the doctor. After registration, the doctor is then given the authority to create new patients and add/view records. Whenever a doctor creates a new patient, the initial data of the patient is added to the blockchain network returning back a unique ID (in a form of QR) which will be the permanent key of the patient.

Whenever creating a new record, the doctor can add multiple values which then are sent to the IPFS [24] which returns a unique hash which will, from here on, be used to access these stored records. The records will not be available to everyone on the network but can only be accessed using the patient's unique ID. The system architecture is shown in the Fig. 2.

3.2 Technology Stack

The public blockchain Ethereum-based framework, called Binance Smart Chain is used to develop the proposed electronic medical records system. Ethereum is an open-source, permissionless Distributed Ledger Technology (DLT). Ethereum provides transparency, security, and immutability to the system. Binance Smart Chain is a clone of original Ethereum blockchain, but provides better security,

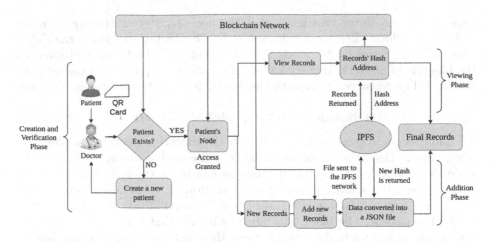

Fig. 2. Proposed system architecture

scalability, and lower transactional costs. The coin used in the BSC (Binance Smart Chain) is called BNB. The proposed system uses BSC as the main blockchain. To handle all the transactions and the functions in the proposed system, smart contracts are required. The proposed system uses Solidity programming language which is a high-level, an object-oriented language for implementing smart contracts and governs the behavior of accounts and nodes within the Binance state [25].

To perform any task on the Binance platform, the user has to call the function corresponding to the required action. If the function call results in a change of state on the blockchain network, then the function call is treated as a transaction. To mine a transaction into a blockchain network, some amount of BNB, in the form of gas, is required. Gas is a denomination of Ether or BNB, also known as wei (smallest denomination of BNB) and its value is 10^{-18} BNB. To handle all of these transactions effectively, a browser extension Metamask is used. Metamask is an Ethereum based wallet that helps in handling and signing transactions [26]. But since testing of the model requires a lot of transactions, using real BNBs doesn't sound feasible.

For the testing purposes, the proposed system uses Binance Testnet which provides us the capability to test our dApps without using real cryptocurrency. The proposed system uses Reactjs [27], a popular Javascript library to create front-end user interfaces, and web3.js [28], a collection of Ethereum Javascript API libraries that enables the front-end to connect to the smart contracts on the Binance blockchain. Since the proposed system is not tied to any particular storage system, IPFS is used to store patient's final records.

3.3   Proposed Algorithms

This section presents details of the algorithms proposed in the system. The precise execution and creation of the doctor is shown in Algorithm 1. The initial requirement for doctor creation is that the node registering the doctor needs to be the deployer. The main requirement for the doctor creation is the public node address. Every doctor needs to have a node address to get registered on the blockchain network. If every added information is up to the standards, the doctor will be registered as an authorized participant in the blockchain network.

$$authAddress[doctor's NodeAddress] = true \tag{1}$$

The process to create a new patient in the blockchain network is shown in Algorithm 2. Here, the initial requirement is the authorization of the doctor's node. After granting access, the doctor now can input the basic details for the patient. Here, the algorithm uses the combination of the patient's name, blood group, age, current timestamp, and the current block difficulty to create a unique ID for the patient. The block difficulty is a metric that calculates the average time to create a block in the network. Here, these values are encoded and hashed using hashing algorithm, keccak256, to create a unique hash ID for the patient.

$$patient's ID = Keccak256(block.timestamp, block.difficulty, name, dob, bGroup) \tag{2}$$

Algorithm 1. Pseudocode to add a new doctor

BEGIN
if user == contract deployer **then**
   if doctor's ID does not exist **then**
      if password == entered password **then**
         enter doctor's initial infomation
         enter node address of the doctor
      end if password is incorrect
   else doctor already exists
   end if
else user needs to be the deployer
end if
New doctor created
END

From here on, the previous records of the patient can easily be accessed using the patient unique ID. The process to add new records to the blockchain network are depicted in Algorithm 3. For input, the patient provides his/her QR Code to the doctor which lets the doctor gain access to the patient's previous records. An authorized doctor can add a request to add new records to the patient's node. After adding, the data is converted into a JavaScript Object Notation (JSON) file and is sent to the InterPlanetary File System (IPFS). IPFS stores the data and returns the hash address to the system. This hash is then stored in the patient's node as a new record address.

Algorithm 2. Pseudocode to add a new patient

```
BEGIN
if doctor == authorized node then
    Enter patient's details
    Generate patient's unique ID using keccak 256
    Data stored in Struct
    map the patient's unique ID to his struct address
else patient cannot be created
end if
New patient is created
END
```

Algorithm 3. Pseudocode to add records

```
BEGIN
Enter patient's ID access patient's node
if the patient exists then
    Request to create new record created
    Add data to the patient's node
    Convert the entered data into a JSON format file
    Send the file to the IPFS and fetch the hash address returned
    Store the hash in the blockchain and show final records
else the patient doesn't exist
end if
New records added
END
```

4   Results and Discussion

In this section, the proposed system is evaluated and results are compared with the transaction costs of various functions involved in the system.

4.1   Simulation Settings

For the test runs, a dataset of 15 diseases is used. Every disease is given a serial number, a name, a summary, and cures prescribed by the doctor. Once the smart contracts are compiled, all the functions and variables are converted into low-level assembly opcodes which can be read by Ethereum Virtual Machine (EVM). These opcodes are then imported into the React framework using the web3 module allowing it to connect to the front-end of the application. Every transaction is recorded in Metamask and mined in the blockchain provided by Binance testnet.

4.2   Experiment

To get a better idea of the transaction costs or gas prices involved in the execution of the functions, gas requirements are obtained and then their costs are estimated. The experiment is performed on BNB testnet where the gas price to perform the transactions was 10 Gwei or 10^{10} wei. It must be noted that 1 Billion Gwei is equal to 1 BNB and the price of 1 BNB at the time of this experiment (November 2021) was around $634.

Table 2 represents functions, the gas costs, and the average transaction costs involved (in USD). Deploying the contract is a one-time process. In the test runs, the cost for deploying the contract came out to be an average of 0.017 BNB or $ 10.77. Adding the doctor is also a one-time process. For this, the deployer needs the public address of the doctor. In the test runs, the average cost for creating a doctor came out to be 0.000908 BNB or $0.57. Adding a patient is also a one-time task. In the test runs, the cost for adding a new patient to the network came out to be 0.009476 BNB or $6.003. Adding a new record to IPFS returns a unique hash that costs 0.0016 BNB or $1.01 to be saved on the blockchain. This means that a patient can get new records entered into his node with a minimal amount of 0.0016 BNB or $1.01, neglecting all the one-time functions.

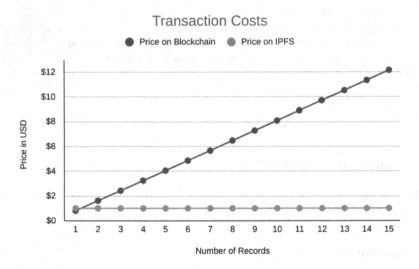

Fig. 3. Transaction costs comparison between blockchain and IPFS

Based on these gas costs, the proposed system is compared with the traditional systems where the data was stored on the blockchain itself. Table 3 shows the comparison of transactional costs between both of the scenarios. As there can be multiple tuples in a single record, the transaction cost in the Fig. 3 is increased proportionally to the number of tuples. But after using the IPFS, the transaction cost came out to be really low. In our results, we found out that for a record with 15 tuples, the transaction cost will remain the same as for the record with 1 tuple.

Table 2. Gas costs and transactions costs for the functions in the proposed system

S. No.	Function	Gas cost	Cost estimate (in BNB)	Cost estimate (in USD)	Number of times to be repeated
1.	Deploying the contract	1736649	0.017	10.77	One time
2	Add a new doctor	90823	0.000908	0.57	One time
3	Add a new patient	947639	0.009476	6.003	One time
4	Store the record hash from IPFS	144816	0.0016	1.01	Once for each record

Table 3. Gas costs and transactions costs for record storage comparison

Patient records	Gas cost	Cost estimate (in BNB)	Cost estimate (in USD)	Number of times to be repeated
On blockchain	129122	0.001291	0.81	Once for each tuple
On IPFS	144816	0.0016	1.01	Once per record

4.3   Discussion and Analysis

Blockchain has revolutionized the creation, storage, and management of data. Its decentralized, distributed, and immutable nature of storage provides a significant upgrade to the traditional centralized system of storage and can help in situations of catastrophic and disaster. This is a huge advantage, considering the fact that data can easily be lost in Medical institutions. In the proposed system, use of multiple contracts ensures improved privacy and security. Because of this, no unauthorized entity will be able to access records of the patient without going through initial contracts.

As discussed in Sect. 4.3, IPFS provides a significantly low cost for the storage of patient's records compared to the scenario where records are stored on the blockchain itself. Storing a hash address is cheaper than storing the whole record of the patient. IPFS also provides added security and avoids the reduced bandwidth problem in the blockchain network, as the major amount of data will be stored off-chain. Thus, IPFS provides a major advantage over the blockchain network.

5   Conclusion

Blockchain technology, combined with other modern technologies, plays an important role in medicine and can transform the current healthcare industry. In this paper, current challenges and issues faced by the healthcare industry are discussed. The proposed system defined algorithms and architecture for an EMR system that achieved privacy, security, and immutability of patient's data. The proposed system is implemented and evaluated using blockchain technology.

The involvement of blockchain eliminates the central authorisation or middle-man from the system and is saves the network from single point of failure. The use of IPFS saves the bandwidth of the system and makes the transactions fast and cheap. For future works, researchers can include smart contracts to add more functionalities like billing, transportation, reports, etc. to create a full-fledged healthcare management system. The researchers should also focus on different blockchain technologies, like Ethereum 2.0 which is estimated to use very low transactional costs with faster mining on the network. Beyond this, researchers can also extend the proposed work by implementing it in a real-time environment by adding real participants to the system.

References

1. Baker, S.B., Xiang, W., Atkinson, I.: Internet of things for smart healthcare: Tech-nologies, challenges, and opportunities. IEEE J. Mag. IEEE xplore. **5**, 26521–26544 (2017). https://ieeexplore.ieee.org/document/8124196
2. Fernandez, F., Pallis, G.C.: Opportunities and challenges of the internet of things for healthcare: Systems engineering perspective. In: 2014 4th International Confer-ence on Wireless Mobile Communication and Healthcare - Transforming Healthcare Through Innovations in Mobile and Wireless Technologies (MOBIHEALTH), pp. 263–266 (2014)
3. Hinings, B., Gegenhuber, T., Greenwood, R.: Digital innovation and transforma-tion: an institutional perspective. Inf. Organ. **28**(1), 52–61 (2018). https://www.sciencedirect.com/science/article/pii/S1471772718300265
4. Huh, S., Cho, S., Kim, S.: Managing IoT devices using blockchain platform. In: 2017 19th International Conference on Advanced Communication Technology (ICACT), pp. 464–467 (2017)
5. Guy, J.S.: Digital technology, digital culture and the metric/nonmetric distinction. Tech. Forecast. Soc. Change **145**, 55–61 (2019). https://www.sciencedirect.com/science/article/pii/S0040162518316159
6. Markides, C.: Disruptive innovation: in need of better theory. J. Prod. Innov. Manage. **23**, 19–25 (2006)
7. Tripathi, G., Ahad, M.A., Paiva, S.: S2hs- a blockchain based approach for smart healthcare system. Healthcare **8**(1), 100391 (2020). https://www.sciencedirect.com/science/article/pii/S2213076419302532
8. Tanwar, S., Parekh, K., Evans, R.: Blockchain-based electronic healthcare record system for healthcare 4.0 applications. J. Inf. Secur. Appl. **50**, 102407 (2020). https://www.sciencedirect.com/science/article/pii/S2214212619306155
9. Chen, J., Ma, X., Du, M., Wang, Z.: A blockchain application for medical information sharing. In: 2018 IEEE International Symposium on Innovation and Entrepreneurship (TEMS-ISIE), pp. 1–7 (2018)
10. Nakamoto, S.: Bitcoin: a peer-to-peer electronic cash system, p. 9 (2009)
11. What is ethereum? - ethereum homestead 0.1 documentation. https://ethdocs.org/en/latest/introduction/what-is-ethereum.html
12. Kabra, N., Bhattacharya, P., Tanwar, S., Tyagi, S.: MudraChain: blockchain-based framework for automated cheque clearance in financial institutions. Future Gener. Comput. Syst. **102**, 574–587 (2020). https://www.sciencedirect.com/science/article/pii/S0167739X19311896

13. Suveen, A., Krumholz, H.M., Schulz, W.L.: Blockchain technology 10(9), e003800. https://www.ahajournals.org/doi/full/10.1161/CIRCOUTCOMES.117.003800
14. Benchoufi, M., Ravaud, P.: Blockchain technology for improving clinical research quality. Trials 18(1), 335 (2017). https://doi.org/10.1186/s13063-017-2035-z
15. Vora, J., et al.: BHEEM: A blockchain-based framework for securing electronic health records. In: 2018 IEEE Globecom Workshops (GC Wkshps), pp. 1–6 (2018)
16. Kaur, H., Alam, M.A., Jameel, R., Mourya, A.K., Chang, V.: A proposed solution and future direction for blockchain-based heterogeneous medicare data in cloud environment. J. Med. Syst. 42(8), 1–11 (2018). https://doi.org/10.1007/s10916-018-1007-5
17. Li, H., Zhu, L., Shen, M., Gao, F., Tao, X., Liu, S.: Blockchain-based data preservation system for medical data. J. Med. Syst. 42(8), 1–13 (2018). https://doi.org/10.1007/s10916-018-0997-3
18. Sun, J., Ren, L., Wang, S., Yao, X.: A blockchain-based framework for electronic medical records sharing with fine-grained access control. PLoS ONE 15(10), e0239946 (2020)
19. Usman, M., Qamar, U.: Secure electronic medical records storage and sharing using blockchain technology. Procedia Comput. Sci. 174, 321–327 (2020). https://www.sciencedirect.com/science/article/pii/S1877050920316136
20. Huang, H., Zhu, P., Xiao, F., Sun, X., Huang, Q.: A blockchain-based scheme for privacy-preserving and secure sharing of medical data. Comput. Secur. 99, 102010 (2020). https://www.sciencedirect.com/science/article/pii/S0167404820302832
21. Shamshad, S., Minahil, Mahmood, K., Kumari, S., Chen, C.M.: A secure blockchain-based e-health records storage and sharing scheme. J. Inf. Secur. Appl. 55, 102590 (2020). https://www.sciencedirect.com/science/article/pii/S2214212620307596
22. Pandey, P., Litoriya, R.: Implementing healthcare services on a large scale: challenges and remedies based on blockchain technology. Health Policy Technol. 9(1), 69–78 (2020). https://www.sciencedirect.com/science/article/pii/S2211883720300046
23. Al Omar, A., Rahman, M.S., Basu, A., Kiyomoto, S.: MediBchain: a blockchain based privacy preserving platform for healthcare data. In: Wang, G., Atiquzzaman, M., Yan, Z., Choo, K.-K.R. (eds.) SpaCCS 2017. LNCS, vol. 10658, pp. 534–543. Springer, Cham (2017). https://doi.org/10.1007/978-3-319-72395-2_49
24. Labs, P.: IPFS powers the distributed web. https://ipfs.io/
25. Solidity - solidity 0.8.3 documentation. https://docs.soliditylang.org/en/v0.8.3/
26. MetaMask.   https://en.wikipedia.org/w/index.php?title=MetaMask&oldid=1023291296, page Version ID: 1023291296
27. React - a JavaScript library for building user interfaces. https://reactjs.org/
28. web3.js - ethereum JavaScript API - web3.js 1.0.0 documentation. https://web3js.readthedocs.io/en/v1.3.4/

Edge-Assisted IoT Architecture: A Case of Air Pollution Monitoring Frameworks

Surleen Kaur[✉] and Sandeep Sharma

Department of Computer Engineering and Technology, Guru Nanak Dev University,
Amritsar, India
{surleencse.rsh,sandeep.cse}@gndu.ac.in

Abstract. With the deployment of Internet of Things systems now becoming much more large scale, there arises a need to see beyond cloud as the number of IoT devices are increasing exponentially which in turn are generating huge quantities of data which needs to be processed in real time. Edge computing provides the required support to handle such huge volumes of data by providing the cloud services at the network edge; which improves the response time, bandwidth consumption, efficiency, reliability of any IoT application. IoT systems can greatly benefit from having cloud-like computational facilities closer to the source of the data. Hence, this paper mainly focuses upon analysing the collaboration of IoT and edge in IoT based air pollution monitoring applications. The survey further provides a comparison between edge-based and cloud-based systems, drawing attention to the advantages edge computing has over cloud computing.

Keywords: Air pollution monitoring · Cloud computing · Edge computing · Internet of Things

1 Introduction

The concept of 'Internet of Things' came into existence when Kevin Ashton first proposed it in 1999 [1]. Ever since, its conception, it has transformed the face of networking. It has provided the world with a dynamic framework where almost everything that can be equipped with sensors, actuators, processors, communication modules can be regarded as a uniquely identifiable 'thing' in this enormous heterogenous network [2]. IoT, in the past decade has been put to use by technologists in almost every sector with an aim to enhance the quality and improve the efficiency in various domains, be it healthcare, agriculture, sustainable cities and infrastructure, autonomous cars, environmental monitoring, supply chain, manufacturing, industry 4.0 and more [3]. This has led to an exponential growth of Internet of Things with millions of devices (things) being added to the network every day. After analysing the current trend and the future potential, it has been estimated that by the end of 2025, there will be approximately 41.6 billion IoT devices. This number is nearly double the previous estimation made by Gartner in 2014 where 26 billion IoT devices were expected to be added by the end of 2020 [4]. These

A. K. Luhach et al. (Eds.): ICAICR 2021, CCIS 1575, pp. 244–256, 2022.
https://doi.org/10.1007/978-3-031-09469-9_21

41.6 billion devices are further expected to generate nearly 79.4 zettabytes (ZB) of data, in other words, trillions of gigabytes of data will be generated worldwide [5].

The advent of a wide range of enabling technologies, such as low-power smart sensors, highly efficient processors, communication protocols (2G/3G/4G/5G, GPS, Wi-Fi), cloud computing, support for security, privacy, data storing, processing and visualization tools, application software have revolutionised Internet of Things. It is the fastest growing trend and will continue to rise with such advanced technologies at our disposal. These technologies have allowed Internet of Things to offer interconnectivity, heterogeneity, interoperability, scalability, safety, energy management, data management and much more [6]. A typical IoT architecture is a layered structure with sensing layer at the lowest level, followed by communication layer, cloud layer and finally the application layer [3]. The sensing layer constitutes of smart devices that collect information in real-time, which can be regarding air quality, motion, temperature, humidity, pollutant concentration, etc. These devices can be standalone sensors or sensors attached to microcontroller boards which have some memory of their own to be able to locally store some data. These devices are also equipped with communication module, so that they are able to transmit the collected data through gateways to cloud (datacentres) where the data can be analysed and processed for further use.

IoT devices produce a huge amount of data and that data in the raw form do not denote much meaning. Hence, there is a need to process and analyse the collected data by applying appropriate machine learning or artificial intelligence algorithms, so that it can be utilised to highlight patterns, trends and can even be used for predictive analysis [7]. As a result, cloud computing has always been an integral part of the core IoT architecture as it provides a centralized storage space where all data obtained by the heterogenous network of devices is sent for further processing [4]. Cloud computing provides the users with shared services which are generally broadly categorised as, Infrastructure as a Service (IaaS), Platform as a Service (PaaS), Software as a Service (SaaS) [8]. However, with the rapid increase in the number of IoT devices and the amount exploding beyond billions of gigabytes, it becomes hard to send all the data to the cloud which could physically be thousands of miles away. The data pipeline traffic increases and so does the cost of centralized storage and analysis of data which is contrary to the main objective of IoT applications, i.e., is faster real-time response. Hence, this calls for local processing of data such that the latency and connectivity issues of IoT devices can be alleviated [5]. This is where edge computing can play a major role as it basically means, processing data at the 'edge' of the network. Edge computing has the capability to transform the way data obtained from billions of devices is stored, processed and analysed, as it ensures much faster and reliable service [9]. In this paper, the contribution of edge computing in the field of Internet of Things has been explored in detail. The main objectives of the paper are as follows:

- To understand in detail the concept of edge computing and its distinct characteristics.
- To examine the role of edge computing in the field of Internet of Things.
- To compare cloud-based and edge-based computing with respect to IoT-enabled air pollution monitoring frameworks.

The rest of the paper has been organised into various sections. In the second section, the concept of edge computing, and its distinct characteristics have been elaborated, which is followed by the third section where the role of edge computing in Internet of Things has been examined. In the fourth section, a comparison has been done between cloud based and edge based IoT frameworks for air pollution monitoring with an aim to highlight the significance of edge in IoT applications that generate large amounts of data. The last section briefly concludes the paper.

2 Edge Computing

2.1 Definition and Characteristics

Edge computing can be regarded as an upgradation of cloud computing which allows storing and processing of data at the edge of the network without having to send the entire data stream to the centralized serves for computational purposes [10]. The 'edge' in such a network is any device that is sitting between the source of the data and the cloud data servers [11]. Figure 1(a) depicts a traditional IoT-cloud architecture and Fig. 1(b) shows a modified architecture with an additional edge layer in between the IoT devices and the cloud. An edge device can be considered as a link between the cloud and the end devices as it has the capability to work on data coming from the cloud as well as the IoT devices [11]. However, the main task of an edge is not only to transfer the data, but infact to store, process and compute the consumed data. In other words, edge computing has the capability to bring the services facilitated by cloud computing much closer to the end user [10] which results in smaller response time and efficient processing of data, as the data is handled locally instead of being transferred all the way to the cloud [12].

Characteristics of Edge Computing. The exponential growth in the number of devices connected to the network and in turn the data being produced by them has reached unprecedented volumes [9]. In addition, with the growth of 5G networks data generation is further expected to increase. Transferring such huge volumes of heterogenous data to the cloud leads to latency, bandwidth, security and reliability issues. Devices these days are more than capable of merely gathering and transferring data, they are equipped with storing and computational capabilities as well [13]. This gives scope to relocate processing tasks closer to the network edge. Hence, there have been numerous studies in the recent times which have utilised edge computing paradigms viz. fog computing [14], cloudlets [15], mobile edge computing [16] in real -time applications to dig up trends and patterns, perform predictive analysis and deep learning tasks. Thus, edge allows one to exploit the connected devices to their maximum potential. Although, edge computing as of now is in its infancy phase as there are various open challenges associated with it like, heterogeneity, standard protocols, availability, mobility, scheduling and load balancing, trust and authentication, pricing [17, 18], etc., but it is estimated that by the end of 2025, 75% of data will be handled at the edge (in today's time, the figure is nearly 10%) [9]. The following are certain unique characteristics of edge which make it an optimal choice for near-real processing of data:

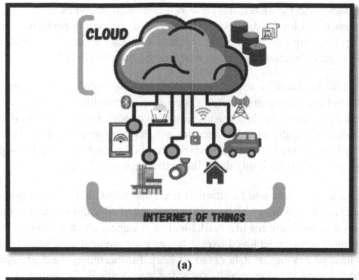

(a)

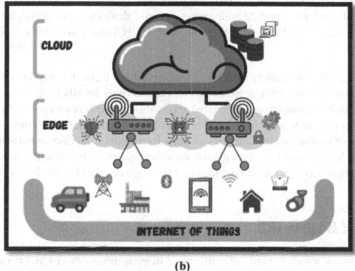

(b)

Fig. 1. (a). Typical IoT-cloud architecture (b) edge-cloud IoT architecture

Reduced Latency. Reduced latency is the prime characteristic of edge computing due to its very nature of performing local processing of data closer to the end devices [19]. It increases network performance as the data doesn't have to travel far and allows delay-sensitive applications to collect and analyse data faster and trigger the required action [20].

Optimized Bandwidth. Normally the data produced by devices is sent back to the centralised servers where analytic tools are applied to draw inferences. However, in majority IoT based applications, thousands of devices are deployed and each device continuously sends data packets to the cloud; the network bandwidth becomes clogged and causes delay and sometimes loss of data as well. Thus, edge computing performs the essential task of pre-processing and filtering out the data first and sending only necessary and compressed data to the cloud, in turn optimising the bandwidth [21].

Enhanced Security. Security management is one of the most critical aspects of any network. Cloud computing architectures are more vulnerable to security attacks and breaches on data since the data travels larger distances to reach centralized server. Although, edge is equally prone to security attacks but the amount of data at risk is considerably less. Owing to the distributed nature of edge architecture, if a single device is compromised, it does not bring down the entire network [18, 21].

Geographical Distribution and Location Awareness. Most IoT applications involve wide-spread sensor networks which demand distributed edge device deployment so that location-based services are readily available. For instance, an environment monitoring system can have sensors deployed over a larger geographical area which might need faster and near processing of data obtained [22]. Furthermore, there are applications which might require location specific data, for e.g., vehicular monitoring or disaster management, here edge architecture allows the end devices to communicate with the nearest edge-node available with the help of GPS (Global Positioning System) like technologies.

Mobility Support. The variety of devices available have tremendously increased ranging from smart phones, tablets, wearables to various other handheld devices which are capable of running computation-intensive applications. These resource-intensive applications often rely on servers for storing and processing purposes. With this increase in the number of mobile devices, arises the need for mobility support in networks. Edge architecture has the ability to provide the necessary support, by enabling direct link of communication between the end devices and the edge device [10, 18, 23, 24].

3   Role of Edge in IoT

IoT is a network which consists of millions of heterogenous devices and networks that are linked by a wide spectrum of supporting technologies like Radio Frequency Identification (RFID), Wireless Sensor Networks (WSNs), cloud computing etc. [25]. The advances in sensors and communication technologies have led to deployment of wide scale smart IoT systems owing to their ability to transmit and analyze the data. The applicability of IoT in areas like healthcare, manufacturing, infrastructure sustainable development, autonomous vehicles, smart cities, pollution monitoring and many more, make it a multidisciplinary interest. As a result, its use is becoming widespread as more and more companies, enterprises, businesses, governments are building intelligent systems for the various abovementioned fields.

3.1 Significance of Edge

The idea behind Internet of Things is a simple concept where sensors are used to obtain physical world data and this data is transmitted to web-based servers (cloud) for storage and processing to further draw inferences and make intelligent decisions for the next course of action. The IoT devices are generally resource-constrained and hence rely on cloud services for computation-intensive tasks [26]. However, with the increase in number of IoT devices and the variety of data collected by them, it is becoming difficult for the cloud to meet all the requirements [23]. Transmission of such huge volumes of data consumes excessive network bandwidth and that increases the associated costs of cloud services [27]. Another issue with traditional cloud computing is the longer response time [26]. Majority of the current IoT applications require computing in real time with minimum possible latency, such that as soon as the data is perceived, the actuation process can be triggered. Applications like heath monitoring where the delay in response can turn into a matter of life and death or applications like industrial and environment monitoring expect a low response time [20].

In such scenarios, edge computing proves beneficial as it delivers computing services closer to the IoT devices with decreased response time and increased efficiency [7]. Edge acts as a small data centre that is physically near the IoT device and provides cloud-like services [28]. İt also promotes efficient data management by pre-processing of data and filtering out the necessary data that needs to be sent to cloud for further analysis [23]. IoT devices are battery powered and by nature have a smaller lifetime; however, edge helps to extend the battery life of IoT devices since the communication between the both happens over a shorter distance. Also, short distance communication reduces the risk of enroute security attacks on the data, hence enhancing the reliability of the network. Edge offers more resilient data communication due to its distributed nature as the failure of a single edge node does not hinder data transfer by IoT devices [7, 27]. Further because of this decentralized storage and processing, edge encourages scalability in IoT networks. Hence, edge computing allows efficient, reliable, secure, cost-effective computing facilitating large scale IoT implementation.

As of now, there are not many IoT applications that depend entirely on edge computing, but lately more and more devices are connecting to the network, making edge computing an important enabler of IoT. Other than reduced latency and bandwidth, local storage and processing, there are still many unknown benefits of edge which are being discovered with the wide spread growth of real-time IoT applications.

4 IoT Enabled Air Pollution Monitoring

Rapid industrialization and urbanisation have had deteriorating effects on our environmental health. The global air quality is worsening due to the pollution created by industries and transportation. Air pollution has been listed as one of the highest risk factors and is responsible for millions of premature deaths each year [29]. The harmful pollutants released into the air by vehicles, industries, buildings have detrimental health impacts and prolonged exposure to these pollutants can cause serious complications such as respiratory issues, reduced lung capacity, asthma, cardiovascular diseases, skin and eye infections and many more [30]. Air pollution also has poor effect on plant and aquatic life. Nearly 90% of the world's population is breathing the air whose pollutant concentrations are more than the standards issued by WHO [31]. Hence, it is absolutely necessary to monitor and control air pollution at a large scale. Governments and pollution control boards have installed stationary air quality monitoring stations; however, these traditional stations are bulky and expensive to install. Moreover, there is usually a single monitoring station in a city, and sometimes these are out of function [32]. A problem as serious as air pollution requires real-time widespread monitoring. There is a need to monitor and control air pollution at street level. This is where, Internet of Things with its wide range of technologies can play an important role. Researchers have undertaken many studies to propose various frameworks that are cost-effective, efficient and can help monitor air pollution in real time.

A typical IoT based air pollution monitoring system has sensors deployed at the lowest layer, which can accurately obtain pollution data, the collected data is then sent to local gateways or cloud for further processing [33]. The next subsection discusses some of the proposed models in the recent years and the technologies utilised by them to monitor and control air pollution.

4.1 Existing Frameworks

In the recent years, many IoT enables frameworks have been proposed for real-time monitoring of air pollution worldwide [34–39]. A wide range of technologies [33], including sensors (such as, MQ-series, MICS- series, SEN-series, particulate matter sensors for sensing wide range of pollutants like carbon dioxide, carbon monoxide, oxides of sulphur, oxides of nitrogen, particulate matter etc.), microcontroller boards (Arduino, Raspberry Pi, NodeMCU etc.), communication technologies (RFID, Bluetooth, Wi-Fi, Cellular etc.) and cloud platforms like (AWS, Microsoft Azure, ThingSpeak, MongoDB etc.) along with machine/deep learning techniques have been utilised in the proposed systems [40]. Air pollution systems generate a lot of data which needs to be stored and processed to take necessary actions. Hence, in recent times, there have been studies which are utilizing the benefits of edge computing to manage the data more efficiently [39, 41, 42]. The pollution sensors used are battery operated with a limited lifetime, and are continuously sensing the environment, their lifetime can be increased significantly by introducing edge computing. Edge also allows quick decision making by applying machine learning on the data where it is generated. Furthermore, cloud and edge have together been used for more advanced systems where the benefits of edge and cloud both can be exploited for developing real-time applications that not only monitor the data, but also generate trends and patterns of pollution data which can prove helpful to curb and control air pollution [37, 38, 43, 44]. Detailed findings of some of the recently proposed systems have been enlisted in Table 1.

Table 1. Summary of various IoT-enabled air pollution monitoring frameworks

Study	Cloud/Edge	Objectives/Findings/Contribution	Limitations/Future scope
[36]	Cloud	A low-cost, low-power system which monitors various pollutants via sensors and sends collected data to cloud for better management of data Stored data is then used to take necessary actions by the authorities to curb air pollution	The collected data can be used to discover long-term pollution patterns and relationship between various pollutants utilizing cloud's resources
[45]	Cloud	A wireless smart air quality monitoring system that uses low-cost sensors and cloud storage to store the records of air pollution in an area and sends message to user whenever unhealthy air quality is observed Easy to install system provides real time web-based application that displays pollution data	Real time functionality dependent on the availability of wireless communication for cloud storage Network communication area needs to be explored for wider application
[35]	Cloud	Portable low-cost system proposed for real time monitoring particulate matter with high spatial resolution The system developed produces statistically equal results when compared to existing high-cost stationary monitoring stations	Improvements in data reliability can be done and power consumption of sensor nodes can be reduced Further, street level resolution can be provided such that pollution sources are identified and predictions can be made
[46]	Cloud	An environment monitoring system which uses LoRa (long range) wireless communication technology to facilitate communication over larger area State-of -the-art sensor technologies used to improve sensing reliabilities and extend battery life and reduce system costs	Higher accuracy of sensor data can be achieved by applying machine/deep learning algorithms Distributed architecture can be implemented to further extend the area being monitored

(*continued*)

Table 1. (*continued*)

Study	Cloud/Edge	Objectives/Findings/Contribution	Limitations/Future scope
[34]	Cloud	A cloud-based air quality monitoring system which shows the concentrations of certain pollutants in the surrounding area to the user via a mobile application. Designed for visualising real time data on geographical maps from anywhere in the city	A dedicated cloud server has been deployed for the obtained data; however, more processing can be performed on the data to draw meaning and generate trends instead of just storing the data
[39]	Edge	Reduced computational burden of battery powered sensing nodes up to 70% with edge computing. Data transmission strategies applied to minimize network traffic. Power consumption reduced to up to 23% with minimum cost	Supports only static sensor networks
[38]	Edge-cloud	Real-time pollution monitoring in highly polluted areas on the city by deploying low-cost edge devices with sensors. On location processing done to find out any patterns in air pollution gives contextual information	Some issues related to edge need to be addressed, for e.g., number of IoT devices connected and their power limitations. Restrictions on communication protocols utilized for sending data to the cloud
[41]	Edge	High accuracy, low cost. Real time pollution monitoring and prediction system using edge reducing dependence on cloud. Increased accuracy of pollution sensors by application of Kalman Filter algorithm on edge. Putting machine learning on the edge reduces transmission delay and enhances better decision making	Edge layer designed to be too centralized, hence any disaster can lead to data loss. Early warning mechanism of the edge layer can be improved further by considering external environmental factors

(*continued*)

Table 1. (*continued*)

Study	Cloud/Edge	Objectives/Findings/Contribution	Limitations/Future scope
[43]	Edge-cloud	Air quality monitoring methodology proposed where sensors collect data and transfer to the fog nodes for quick service Non-actionable data is refined at fog nodes and sent to cloud for longer storage (months, years) duration and batch analytics Algorithms applied to decrease network traffic and power consumption	Data worth years of monitoring can be put to use by applying better analytics and visualization techniques to understand the trend of air pollution over the years and make predictions
[37]	Edge-cloud	Combination of edge and cloud computing to develop intelligent air pollution monitoring system Integration of various technologies such as OpenStack, Kubernetes, Docker, and Ceph to implement edge monitoring architectures System collects memory, network information to monitor power consumption	Integrating more open-source software for better edge implementation, for IoT devices Machine learning and deep learning technologies can also be integrated to enhance efficiency of systems
[44]	Edge-cloud	Architecture for both static and mobile sensor networks Basic processing of the data performed at the edge by sensors and more complex processing is carried out at cloud on the aggregated data	Real time statistics can be applied on the aggregated data to make sense out of it for future use
[42]	Edge	A quick responding system to air pollution in remote areas with low bandwidth availability Applies hybrid prediction architecture by implementing machine learning algorithms at the edge to achieve a balance between accuracy and speed Implementing edge helps get a quicker response in areas with poor internet connection	Evaluation prediction performance should be focussed upon Samples of pollution data can be reduced from 8-h format for better prediction Multiple nodes performing local and prediction processing can be deployed for distributed computing

5 Conclusion

The paper explores the use of edge computing paradigm in Internet of Things applications. Edge computing has gained a lot of attention in the recent years due to the benefits it offers in implementation of IoT based systems. In this paper a survey has been conducted on IoT enabled air pollution monitoring systems and it has been found that in the past three to four years, there has been an increase in the number of studies which are relying more on edge computing paradigm due to its ability to address some of the most prevalent problems in existing systems, such as latency concerns, bandwidth costs, IoT devices battery life. A lot of systems still depend on cloud for computing purposes; however, the use of edge has seen an upward trend in the recent years. It has further been observed that in a few studies researchers have suggested the use of hybrid edge-cloud systems to enhance network performances, improve computational capability where edge provides real-time analysis and cloud offers centralized services for large scale analysis. For future work, the aim is to propose a robust real-time edge-cloud assisted air pollution monitoring system for large scale implementation.

References

1. Li, S., Xu, L.D., Zhao, S.: The internet of things: a survey. Inf. Syst. Front. **17**(2), 243–259 (2014). https://doi.org/10.1007/s10796-014-9492-7
2. Sabry, S.S., Qarabash, N.A., Obaid, H.S.: The road to the internet of things: a survey. In: IEMECON 2019 - 9th Annual Information Technology, Electromechanical Engineering and Microelectronics Conference (2019)
3. JabraeilJamali, M.A., Bahrami, B., Heidari, A., Allahverdizadeh, P., Norouzi, F.: IoT architecture. In: JabraeilJamali, M.A., Bahrami, B., Heidari, A., Allahverdizadeh, P., Norouzi, F. (eds.) Towards the Internet of Things. EAI/Springer Innovations in Communication and Computing, pp. 9–31. Springer, Cham (2020). https://doi.org/10.1007/978-3-030-18468-1_2
4. Lee, I., Lee, K.: The internet of things (IoT): applications, investments, and challenges for enterprises. Bus. Horiz. **58** (2015). https://doi.org/10.1016/j.bushor.2015.03.008
5. Immerman, G.: The importance of edge computing for the IoT (2020). https://www.machinemetrics.com/blog/edge-computing-iot. Accessed 12 Sept 2021
6. Patel, K.K., Patel, S.M., Scholar, P.G.: Internet of things-IOT: definition, characteristics, architecture, enabling technologies, application & future challenges. Int. J. Eng. Sci. Comput. **6** (2016). https://doi.org/10.4010/2016.1482
7. GSMA: Opportunities and use cases for edge computing in the IoT (2018). https://www.gsma.com/iot/resources/edge-computing-iot-report/. Accessed 12 Sept 2021
8. Antonopoulos, N., Gillam, L.: Cloud Computing: Principles, Systems and Applications, 2nd edn. Springer, Cham (2017). https://doi.org/10.1007/978-1-84996-241-4
9. IBM: What is edge computing? https://www.ibm.com/in-en/cloud/what-is-edge-computing. Accessed 12 Sept 2021
10. Khan, W.Z., Ahmed, E., Hakak, S., et al.: Edge computing: a survey. Futur. Gener. Comput. Syst. **97**, 219–235 (2019). https://doi.org/10.1016/j.future.2019.02.050
11. Shi, W., Dustdar, S.: The promise of edge computing. Computer **49**, 78–81 (2016). https://doi.org/10.1109/MC.2016.145
12. REDHAT: Why IoT and edge computing need to work together (2021). https://www.redhat.com/en/topics/edge-computing/iot-edge-computing-need-to-work-together. Accessed 12 Sept 2021

13. Gyarmathy, K.: The benefits, potential, and future of edge computing (2021). https://www.vxchnge.com/blog/the-5-best-benefits-of-edge-computing. Accessed 12 Sept 2021
14. Bao, W., Yuan, D., Yang, Z., et al.: Follow me fog: toward seamless handover timing schemes in a fog computing environment. IEEE Commun. Mag. **55**, 72–78 (2017). https://doi.org/10.1109/MCOM.2017.1700363
15. Shaukat, U., Ahmed, E., Anwar, Z., Xia, F.: Cloudlet deployment in local wireless networks: motivation, architectures, applications, and open challenges. J. Netw. Comput. Appl. **62** (2016)
16. Ahmed, E., Rehmani, M.H.: mobile edge computing: opportunities, solutions, and challenges. Future Gener. Comput. Syst. **70** (2017)
17. Naveen, S., Kounte, M.R.: Key technologies and challenges in IoT edge computing. In: Proceedings of the 3rd International Conference on I-SMAC IoT in Social, Mobile, Analytics and Cloud, I-SMAC 2019 (2019)
18. Hassan, N., Gillani, S., Ahmed, E., et al.: The role of edge computing in internet of things. IEEE Commun. Mag. **56**, 110–115 (2018). https://doi.org/10.1109/MCOM.2018.1700906
19. Ren, J., Yu, G., He, Y., Li, G.Y.: Collaborative cloud and edge computing for latency minimization. IEEE Trans. Veh. Technol. **68**, 5031–5044 (2019). https://doi.org/10.1109/TVT.2019.2904244
20. Pan, J., McElhannon, J.: Future edge cloud and edge computing for internet of things applications. IEEE Internet Things J. **5**, 439–449 (2018). https://doi.org/10.1109/JIOT.2017.2767608
21. STL PARTNERS: IoT and edge computing – requirements, benefits and use cases. https://stlpartners.com/edge_computing/iot-and-edge-computing-requirements-benefits-and-use-cases/. Accessed 12 Sept 2021
22. Bonomi, F., Milito, R., Zhu, J., Addepalli, S.: Fog computing and its role in the internet of things. In: MCC 2012 - Proceedings of the 1st ACM Mobile Cloud Computing Workshop (2012)
23. Yu, W., Liang, F., He, X., et al.: A survey on the edge computing for the internet of things. IEEE Access **6** (2017)
24. Bi, Y., Han, G., Lin, C., et al.: Mobility support for fog computing: an SDN approach. IEEE Commun. Mag. **56**, 53–59 (2018). https://doi.org/10.1109/MCOM.2018.1700908
25. Mazhelis, O., Luoma, E., Warma, H.: Defining an internet-of-things ecosystem. In: Andreev, S., Balandin, S., Koucheryavy, Y. (eds.) NEW2AN/ruSMART - 2012. LNCS, vol. 7469, pp. 1–14. Springer, Heidelberg (2012). https://doi.org/10.1007/978-3-642-32686-8_1
26. Premsankar, G., di Francesco, M., Taleb, T.: Edge computing for the internet of things: a case study. IEEE Internet Things J. **5**, 1275–1284 (2018). https://doi.org/10.1109/JIOT.2018.2805263
27. Sittón-Candanedo, I., Alonso, R.S., Rodríguez-González, S., García Coria, J.A., De La Prieta, F.: Edge computing architectures in industry 4.0: a general survey and comparison. In: Martínez Álvarez, F., TroncosoLora, A., SáezMuñoz, J.A., Quintián, H., Corchado, E. (eds.) SOCO 2019. Advances in Intelligent Systems and Computing, vol. 950, pp. 121–131. Springer, Cham (2020). https://doi.org/10.1007/978-3-030-20055-8_12
28. Shi, W., Cao, J., Zhang, Q., et al.: Edge computing: vision and challenges. IEEE Internet Things J. **3**, 637–646 (2016). https://doi.org/10.1109/JIOT.2016.2579198
29. Balakrishnan, K., Dey, S., Gupta, T., et al.: The impact of air pollution on deaths, disease burden, and life expectancy across the states of India: the Global Burden of Disease Study 2017. Lancet Planetary Health **3**, e26–e39 (2019). https://doi.org/10.1016/S2542-5196(18)30261-4
30. Health Effects Institute: State of Global Air 2019. Health Effects Institute (2019). https://www.stateofglobalair.org/sites/default/files/soga_2019_report.pdf
31. WHO: Ambient (outdoor) air pollution (2018). https://www.Who.Int/En/News-Room/Fact-Sheets/Detail/Ambient-(Outdoor)-Air-Quality-and-Health

32. Nagpure, A.S., Gurjar, B.R.: Development and evaluation of vehicular air pollution inventory model. Atmos. Environ. **59**, 160–169 (2012). https://doi.org/10.1016/j.atmosenv.2012.04.044

33. Idrees, Z., Zheng, L.: Low cost air pollution monitoring systems: a review of protocols and enabling technologies. J. Ind. Inf. Integr. **17**, 100123 (2020). https://doi.org/10.1016/j.jii.2019.100123

34. Purkayastha, K.D., Mishra, R.K., Shil, A., Pradhan, S.N.: IoT based design of air quality monitoring system web server for android platform. Wirel. Pers. Commun. **118**(4), 2921–2940 (2021). https://doi.org/10.1007/s11277-021-08162-3

35. İçöz, E., Malik, F.M., İçöz, K.: High spatial resolution IoT based air PM measurement system. Environ. Ecol. Stat. **28**(4), 779–792 (2021). https://doi.org/10.1007/s10651-021-00494-4

36. Kumar, S., Jasuja, A.: Air quality monitoring system based on IoT using Raspberry Pi. In: Proceeding - IEEE International Conference on Computing, Communication and Automation, ICCCA 2017 (2017)

37. Kristiani, E., Yang, C.-T., Huang, C.-Y., Wang, Y.-T., Ko, P.-C.: The implementation of a cloud-edge computing architecture using openstack and kubernetes for air quality monitoring application. Mob. Netw. Appl. **26**(3), 1070–1092 (2020). https://doi.org/10.1007/s11036-020-01620-5

38. Biondi, K., Al-Masri, E., Baiocchi, O., et al.: Air pollution detection system using edge computing. In: International Conference in Engineering Applications (ICEA), Sao Miguel, Portugal 2019, pp. 1–6 (2019)

39. Idrees, Z., Zou, Z., Zheng, L.: Edge computing based IoT architecture for low cost air pollution monitoring systems: a comprehensive system analysis, design considerations & development. Sensors (Switzerland) **18**, 3021 (2018). https://doi.org/10.3390/s18093021

40. Mokrani, H., Lounas, R., Bennai, M.T., et al.: Air quality monitoring using IoT: a survey. In: Proceedings - 2019 IEEE International Conference on Smart Internet of Things, SmartIoT 2019 (2019)

41. Lai, X., Yang, T., Wang, Z., Chen, P.: IoT implementation of Kalman filter to improve accuracy of air quality monitoring and prediction. Appl. Sci. (Switzerland) **9**, 1831 (2019). https://doi.org/10.3390/app9091831

42. Moursi, A.S., El Fishawy, N., Djahel, S., Shouman, M.A.: An IoT enabled system for enhanced air quality monitoring and prediction on the edge. Compl. Intell. Syst. **7**(6), 2923–2947 (2021). https://doi.org/10.1007/s40747-021-00476-w

43. Senthilkumar, R., Venkatakrishnan, P., Balaji, N.: Intelligent based novel embedded system based IoT enabled air pollution monitoring system. Microprocess. Microsyst. **77**, 103172 (2020). https://doi.org/10.1016/j.micpro.2020.103172

44. Kalajdjieski, J., Stojkoska, B.R., Trivodaliev, K.: IoT based framework for air pollution monitoring in smart cities. In: 2020 28th Telecommunications Forum, TELFOR 2020 - Proceedings. Institute of Electrical and Electronics Engineers Inc. (2020)

45. Azma Zakaria, N., Zainal Abidin, Z., Harum, N., et al.: Wireless internet of things-based air quality device for smart pollution monitoring (2018)

46. Truong, T.P., Nguyen, D.T., Truong, P.V.: Design and deployment of an IoT-based air quality monitoring system. Int. J. Environ. Sci. Dev. **12**, 139–145 (2021). https://doi.org/10.18178/IJESD.2021.12.5.1331

Capsule Network Based Speech Emotion Recognition for Efficient Capturing of Spatial Features

Yalamanchili Bhanusree[1]([✉]), Ummenthala Srimanth Reddy[2], Gunuganti Jeshmitha[3], Dontha Bharadwaj[4], and Kalva Sravani[5]

[1] Department of CSE, VNRVJIET, Hyderabad, India
bhanusree_y@vnrvjiet.in
[2] ServiceNow Software Development India Pvt Ltd, Hyderabad, India
[3] MS Computer Science, University of Cincinnati, Cincinnati, USA
[4] JP Morgan Chase Services India Pvt Ltd, Hyderabad, India
[5] Metricstream Infotech India Private Limited, Hyderabad, India

Abstract. Speech Emotion Recognition aims at perceiving the hidden emotional state of an individual from their speech signals, regardless of the semantic content. This paper presents deep learning techniques to classify emotions. Audio recordings from the IEMOCAP (Interactive Emotional Dyadic Motion Capture) Dataset and RAVDESS (Ryerson audio-visual dataset of emotional speech and songs) are used as speech signals. MFCC (Mel Frequency Cepstral Coefficients) features are extracted from speech signals and used as input features for training the deep learning models. Models such as CNN, LSTM are generally a better fit in performing tasks like emotion recognition. However, considering the spatial features of audio will better predict the emotion which can be achieved using CapsuleNets. On comparing the CNN-LSTM model with CapsuleNets and evaluating them using metrics such as accuracy, precision, recall, and F1-score on IEMOCAP and RAVDESS datasets, CapsuleNets attained an accuracy of 94.01 & 84.2 respectively. Additionally, Loss and Accuracy curves are analyzed to understand the learning performance of models over time.

Keywords: Speech emotion recognition · CapsuleNets · CNN · LSTM · Spatial features · MFCC

1 Introduction

Signal processing techniques have enabled systems to reply to people via speech signals, but their inability to identify the emotional state remains to be a concern. Thus, Emotion Recognition emerged as an active field of research to promote human-machine interaction.

Speech emotion recognition is a system that uses speech signals to interpret emotions. One of the most natural means for humans to convey their emotions is through speech. Variations in the autonomic nervous system can impact a person's voice in an indirect

© Springer Nature Switzerland AG 2022
A. K. Luhach et al. (Eds.): ICAICR 2021, CCIS 1575, pp. 257–268, 2022.
https://doi.org/10.1007/978-3-031-09469-9_22

manner, and technology can use this data to discern emotion. This technology i.e., Speech emotion recognition can be utilized in a variety of areas. For example, it can assist call center agents in perceiving emotions of their customers. Also, most of the youth are suffering from emotional distress, causing suicides. Speech emotion recognition allows us to recognize an individual's emotional state and thereby take appropriate action [16].

Interpreting emotion through speech signals is a challenging task as it involves diverse languages, contexts, accents and sometimes humans might exhibit multiple emotions in the same speech signal [17]. Another issue with speech emotion recognition is determining input features that would best reflect the underlying emotional state. Speech signals comprise numerous frequencies associated aspects that are spectral features, out of which MFCCs (Mel Frequency Cepstral Coefficients) are usually utilized in speech emotion recognition with remarkable accuracy [18].

In this study, proposed models include CNN-LSTM and CapsuleNets. This blend of CNN and LSTM is particularly effective since it incorporates capabilities of both neural networks. However, CNN is unaffected by spatial or orientational information. Recently, CapsuleNets have been recognized to address the limitation of CNNs in capturing spatial features [19]. Therefore, comparing these two models allows us to select a suitable architecture for performing speech emotion recognition.

The rest of the paper is organized as follows: Sect. 2 discusses similar research works; Sect. 3 describes the datasets used. Section 4 explains the methodology, implementation, results and offers a comparative study. Section 5 summarizes the research work and presents the future scope.

2   Literature Review

CNN is capable of modelling two-dimensional inputs such as voice and picture well which are difficult to describe adequately using conventional models such as SVM. It presents a comparison of CNN with SVM, with SVM serving as the base model. Anger, sadness, fear, surprise, and happiness are five emotions that are identified. SVM has a 94.17% accuracy and CNN has a 95.5% accuracy in image recognition where CNN gave better accuracy comparatively and required less time [1]. Excitation parameters such as immediate fundamental frequency, excitation intensity, and excitation energy of speech were taken into consideration for calculating Kullback-Leibler distance which determines deviations between neutral and emotional speech on IIIT-H and EMO-DB database. Kullback-Leibler distance is used to compare the correlation between neutral and emotional feature patterns [2]. CNN and LSTM were integrated to develop a novel spontaneous SER technique and AFEW 5.0 and BAUM-datasets were used for evaluating the implemented model. CNN model is used to generate high-level segment characteristics from image-like spectrograms, and these are used to model long-term temporal dependency by LSTM [3]. The K-means algorithm is used to choose an optimal speech pattern, which uses the STFT algorithm to convert into spectrograms. Using Resnet, discriminative and significant features are extracted from spectrograms of speech signals, normalized them, and input them into BiLSTM to discover hidden patterns, detect the end state of pattern, and identify the emotional state. Standard Datasets such as IEMOCAP, EMO-DB, and RAVDESS which achieved accuracies of 72.25%,

85.57%, 77.02%. respectively were used for determining the model's reliability [4]. Novel approach for recognizing emotional states is developed, which is based on deep and acoustic features. spectrograms and acoustic features are retrieved from speech signals, and deep features are extracted from the retrieved images of spectrogram using six popular CNN Algorithms: ResNet50, VGG16, ResNet101, ResNet18, DenseNet201, and Squeeze Net. ReliefF can be utilized to identify features from a hybrid vector space composed of deep and acoustic features. This model is then tested on the IEMOCAP, RAVDESS, and EMO-DB datasets using SVM for classification and accuracies achieved by IEMOCAP, RAVDESS, and EMO-DB datasets were 79.41%, 90.21%and 85.37% [5]. Multiple CNNs are utilized to learn deep segment level binaural interpretations from the Mel spectrograms which are extracted images. Block based temporal feature pooling technique is introduced for combining learnt segment-level characteristics into fixed length utterance-level features and these features served as the basis for using SVM for emotion recognition. Experiments on the AFEW 5.0 and BAUM-1s datasets were used to assess the model's efficiency [6].

A speaker and text independent emotion identification system is developed to recognize emotions using a novel technique which is a combination of a Gaussian mixture and deep neural network model. On the "Emirati speech database," this novel classifier was tested for emotion identification with different emotions. The performance of this classifier which has achieved an accuracy of 83.7% has been compared to support vector machines and multilayer perceptron classifiers which achieved accuracies of 80.33% and 69.78% respectively [7]. Deep Learning is a relatively latest study domain in machine learning that has received a lot of focus in recent years. Deep learning approaches for SER provide a lot of benefits, such as the capacity to identify complicated structures and features without requiring feature extraction and optimization manually. The categorization of various environmental emotions such as happy, joy, sorrow, neutral, boredom, disgust, surprise and fear are used to illustrate these deep learning approaches and associated layer-wise structures. Deep learning approaches have several drawbacks, including a complex layer-wise internal structure, lower accuracy for dynamically changing input data [8]. CNN is recognized as the better model compared to various other models. The proposed model distinguishes between a female and male voice and recognizes various emotions such as sad, neutral state, happy, surprise, anger etc. It obtained an accuracy of 71% [9]. Features of speech such as Zero crossing rate, Fundamental frequency, MFCC, Linear Predictive Coding are considered to classify the emotion. SVM model is applied and is evaluated on three different linguistic databases namely Japan, Thai, Berlin databases [10]. This study [11] gives an overview of various methods used to extract audio features from a particular speech sample and different classifiers like SVM, HMM (Hidden Markov Model), KNN (K-Nearest Neighbors), AdaBoost Algorithm whose accuracy depends on the classification algorithm used, combination of features extracted, and speech database used. This paper [12] takes in each audio file from Berlin Database, that were split into 20 ms audio segments and each of these were used to train the deep neural network which is optimized using Stochastic Gradient Descent. The model classifies the audio samples into 3 classes namely sad, neutral, angry. A study on SER using CNN [13] for which spectrograms were fed as input obtained from Berlin emotions dataset. The model classifies the speech into seven distinct emotions. Also, a pre-trained AlexNet model was used to assess the efficiency of transfer learning. Another experiment done as a part of this study compares finely tuned models and freshly trained models.

3 Dataset

In this paper, RAVDESS (Ryerson audio-visual dataset of emotional speech and songs) and IEMOCAP (Interactive emotional dyadic motion capture dataset) are used. The description of these datasets are as follows.

3.1 IEMOCAP

The IEMOCAP dataset [14] contains two kinds of dialogues: improvised and scripted and is often used for emotion recognition by speech. The audiovisual data set contains 12 h of audio, speech, facial motion, videos, and text transcriptions. Each session in the dataset has two actors (one female and one male) recording a script that depicts emotion which is 3–15 s long and has a sample rate of 16 kHz. There are five such sessions. Surprise, sad, anger, neutral, happy, excited, frustrated, fearful and disgusting emotions are classified in each session and annotated by three experts. Pronunciations that two experts agreed on after individually labelling the data are used. It compares the system to happiness, neutral, anger and sadness emotions, which are commonly utilized in the literature (Table 1).

Table 1. Frequencies and percentage of participation of each emotion in IEMOCAP database.

Emotion	Frequency	Percentage of participation (%)
Happy	1636	29.58
Anger	1103	19.94
Sad	1084	19.6
Neutral	1708	30.88

3.2 RAVDESS

The RAVDESS dataset [15] is an enacted dataset which is widely utilized for dialog reactions and expressive music. The dataset consists of 24 actors (12 female and 12 male) exhibiting 8 emotions namely: Surprise, sad, anger, neutral, happy, fearful and disgusting with 60 trials per each actor. There are 1440 audio files in total: 60 trials per actor × 24 actors = 1440 with 48000 Hz sampling rate (Table 2).

Table 2. Frequencies and percentage of participation of each emotion in RAVDESS database.

Emotion	Frequency	Percentage of participation (%)
Happy	192	13.33
Sadness	192	13.33
Neutral	96	6.667
Anger	192	13.33
Fear	192	13.33
Surprise	192	13.33
Disgust	192	13.33

4 Proposed Methodology

4.1 Implementation

4.1.1 Combination of CNN and LSTM

The Long Short-Term Memory (LSTM) network is possibly the most successful RNN (Recurrent Neural Network) because it conquers the challenges of training a recurrent network and is being used on a wide range of applications. LSTMs and RNNs in general have been successful with NLP (natural language processing) (Fig. 1).

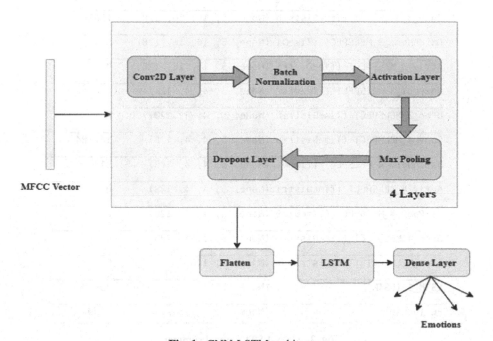

Fig. 1. CNN-LSTM architecture

This includes patterns of speech, text and patterns of language represented in the form of time series. For LSTMs, to derive insights from high-dimensional data is a tedious task. Convolutional Neural Networks (CNNs) are handy in bringing down the dimensionality

Layer (type)	Output Shape	Param #
Input_MELSPECT (InputLayer)	[(None, 5, 128, 128, 1)]	0
Conv_1_MELSPECT (TimeDistrib	(None, 5, 128, 128, 64)	640
BatchNorm_1_MELSPECT (TimeDi	(None, 5, 128, 128, 64)	256
Activ_1_MELSPECT (TimeDistri	(None, 5, 128, 128, 64)	0
MaxPool_1_MELSPECT (TimeDist	(None, 5, 64, 64, 64)	0
Drop_1_MELSPECT (TimeDistrib	(None, 5, 64, 64, 64)	0
Conv_2_MELSPECT (TimeDistrib	(None, 5, 64, 64, 64)	36928
BatchNorm_2_MELSPECT (TimeDi	(None, 5, 64, 64, 64)	256
Activ_2_MELSPECT (TimeDistri	(None, 5, 64, 64, 64)	0
MaxPool_2_MELSPECT (TimeDist	(None, 5, 16, 16, 64)	0
Drop_2_MELSPECT (TimeDistrib	(None, 5, 16, 16, 64)	0
Conv_3_MELSPECT (TimeDistrib	(None, 5, 16, 16, 128)	73856
BatchNorm_3_MELSPECT (TimeDi	(None, 5, 16, 16, 128)	512
Activ_3_MELSPECT (TimeDistri	(None, 5, 16, 16, 128)	0
MaxPool_3_MELSPECT (TimeDist	(None, 5, 4, 4, 128)	0
Drop_3_MELSPECT (TimeDistrib	(None, 5, 4, 4, 128)	0
Conv_4_MELSPECT (TimeDistrib	(None, 5, 4, 4, 128)	147584
BatchNorm_4_MELSPECT (TimeDi	(None, 5, 4, 4, 128)	512
Activ_4_MELSPECT (TimeDistri	(None, 5, 4, 4, 128)	0
MaxPool_4_MELSPECT (TimeDist	(None, 5, 1, 1, 128)	0
Drop_4_MELSPECT (TimeDistrib	(None, 5, 1, 1, 128)	0
Flat_MELSPECT (TimeDistribut	(None, 5, 128)	0
LSTM_1 (LSTM)	(None, 256)	394240
FC (Dense)	(None, 7)	1799

Fig. 2. CNN-LSTM model summary

by retaining the important features. The suggested model is a combination of CNNs and LSTM.

This model (Fig. 2) constitutes four convolution layers with ELU (Exponential linear unit) as the activation function which helps to bring down the dimensionality followed by an LSTM network. The dimension of the input is 128 × 128 x 1. The convolution layers in front of the CNN's fully linked layers are sliced and appended to a 256-cell LSTM layer. As a result, following the convolutional portion, the 128 × 128 × 1 input is scaled to a 128 × 1 feature vector and finally passed on to layers of LSTM. The LSTM output is fed to the Dense layer with SoftMax as an activation function giving out the predicted emotion as the output label.

4.1.2 CapsNet

Viewpoint invariance can be attained in the activities of neurons, a capsule is a better depiction of neurons than convolution. Capsule Networks (CapsNet) are networks that can retrieve spatial information and other key properties in order to avoid data loss during pooling operations. A vector is produced by a capsule which represents a generalized related attribute, whereas a neuron produces a scalar. A capsule tries to capture many characteristics of an object inside an image, such as velocity, position, texture, size, deformation, angle of view and so on, in order to determine the likelihood of the existing entity. When compared to ConvNets, CapsuleNets need less data to train.

In this model, the input is fed into a conventional Convolution layer followed by the primary capsule Layer (Conv2D layer with "squash" as activation function which is represented as Equations below where c_{ij} are coupling coefficients and transformation matrix being w_{ij}).

$$v_j = \frac{\|s_j\|^2}{1 + \|s_j\|^2} \frac{s_j}{\|s_j\|} \tag{1}$$

$$s_j - \sum_i c_{ij} \hat{u}_{j|i}, \hat{u}_{j|i} - w_{ij} u_i \tag{2}$$

The Primary capsule layer is connected to the digit capsule layer where the dynamic routing between the capsules happens(routing-by-agreement). During training, the decoder receives the output of the digit capsule layer, which is masked with the original labels. That is, all vectors except the one corresponding to the correct label will be multiplied by zero. Thus, only the correct digit capsule can be used to train the decoder. The same output from the digit capsule layer will be fed into the decoder during testing, but it will be masked with the longest vector in that layer (Figs. 3 and 4).

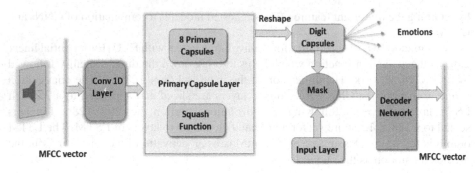

Fig. 3. CapsNet architecture

Layer (type)	Output Shape	Param #	Connected to
input_1 (InputLayer)	[(None, 58, 1)]	0	
conv1 (Conv1D)	(None, 50, 128)	1280	input_1[0][0]
primarycap_conv2d (Conv1D)	(None, 21, 256)	295168	conv1[0][0]
primarycap_reshape (Reshape)	(None, 672, 8)	0	primarycap_conv2d[0][0]
primarycap_squash (Lambda)	(None, 672, 8)	0	primarycap_reshape[0][0]
digitcaps (CapsuleLayer)	(None, 4, 16)	344064	primarycap_squash[0][0]
input_2 (InputLayer)	[(None, 4)]	0	
mask (Mask)	(None, None)	0	digitcaps[0][0] input_2[0][0]
capsnet (Length)	(None, 4)	0	digitcaps[0][0]
decoder (Sequential)	(None, 58, 1)	3770	mask[0][0]

Fig. 4. CapsNet model summary

4.2 Comparative Analysis

This section presents a comparative analysis between CapsNet and CNN-LSTM. Each model is trained and tested on IEMOCAP and RAVDESS dataset. Among the models CapsNet has achieved higher accuracy i.e., 94.01%, 84.2% on IEMOCAP, RAVDESS datasets respectively. However, the CNN-LSTM model has proved to be less accurate with 63.94%, 62.02% on IEMOCAP, RAVDESS datasets respectively. F1-score being a descriptor for both precision and recall tells us that the CapsNet model is substantially better than CNN-LSTM (Fig. 5 and Table 3).

Table. 3. The performances of proposed models for SER with IEMOCAP and RAVDESS datasets.

Model/Metric	Dataset	Accuracy	Precision	Recall	F1-score
CapsNet	IEMOCAP	94.01	95.75	98.1	96.91
CNN-LSTM	IEMOCAP	63.94	82.48	79.91	77.48
CapsNet	RAVDESS	84.2	83.65	85.31	84.47
CNN-LSTM	RAVDESS	62.02	59.55	56.3	57.88

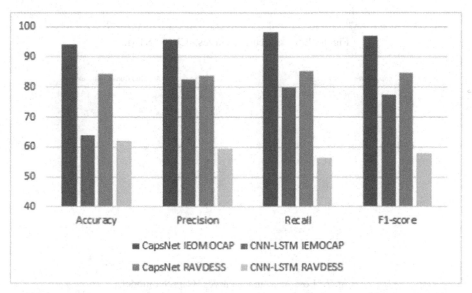

Fig. 5. Comparison of proposed models with existing models on RAVDESS and IEMOCAP datasets.

4.3 Results

A model is said to be good fit if the training loss plot declines until it reaches a point of equilibrium and the validation loss plot reaches a point of steadiness, with a tiny gap between it and the training loss.

On comparing the results from both the models, the CapsNet model performed better in comparison to the CNN-LSTM model, with the increase in epochs the CapsNet model validation loss curve tends to approach training loss curve in a steady fashion. On the other hand, CNN-LSTM model is not as stable as the CapsNet model in all aspects (Figs. 6 and 7).

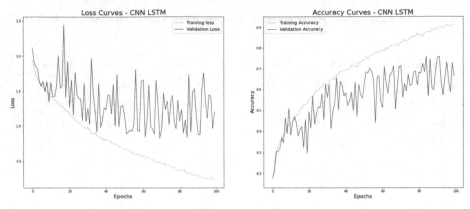

Fig. 6. Loss & accuracy curves - CNN-LSTM.

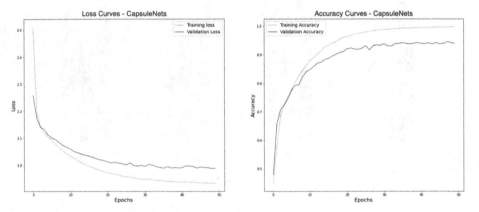

Fig. 7. Loss & accuracy curves -CapsNet model.

5 Conclusion and Future Scope

In this research, CNN LSTM and CapsuleNets models are implemented to predict the emotion of an individual from their speech data with an accuracy of 84.20 and 94.01 using the RAVDESS and IEMOCAP datasets respectively. As CapsuleNets have achieved state-of-art performance over Image data, it out-performed traditional models considering the impact of Spatial features in Speech data as well. This prediction analysis can assist individuals in analyzing their emotional state using their voice input. This CapsNet model is consistent in performing better over the other models despite the nuances in the dataset. CapsuleNets are potential in handling the realistic data with higher accuracy.

This approach may be applied to several situations, including customer service and marketing contact centers, voice-based virtual assistants or chatbots, and linguistic research. An accurate implementation of the speech pace can be investigated to see if it can assist the model perform better. In some circumstances, the display of emotion is contextual rather than vocal, so taking a lexical features-based approach to SER and combining an ensemble of lexical and acoustic models will increase the system's accuracy.

References

1. Zhang, B., Quan, C., Ren, F.: Study on CNN in the recognition of emotion in audio and images. In: 2016 IEEE/ACIS 15th International Conference on Computer and Information Science (ICIS), pp. 1–5. IEEE, June 2016
2. Kadiri, S.R., Alku, P.: Excitation features of speech for speaker-specific emotion detection. IEEE Access **8**, 60382–60391 (2020)
3. Zhang, S., Zhao, X., Tian, Q.: Spontaneous speech emotion recognition using multiscale deep convolutional LSTM. IEEE Trans. Affect. Comput. (2019)
4. Sajjad, M., Kwon, S.: Clustering-based speech emotion recognition by incorporating learned features and deep BiLSTM. IEEE Access **8**, 79861–79875 (2020)
5. Er, M.B.: A novel approach for classification of speech emotions based on deep and acoustic features. IEEE Access **8**, 221640–221653 (2020)
6. Zhang, S., Chen, A., Guo, W., Cui, Y., Zhao, X., Liu, L.: Learning deep binaural representations with deep convolutional neural networks for spontaneous speech emotion recognition. IEEE Access **8**, 23496–23505 (2020)
7. Shahin, I., Nassif, A.B., Hamsa, S.: Emotion recognition using hybrid Gaussian mixture model and deep neural network. IEEE access **7**, 26777–26787 (2019)
8. Khalil, R.A., Jones, E., Babar, M.I., Jan, T., Zafar, M.H., Alhussain, T.: Speech emotion recognition using deep learning techniques: a review. IEEE Access **7**, 117327–117345 (2019)
9. Huang, Z., Dong, M., Mao, Q., Zhan, Y.: Speech emotion recognition using CNN. In: Proceedings of the 22nd ACM International Conference on Multimedia, pp. 801–804, November 2014
10. Seehapoch, T., Wongthanavasu, S.: Speech emotion recognition using support vector machines. In: 2013 5th International Conference on Knowledge and Smart Technology (KST), pp. 86–91. IEEE, January 2013
11. Joshi, A., Kaur, R.: A study of speech emotion recognition methods. Int. J. Comput. Sci. Mob. Comput. (IJCSMC) **2**(4), 28–31 (2013)
12. Harár, P., Burget, R., Dutta, M.K.: Speech emotion recognition with deep learning. In: 2017 4th International Conference on Signal Processing and Integrated Networks (SPIN), pp. 137–140. IEEE, February 2017
13. Badshah, A.M., Ahmad, J., Rahim, N., Baik, S.W.: Speech emotion recognition from spectrograms with deep convolutional neural network. In: 2017 International Conference on Platform Technology and Service (PlatCon), pp. 1–5. IEEE, February 2017
14. Busso, C., et al.: IEMOCAP: interactive emotional dyadic motion capture database. Lang. Resour. Eval. **42**(4), 335–359 (2008)
15. Livingstone, S.R., Russo, F.A.: The Ryerson audio-visual database of emotional speech and song (Ravdess): a dynamic, multimodal set of facial and vocal expressions in North American English. PLoS ONE **13**(5) (2018)
16. Yoon, W.-J., Park, K.-S.: A study of emotion recognition and its applications. In: Torra, V., Narukawa, Y., Yoshida, Y. (eds.) MDAI 2007. LNCS (LNAI), vol. 4617, pp. 455–462. Springer, Heidelberg (2007). https://doi.org/10.1007/978-3-540-73729-2_43
17. Byun, S.W., Lee, S.P.: A study on a speech emotion recognition system with effective acoustic features using deep learning algorithms. Appl. Sci. **11**(4), 1890 (2021)

18. Wanli, Z., Guoxin, L.: The research of feature extraction based on MFCC for speaker recognition. In: Proceedings of 2013 3rd International Conference on Computer Science and Network Technology, pp. 1074–1077. IEEE, October 2013
19. Deka, J.: Image captioning: capsule network vs CNN approach. Doctoral dissertation, Dublin, National College of Ireland (2020)

Application of IoT in 5G Wireless Communication: A Detailed Review

Bharti Bhardwaj, Vanita, and Suresh Kumar(✉)

University Institute of Engineering and Technology, MD University, Rohtak, Haryana, India
sureshvashist.uiet.ece@mdurohtak.ac.in

Abstract. Internet Of Things (IoT) based wireless technologies have gained a lot of popularity recently all around the world and 5G technology has emerged as a particularly difficult and intriguing research field. This article examines 5th Generation (5G) wireless technologies based on IoT. Internet in 5G is the coming future. Cutting-edge Wi-Fi infrastructure and automation will be enabled by this. Recent cellular networks, such as LTE, will be insufficient or inefficient in meeting the needs of connection to more than one devices with higherrate of data transmission, increased capacity, and lower latency. High-quality service with minimal disruption. 5G technology is the most promising solution to these all issues. This paper gives an in-depth study of the obstacles and future objectives of several communication businesses in the context of 5G. Many features of 5G systems are thoroughly discussed and examines in depth emerging and enabling technologies, which enables the IoT. Control techniques, wider area with low power networks and security considerations are also considered. This paper discusses the role of augmented reality in the 5G future. It also goes into details of IoT application areas in 5G.

Keywords: IoT · Wireless sensor network · 5G system · Security · LTE

1 Introduction

IoT is a system in which physical objects-gadgets are connected to each other and can be remotely controlled. Here vehicles, different structureshaving hardware, programmable sensors and system connected tonetworks are involved. All this helps to collect and analyse information. The IoT allows items to be sensed and give access to control them at a remote location across connected system foundation, making them available for more reconciliation of physical things into digital based infrastructures and giving better proficiency, accuracy, precision at lower costs [1].

1.1 Basics of IoT

Devices containing sensors, computer power, software, and other technologies are referred to as IoT. These devices may connect with one another through the Internet or another communication network. IoT is now being used in 5G system research. In

© Springer Nature Switzerland AG 2022
A. K. Luhach et al. (Eds.): ICAICR 2021, CCIS 1575, pp. 269–279, 2022.
https://doi.org/10.1007/978-3-031-09469-9_23

this study, a wireless sensor network was analyzed in order to make decisions based on a trained network. In order to create a dependable and adaptable solution for 5G wireless system, the study employs wireless network model for 5G system in the current IoT system [2, 3]. The main constituents of IOT are shown below in Fig. 1.

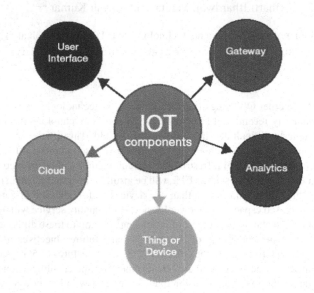

Fig. 1. Major components of IoT

1.2 Need of IoT

Sensors and other IoT devices are most often utilized in the industrial, transportation, and utility sectors. They have also found uses in agriculture, infrastructure, and home automation, contributing to the digital transformation of certain organizations [4]. Secure and pleasant environment is the goal of IoT [5]. This aspires to connect every possible object to the internet, as much as feasible, the IoT links us all.The various networks connected via IoT are shown in Fig. 2.

Embedded computer equipment would be affected by the internet. A recent developed universe of Information Technology (IT) has been created by IoT. In the server room, PCs, and PDAs, data mechanization has not slowed down. Currently, it can be found in every object around us. The vast majorities of the devices we use every day are either now linked or will be in the near future. Many different types of valuable data will be available for them to discover and sell with the help of technologically smart program. The use of media, databases, and apps in our daily lives is becoming more pervasive. Our lives will be covered in a type of technological net or skin as a result. Unexpectedly one may even claim, "No Net, No Planet.

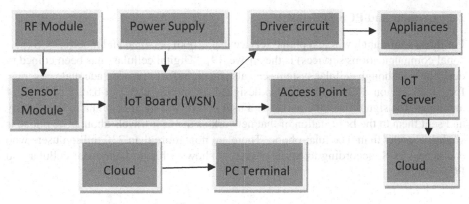

Fig. 2. IoT with network

1.3 Sensor Network Using Wireless Systems

Sensor network with wireless systems or WSN is a network that are scattered over a large area and monitor and record environmental parameters before transferring data to central point [6]. Humidity, wind speed, and temperature and direction are just a few of the variables that WSNs can track. A network of sensors that collect and transfer data on physical or environmental components like sound pressure, motion velocity, or pollutants to a central location is characterized as a self-configured and infrastructure-free wireless sensor network.

Sensors with built-in Wi-Fi may keep tabs on a variety of environmental parameters and relay that data to a central location for analysis [7]. WSNs may be used to collect data on environmental parameters as noise levels, pollution levels, humidity levels, and wind speeds.

2 Applications of 5G in Various Wireless Systems

2.1 Terrestrial Microwave

Wireless microwave networking technique, terrestrial microwave employs line-of-sight communication between transmitters and receivers which are on earth using 5G network [8]. For cost reasons, microwave transmitter and receivers are often located far above the earth on towers or mountaintops.terrestrial microwave link is shown in Fig. 3.

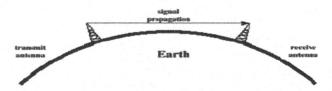

Fig. 3. Terrestrial microwave

In order to transfer data, pairs of Earth-based transmitters and receivers employ line-of-sight communications to establish a terrestrial microwave network.

2.2 Cellular and PCS Systems

For those who want a wireless phone service that is both personal and mobile, PCS (personal communications services) is the answer [9]. "Digital cellular" has been coined to describe it (although cellular systems can also be digital). To provide adequate coverage for a large region, PCS, which is also designed for mobile users, utilises a plethora of antennae. The signal from the phone of a user is received by an antenna in the vicinity and sent them to the base station of that network as the user travels about. The phone is slightly smaller than a cellular phone. There are now more than 230 million users who can access PCS, according to Sprint. Figure 4 shows a block diagram of cellular and PCS systems.

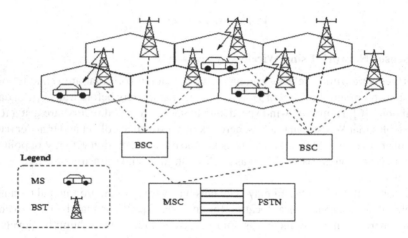

Fig. 4. Cellular & PCS systems

2.3 Radio and Spread Spectrum Technologies

Telecommunications and communication using radio frequenciesuses techniques of spreading a signal with a given bandwidth in the frequency domain, creating a signal with a broader bandwidth [10, 11]. Thus signal structure resembling noise is used to widened a low band signal on a wide frequency band in a spread spectrum approach as shown in Fig. 5.

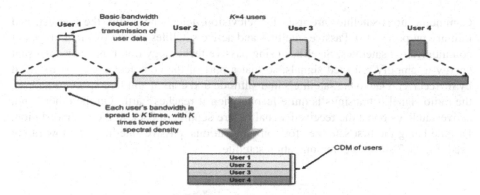

Fig. 5. Radio & spread spectrum technologies

2.4   Free Space Optical (FSO) Communication

Data may be sent wirelessly across long distances using a modulated optical beam aimed towards free space, without the need of conventional optical technologies such as fibre optics. Light (or smoke) signals were employed in ancient times to communicate information [12]. Infrared laser light can be used to build point-to-point optical communications in free space, but LEDs can also be used for low-data-rate communication over short distances [13]. Communications between spacecraft can be made using free-space optics depicted below in Fig. 6.

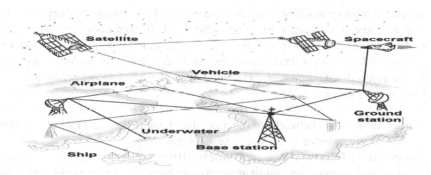

Fig. 6. Free space optical communication

This type of free-space optical communication is known as Infrared Data Association (IrDA). When it comes to optical wireless communications applications, FSO technology is included [14].

2.5   Communication Satellite

One kind of communications satellite is a transponder-based artificial satellite that transmits data from a remote transmitter to a receiver located in another part of the world.

Communications satellites are used for television, telephone, radio, the internet, and military purposes [15]. Passive satellites and active satellites are the two main types of communication satellites. Satellites using passive technology don't use their own sent energy to amplify reflected signals, so that a part of the complete energy is received by thereceiver. Due to the satellite's high altitude and consequent free-space route loss, the radio signal it transmits is quite feeble when it reaches Earth. On the other hand, active satellites boost the received signal before sending it back to the ground station. Despite being the first satellites for communications, passive satellites are now rarely used. Figure 7 shows a communication satellite.

Fig. 7. Communication satellite

3   Challenges and Vision oF 5G IoT

As cellular technology has progressed over the years, it has become more common. Since 1G was introduced, there have been a number of challenges in design of physical & network layers and the areas in which they are used. In light of all of these issues with current networks, 5G has ushered in a major shift in wireless technologybased on IoT [16]. The research difficulties on 5G technology, according to the study, are mostly focused on the following topics.

- In order for real-time networks to function, data must be sent at a rate of 110 GBPS, which is ten times faster than existing technology.
- As opposed to LTE networks, latency must be 10 times lower in order for it to function.
- Using MIMO antennas and millimetre wave technology, 5G networks may achieve high bandwidth and spectrum efficiency, while cognitive radio allows users to access both licenced and unlicensed spectrum bands, respectively [17].
- Forlow-cost sensors and devices, as well as low-cost deployment, should be part of IoT.
- As technology improves so will the amount of power it consumes, demanding greater battery storage and backup.
- Energy usage in 5G networks, which are capable of massive connections and high data speeds, might fall by over 90% if green technologies are adopted [18].

    Wireless communication firms and academic institutions are launching & collaborating, research initiatives in many areas of 5G in response to the seven primary concerns listed above. 5G wireless technology is expected to be widely available by 2025 thanks to research and field testing by some of the world's major cellular, semiconductor, and service companies. At a number of world-class research organizations, 5G research and experimentation is taking place. Long-distance communication, longer battery life, the capacity to talk to billions of devices, and faster internet speeds are all anticipated to be satisfied by new cellular technology advances. IoT in a 5G framework has the potential to be most transformative technology in information technology industry, according to experts. 5G technology is expected to be widely available by 2025, a study has shown.

4 Latest Research Work

An in-depth talk by Ali A. Zaidi was given on the aspects of NR OFDM numerology that are required for eMBB, IoT, and MBSFN. The 3rd Generation Partnership Project is presently standardising NR (3GPP). It has been authorised using 3GPP in NR physical layer architecture to accommodate a wide range of situations and deployments.

His presentation at the Mobile World Congress focused on the impact of PTM on 5G network slicing, which allows for network resources to be dynamically adjusted accommodatingvarious services while considering user density.It is possible that 5G PTM broadcasts may be designed to break with the present paradigm of 4G Long Term Evolution, where firstly PTMbroadcast transmissions were planned as an additional and pre-positioned service.

Morteza Hashemi presented a mmWave design operating at less than 6 GHz. Our technology takes advantage of the spatial correlations between the mmWave and sub-6 GHz interfaces for beamforming and data transfer. Because of spatial correlations with the sub-6 GHz frequency region, our extensive tests in both indoor and outdoor environments show that analogue beamforming may be implemented in mmWave without incurring a substantial overhead [19].

By using 5G millimetre wave installations, Dmitrii Solomitckii claims that amateur drones might be tracked We believe that the projected 5G infrastructure contains all of the components essential for drone monitoring and identification. It's consequently important to consider density of base stations as well as their directional antennae & available bandwidth when designing new technologies and systems. Our ray-based modelling techniques are used to quantify the effects of these variables [20].

LTE, which uses OFDM for synchronous communication, and machinetype DUE, which use a different waveform when executing asynchronously, were the focus of Conor Sextan's study. In the synchronous OFDM case, offset-QAM achieves an average rate marginally higher than the baseline case and around 43% higher than the asynchronous OFDM situation [21].

Specifically, Godfrey A. Akpakwu focused on 5G mobile networks, which are predicted to manage exponential traffic growth and allow the Internet of Things, in a thorough analysis of emerging. When developing a context-aware congestion management mechanism, the constraints & open research paths relevant to deployment of large-scale to crucial IoT applications are also highlighted [22].

To help people better comprehend the current stage of IoT development, Jie Lin gave a discussion. Also, it studies the relationships between IoT and fog/edge computing, as well as the difficulties related to this type of IoT. Cyber-physical systems and IoT play a crucial role in achieving an intelligent cyber-physical world, which is the focus of this research study. This is followed by a discussion of the current state-of-art in Internet of Thing designs, technology, and security and privacy concerns. To better understand fog computing-based IoT, authors of this study look at the connection between fog computing and IoT as well as some of the challenges associated with this kind of IoT [23].

Energy management and smart city issues were briefly discussed by W. Ejaz. Finally, they provide a single framework for Internet of Thing based smart city energy-efficient scheduling and optimization. For example, they address how to prolong the life of low-power gadgets using energy harvesting in smart cities and its associated issues. Two examples are given. One focuses on maximising energy efficiency in smart homes, while the other addresses wireless power transmission for IoT devices in urban environments [24].

New mobile technologies on cloud-based IoT systems have unique security and privacy requirements. Hence, J. Zhou created an efficient aggregation without public key homomorphism encryption. Finally, number of intriguing open issues & possible concepts are presented to stimulate more study in this burgeoning fields [25].

Research and design challenges for IoT and machine-to-machine communications necessitate fundamental network paradigm shifts to meet the predicted high traffic and low latency requirements. The massive deployment of tiny cells in the millimeter-wave spectrum is one of these possibilities. 5G will be the most intelligent and dominating wireless technology yet as a result of the many smart features and applications that will be included into future wireless networks [26].

5 Research Gaps

5G technology is designed to deliver data rates up to 20 Gbps and much lower latency for a more immediate response. Even with the users moving around, it provides an overall more uniform user experience so that the data rates stay consistently high. 5G offers downloading speed of 20 Gb/s (gigabits per second) and uploading speed of 10 Gb/s respectively. Significant problem that the emerging nations suffer is security management. With uncertainty about existing safeguards, the cybersecurity protections available to citizens and governments amid 5G rollout is a matter of concern. The existing studies reveal that providing security reduces overall performance by 7% to 20%. Another issue is its accessibility 24 × 7. Presently, users need access to information any time at any location. Another key challenge with 5G is its short range. Trees and buildings cause significant signal obstruction, necessitating numerous cell towers to avoid signal path losses. The present work aims at improving the performance of the network by expanding the capacity of 5G connectivity and addressing signal path challenges.

6 Future Scope

In the future, academic institutions and the telecoms industry will focus on 5G and beyond initiatives. IoT research might improve social services in low-income nations and the rest of the world. These study categories include millimeter wave communication technologies as well as other 5G physical layer research areas like as security and data traffic management. For our analysis, we have included NR, LPWAN networks, as well as high-tech sensors capable of supporting 5G networks. Additional numerology values are included in the physical layer specification for 5G New Radio (NR) in addition to the standard values. Cloud computing and augmented realities, along with the ramifications for 5G (IoT), have also been discussed in detail. Cyber security and privacy are major problems with 5G networks. We looked at the rise in cyber attacks and the corresponding decrease in cyber security and privacy measures in-depth.

7   Conclusion

The integration of 5G with IoT enables to connect as many devices as possible into single network. Several applications that have fueled the Internet revolution include smart agriculture, internet-enabled vehicles, smart manufacturing, smart healthcare, smart cities and many more. NR, MIMO, millimeter wave connectivity and cloud computing are proposed in the 5G IoT architecture. The present work provides a detailed review of IoT, its applications in 5G technology and the upcoming issues in the technology. Several technologies that are critical to the IoT have been overlooked in the present paper on 5G. Cyber security and privacy are major problems with 5G networks. The other issues of concern are its accessibility, short range and reduced performance. These can be resolved by compensating signal path losses and by incorporating effective techniques that increases the capacity of 5G.

References

1. Hashemi, M., Koksal, C.E., Shroff, N.B.: Out-of-band millimeter wave beamforming and communications to achieve low latency and high energy efficiency in 5G systems. IEEE Trans. Cummun. (2017). ieeexplore.ieee.org. https://doi.org/10.1109/TCOMM.2017.2771308
2. Zaidi, A.A., Baldemair, R., Moles-Cases, V., He, N., Werner, K., Cedergren, A.: OFDM numerology design for 5G new radio to support IoT, eMBB, and MBSFN. IEEE Commun. Stand. Mag. 2(2), 78–83 (2018). https://doi.org/10.1109/MCOMSTD.2018.1700021
3. Gomez-Barquero, D., Navrátil, D., Appleby, S., et al.: Google Scholar. https://scholar.goo gle.com/scholar?hl=en&as_sdt=0%2C5&q=3.%09David+Gomez-Barquero%2C+David+ Navrátil%2C+Steve+Appleby%2C+and+Matt+Stagg%2C+"Point-to-Multipoint+Commun ication+Enablers+for+the+Fifth+Generation+of+Wireless+Systems"%2C+IEEE+Commun ications+Standards+Magazine%2C+March+2018.&btnG. Accessed 06 Dec 2021
4. Sexton, C., et al.: Enabling asynchronous machine-type D2D communication using multiple waveforms in 5G. 5(2), 1307–1322 (2018). ieeexplore.ieee.org. https://doi.org/10.1109/JIOT. 2018.2806184
5. Akpakwu, G., Silva, B., Hancke, G.P., Abu-Mahfouz, A.M.: A survey on 5G networks for the Internet of Things: communication technologies and challenges (2017). https://ieeexplore. ieee.org/abstract/document/8141874/. Accessed 08 Dec 2021
6. Lin, J., Yu, W., Zhang, N., Yang, X.: Zhang, H., Zhao, W.: A survey on internet of things: architecture, enabling technologies, security and privacy, and applications, 4(5), 1125 (2017). ieeexplore.ieee.org. https://doi.org/10.1109/JIOT.2017.2683200

7. Solomitckii, D., Gapeyenko, M., Semkin, V., Andreev, S., Koucheryavy, Y.: Technologies for efficient amateur drone detection in 5G millimeter-wave cellular infrastructure (2021). https://ieeexplore.ieee.org/abstract/document/8255736/. Accessed 08 Dec 2021

8. Medjahdi, Y., Traverso, S., Gerzaguet, R., et al.: On the road to 5G: comparative study of physical layer in MTC context (2017). https://ieeexplore.ieee.org/abstract/document/811 0615/. Accessed 08 Dec 2021

9. Al-Falahy, N., Alani, O.Y.: Technologies for 5G networks: challenges and opportunities. It Professional (2017). ieeexplore.ieee.org. https://doi.org/10.1109/MITP.2017.9

10. Hong, W., Baek, K., Ko, S.: Millimeter-wave 5G antennas for smartphones: overview and experimental demonstration. IEEE Trans. Antennas Propag. (2017). https://ieeexplore.ieee.org/abstract/document/8012469/. Accessed 08 Dec 2021

11. Dawy, Z., Saad, W., Ghosh, A., Andrews, J.G., Yaacoub, E.: Toward massive machine type cellular communications (2021). https://ieeexplore.ieee.org/abstract/document/7736615/. Accessed 08 Dec 2021

12. Wang, Y., Lin, X., Adhikary, A., Grovlen, A., et al.: A primer on 3GPP narrowband Internet of Things (2017). https://ieeexplore.ieee.org/abstract/document/7876968/. Accessed 08 Dec 2021

13. Pierpoint, M., Rebeiz, G.-M.: Paving the way for 5G realization and mmWave communication systems (2016). https://www.keysight.com/us/en/assets/7018-05254/article-reprints/5992-1578.pdf. Accessed 08 Dec 2021

14. Bockelmann, C., et al.: Massive machine-type communications in 5G: physical and MAC-layer solutions (2021). https://ieeexplore.ieee.org/abstract/document/7565189/. Accessed 08 Dec 2021

15. Wang, H., Fapojuwo, A.O.: A survey of enabling technologies of low power and long range machine-to-machine communications. IEEE Commun. Surv. Tutor. (2017). https://ieeexplore.ieee.org/abstract/document/7962157/. Accessed 08 Dec 2021

16. Ejaz, W., Naeem, M., Shahid, A., et al.: Efficient energy management for the internet of things in smart cities. IEEE Commun. Mag. (2017). ieeexplore.ieee.org. https://doi.org/10.1109/MCOM.2017.1600218CM

17. Zhou, J., Cao, Z., Dong, X., et al.: Security and privacy for cloud-based IoT: challenges. IEEE Commun. Mag. (2017). https://ieeexplore.ieee.org/abstract/document/7823334/. Accessed 08 Dec 2021

18. M. Elkhodr, S. Shahrestani, Cheung, H.: The internet of things: new interoperability, management and security challenges, **8**(2), 85–102. arxiv.org preprint arXiv:1604.04824 (2016). https://doi.org/10.5121/ijnsa.2016.8206

19. Nokia: LTE evolution for IoT connectivity. Google Scholar. https://scholar.google.com/scholar?q=20.+Nokia,+%60%60LTE+evolution+for+IoT+connectivity,%27%27+Nokia,+Espoo,+Finland,+White+Paper,+2017,+pp.+1_18.&hl=en&as_sdt=0,5. Accessed 08 Dec 2021

20. Painuly, S., Kohli, P., Matta, P., Sharma, S.: Advance applications and future challenges of 5G IoT. In: 2020 3rd International Conference on Intelligent Sustainable Systems (ICISS) (2020). https://ieeexplore.ieee.org/abstract/document/9316004/. Accessed 08 Dec 2021

21. Gupta, N., Sharma, S., Juneja, P.K., Garg, U.: SDNFV 5G-IoT: a framework for the next generation 5G enabled IoT. In: 2020 International Conference on Advances in Computing, Communication & Materials (ICACCM) (2020). https://ieeexplore.ieee.org/abstract/document/9213047/. Accessed 08 Dec 2021

22. Zafeiropoulos, A., et al.: Benchmarking and profiling 5G verticals' applications: an industrial IoT use case. ieeexplore.ieee.org. https://doi.org/10.1109/NetSoft48620.2020.9165393

23. Soos, G., Ficzere, D., Varga, P.: Towards traffic identification and modeling for 5G application use-cases. Electronics (2020). mdpi.com. https://doi.org/10.3390/electronics9040640

24. Kohli, P., Painuly, S., Matta, P., Sharma, S.: Future trends of security and privacy in next generation VANET. In: 2020 3rd International Conference on Intelligent Sustainable Systems (ICISS) (2020). https://ieeexplore.ieee.org/abstract/document/9316043/. Accessed 08 Dec 2021
25. Sharma, S., Agarwal, P., Mohan, S.: Security challenges and future aspects of fifth generation vehicular adhoc networking (5G-VANET) in connected vehicles. In: 2020 3rd International Conference on Intelligent Sustainable Systems (ICISS) (2020). https://ieeexplore.ieee.org/abstract/document/9315987/. Accessed 08 Dec 2021
26. Painuly, S., Sharma, S., Matta, P.: Future trends and challenges in next generation smart application of 5G-IoT.In: 2021 5th International Conference on Computing Methodologies and Communication (ICCMC) (2021). https://ieeexplore.ieee.org/abstract/document/9418471/. Accessed 08 Dec 2021

Author Index

Printed in the United States
by Baker & Taylor Publisher Services